Soul-Making by Grace

Soul-Making by Grace

Purgatory's Past, Present, and Future

MATTHEW S. HENDZEL, SJ

Foreword by Michael Stoeber

◆PICKWICK *Publications* · Eugene, Oregon

SOUL-MAKING BY GRACE
Purgatory's Past, Present, and Future

Copyright © 2024 Matthew S. Hendzel, SJ. All rights reserved. Except for brief quotations in critical publications or reviews, no part of this book may be reproduced in any manner without prior written permission from the publisher. Write: Permissions, Wipf and Stock Publishers, 199 W. 8th Ave., Suite 3, Eugene, OR 97401.

Pickwick Publications
An Imprint of Wipf and Stock Publishers
199 W. 8th Ave., Suite 3
Eugene, OR 97401

www.wipfandstock.com

PAPERBACK ISBN: 978-1-6667-5424-7
HARDCOVER ISBN: 978-1-6667-5425-4
EBOOK ISBN: 978-1-6667-5426-1

Cataloguing-in-Publication data:

Names: Hendzel, Matthew S., SJ [author]. | Stoeber, Michael [foreword writer].

Title: Soul-making by grace : Purgatory's past, present, and future / Matthew S. Hendzel, SJ.

Description: Eugene, OR: Pickwick Publications, 2024 | Includes bibliographical references and index.

Identifiers: ISBN 978-1-6667-5424-7 (paperback) | ISBN 978-1-6667-5425-4 (hardcover) | ISBN 978-1-6667-5426-1 (ebook)

Subjects: LCSH: Purgatory—History of doctrines. | Future life—Christianity. | Purgatory. | Catholic Church—Doctrines. | Eschatology.

Classification: BT842 H46 2024 (paperback) | BT842 (ebook)

04/29/24

For their unfailing support and encouragement, this book is lovingly dedicated to my parents, Leonard and Sharon Hendzel, and to my aunt, Marilyn Hendzel.

"... remade, as new trees are renewed when they bring forth new boughs, I was pure and prepared to climb unto the stars."

—Dante, *Purgatorio* (Mandelbaum), Canto 33:143–45

Contents

Foreword by Michael Stoeber | ix

Preface | xi

Acknowledgments | xiii

Introduction | 1

1. Historical Development of the Doctrine of Purgatory from Its Origins to the Second Vatican Council | 14

2. Doctrinal and Popular Status of Purgatory Since the Second Vatican Council | 55

3. "Soul-Making" and the Western Theological Tradition | 85

4. Soul-Making Influences within a Catholic Context | 118

5. Challenges with Hick's Understanding of Soul-Making and Further Developments within a Protestant Context | 151

6. A Soul-Making Concept of Purgatory within a Contemporary Catholic Context | 185

Conclusion | 210

Bibliography | 217

Index | 223

Foreword

"AND THOUGH THE LORD GIVE YOU the bread of adversity, and the water of affliction, yet shall not thy teachers be removed into a corner any more, but thine eyes shall see thy teachers" (Isa 30:20 KJV).

Simone Weil spoke of *malheur* (affliction) as an extreme form of undeserved and destructive suffering, which include harshly traumatic physical contexts, as well as severe psychological and social pain. In terms of community, she observes how people tend to attack those who become overwhelmed by their affliction, just as chickens will kill the wounded of their hen house, quite naturally it seems. Only those who have experienced this reality first-hand can begin to appreciate the extent of this animosity, the deeply embedded human inclination to take advantage of the powerless, and to scape-goat them. Otherwise, as Isaiah well knew, our teachers lie hidden in the corners of theoretical theodicy, where we tend to take comfort in conceptual responses to theological conundrums associated with transformative or meaningful suffering, rather than with destructive "affliction": How and why is there evil and suffering in a world that was created solely good? How do we distance God from it? Why me, God? Stephen Mitchell points out how, for Job and William Blake, these are all the wrong questions. Deep truths of theodicy are revealed only via first-hand experiences of affliction.

Recently, I encountered my "teachers" of *malheur* in a two-week intensive "Art-Spirituality" class I have taught regularly over many years. In this course, we creatively draw out our emotional-spiritual contexts through sketching and supportive reflection, in the areas of art therapy, spiritual direction, meditation, and prayer. Students in this particular class had suffered much: crippling eye cataracts, life-threatening blood clots, cancer, paralyzing stroke, war-time displacement, and tragic loss of children, parents, and spouses. They were unusually candid about their sufferings, potential healing methods, and processes, and some of it seemed clearly to be affliction.

Their scars were deep. Although such destructive suffering does not contribute to positive outcomes for people who are struck down by it, one can nevertheless in some cases find or receive healing for it, and perhaps even help others adjust to such radical displacement and traumatic distress. "Students" of mine became for me Isaiah's "teachers" in affliction. They pointed me authoritatively in various directions of healing: towards angels, saints, ancestors, children, and grandchildren; to Tobias's homeopathic fish and dog, our own magical pets, and other healing marvels of nature; towards graceful friends, family, medical people, and hospice specialists; as well as to Jesus's marvelous, miraculous work.

In his book, Matthew Hendzel reflects speculatively about healing possibilities *beyond* such spiritual contexts of this world and lifetimes, with special reference to the ground-breaking work of John Hick's "soul-making theodicy," where purgatory is envisioned as a spiritually transformative process that goes well beyond retributive punishment—the traditional go-to theological explanation for all our troubles. The emphasis is on compassionate healing, even from traumas of destructive affliction, within the context of ongoing grace-filled spiritual movements. This is not to say that much of our suffering is not punishment, but it is to insist that such retribution always has some *reformative* component—it needs to be "soul-making." Moreover, affliction is *never* punishment. God is no torturer and not all suffering is punishment! As Jesus responded to the question of the source of the man's blindness from birth: "Neither hath this man sinned, nor his parents: but that the works of God should be made manifest in him" (John 9:3 KJV). Affliction makes no "justifiable" sense for the devastated person, from the vantage point of theoretical theodicy, though it can initiate a person into a community of like-minded teachers and healers.

It seems to me that Matthew's major contribution here is the creative connections he makes ecumenically, of significant Protestant theology with the "Catholic tradition" of theodicy, where Saint Augustine too can be linked to a contemporary "sanctification-purifying" model of purgatory, one that might be colored somewhat by John Hick's soul-making insights. In analyzing current issues of theodicy, Matthew also provides a very fine historical outline of the doctrine and illustrates vividly how it is not a reality we can quietly forget, as Dermot Lane queries. There is simply far too much suffering in *this* world, both destructive and transformative, to let go of our speculations about purgatory.

Michael Stoeber
Feast of the Queenship of the Blessed Virgin Mary
August 22, 2023

Preface

AT THE TIME OF writing, I will be entering into the eleventh year of my life as a member of the Society of Jesus, a Catholic missionary order of priests and brothers. For four of those years, much of my time was devoted towards writing my doctoral dissertation, which serves as the basis for this present book. And during that time, whenever the topic of my writing came up in conversation, I almost always received the same response from whomever I was talking to: interest. For it seemed that no matter their cultural background, age, or level of religiosity, everyone possessed opinions, or questions, or concerns about the afterlife.

These conversations were often eye-opening, as they offered an unvarnished glimpse into what people believed actually happened in the afterlife . . . or what they would like to believe happened in the afterlife . . . or what they heard happened in the afterlife. Over the years, these responses have left me alternately touched, inspired, confused—even shocked, and I quickly came to realize that many persons have lacked opportunities for concrete instruction, nor have they had opportunities for meaningful spiritual conversations, on such important subjects as death and the afterlife.

This book emerges, therefore, from a desire to offer some clarity on how one aspect of our afterlife beliefs may be understood today. In effect, I hope that it is somehow able to offer some sort of response to some of those questions that I encountered in my conversations. For beyond my academic interests in the subjects of eschatology and theodicy, what helped me to decide to write my dissertation on purgatory was a hope that I might be able to show how this now oft-maligned doctrine—an occasional source of confusion and incredulity, even to many Catholics—is still credible, and can still be relevant in Christian consideration of the afterlife. Looking at new approaches to how purgatory can be understood from theologians of various denominational backgrounds, I have sought to demonstrate how some of these ideas can both offer positive insights into how purgatory can be understood today while still remaining faithful to purgatory's history and its defined role within the Catholic theological tradition. Ultimately, I have sought to demonstrate that purgatory indeed deserves to remain in our geography of the afterlife, and that it exists as manifestation of God's love and care for God's people—capable not only of responding to their hopes and needs, but also able to tend to their deepest wounds.

Matthew S. Hendzel, SJ
Montreal, August 2023

Acknowledgments

THIS HAS BEEN A project many years in the making. Instrumental to it all has been Professor Michael Stoeber, my dissertation director. His assistance in helping me develop my ideas and then guiding me through the process of putting them onto paper is very deeply appreciated.

I must also thank Professor Marion Taylor, who moderated my dissertation defense and, many years later, volunteered my name to Wipf and Stock Publishers and suggested that it might make for an interesting book. I sincerely doubt that it would ever have been published without her intervention. At Wipf and Stock, I am indebted to the support offered by Matt Wimer, managing editor for Wipf and Stock, for diligently responding to all of my questions and concerns, as well as Elisabeth Rickard and Robin Parry, my editors for this project. Any errors that remain are mine.

Finally, without the care of my friends and family, I would never have been able to see this project through. Thanks especially goes to my brother Jesuits with whom I've lived over the years and who have had to endure my stories, complaints, and bad moods as I've tried to get my dissertation—and now my book—finished. Special thanks must also go to my previous superiors Gilles Mongeau, SJ, Joseph Schner, SJ, and Mike Rosinski, SJ, whose patience and encouragement throughout these years have been immeasurable. I also thank my friends during this time, Jesuit or otherwise, who have never failed in keeping me supported, consoled, distracted, and (especially) humble, whenever I was most in need.

Introduction

THROUGHOUT ITS LONG HISTORY, the doctrinal development of purgatory's theological role and function has often been marked by change and controversy. Its origins can be found amongst the early faithful, as an object of popular belief.[1] In this capacity, it existed as an undefined, post-mortem realm of existence—a "middle-place" distinct from heaven and hell, to be experienced by a person for some duration between the moments of their bodily death and the final judgment. Premised upon the notion that nothing impure can exist in heaven,[2] purgatory was understood to provide an opportunity for persons to be definitively cleansed from any lingering effects of past venial and absolved mortal sins, thereby broadening the hope of salvation to a greater number of people—particularly those who might have had some anxiety over whether or not they (or their loved ones) had fully atoned for their respective sins during their earthly lives.

It was only during the thirteenth century that purgatory's role and function would be formally defined within the Roman Catholic Church,[3] confirming its originally understood role: the purification of the lingering effects of the various sins that a person may have committed during their earthly life. However, as we shall soon see, how purgatory was understood to function in this role would be articulated according to an established Western Christian intellectual framework that held to clearly defined cultural and theological conceptions of God, church, and society. The historian Jacques Le Goff would characterize this particular framework as being essentially juridical in nature, in which preexisting notions of obligation, debt, and satisfaction would go on to project into the afterlife "a highly sophisticated legal and penal system."[4] The result, for Le Goff, is an understanding

---

1. Le Goff, *Birth of Purgatory*, 3.
2. Walls, *Purgatory*, 4.
3. Le Goff, *Birth of Purgatory*, 239.
4. Le Goff, *Birth of Purgatory*, 5.

of purgatory in which "every human soul becomes involved in complex judicial proceedings concerning the possible mitigation of penalties, the possible commutation of sentences, subject to the influence of a variety of factors."[5] Concepts such as "satisfaction" and "punishment" came to dominate any reflection on these proceedings, in which the dynamics of purgation increasingly took on the trappings of a secular court system.

It was this conception of purgatory that existed for several centuries; yet, with the reforms of the Second Vatican Council, the juridical framework according to which purgatory was understood to function in that role diminished as the Council's proceedings signaled a decisive shift in emphasis in Catholic eschatological reflection, a shift markedly away from many of the previous theological assumptions that undergirded the historical understanding of the doctrine. Yet while the Council chose instead to emphasize a more relational understanding of the human person, recognized the existence of sin as a universal phenomenon experienced and perpetuated by every person, and articulated an understanding of a God who desires all of humanity to be saved, showing it mercy and compassion above everything else, the doctrine of purgatory was not explicitly explored in light of these developments, and as such, a clear and comprehensive alternative vision for the doctrine was not clearly articulated at that time.[6] Thus, while the Council offered a very different set of assumptions that could potentially form the basis for a reevaluation of how purgatory might be understood to function within its established eschatological role, it also provided very little direction in how such an understanding of purgatory might be so conceived. Take for example, the definition provided by the most recent edition of the *Catechism of the Catholic Church*, published some decades after the Second Vatican Council had concluded, in which one continues to find concepts and language which, if left uncontextualized, may appear to bear a more than passing resemblance to those utilized in previous explanations of the doctrine.

> To understand this doctrine [purgatory] and practice of the Church [prayers for the dead], it is necessary to understand that sin has a double consequence. Grave sin deprives us of communion with God and therefore makes us incapable of eternal life, the privation of which is called the "eternal punishment" of sin. On the other hand every sin, even venial, entails an unhealthy attachment to creatures, which must be purified either here on earth, or after death in the state called Purgatory. This purification

---

5. Le Goff, *Birth of Purgatory*, 5.

6. For the few oblique references regarding purgatory, see Second Vatican Council, *Lumen gentium*, #49–51.

frees one from what is called the "temporal punishment" of sin. These two punishments must not be conceived of as a kind of vengeance inflicted by God from without, but as following from the very nature of sin. A conversion which proceeds from a fervent charity can attain the complete purification of the sinner in such a way that no punishment would remain. The forgiveness of sin and restoration of communion with God entail the remission of the eternal punishment of sin, but temporal punishment of sin remains. While patiently bearing sufferings and trials of all kinds and, when the day comes, serenely facing death, the Christian must strive to accept this temporal punishment of sin as a grace. He should strive by works of mercy and charity, as well as by prayer and the various practices of penance, to put off completely the "old man" and to put on the "new man."[7]

While it is important to note the *Catechism*'s emphasis upon the "punishments" of purgatory existing as simply the necessary consequence of sin, and not as something directly desired by an offended God, it would nevertheless seem that the stark (if not severe) definition offered above has not yet been allowed to fully engage the more dynamic and hopeful themes expressed by the Second Vatican Council. As a possible consequence of this growing discrepancy between the content of the doctrine and the energies that continued to guide the Catholic Church's post-conciliar eschatological reflection, it would seem that the doctrine of purgatory quickly fell out of both theological and popular favor within Catholicism and has lived a relatively obscure existence up to the present day. This reality has been observed by a number of authors, such as Dermot Lane, who, in *Keeping Hope Alive: Stirrings in Christian Theology*, poses the following question:

> For many the doctrine of Purgatory has lost credibility. The language of "punishment due to sin" and making satisfaction for sin, and of souls suffering for a period of time, sounds to many quite anachronistic. . . . Above all, the image of God portrayed by this language seems to contradict the revelation of the love of God in the life, death and resurrection of Jesus. In a word, the question must be asked: Is the doctrine of Purgatory worth retrieving or can it not be quietly forgotten about?[8]

With this question in mind, it may be helpful to return to the definition offered by the *Catechism*. For while it may indeed be characterized

---

7. Catholic Church, *Catechism of the Catholic Church*, 1472–73.

8. Lane, *Keeping Hope Alive*, 146. For a similar assessment, see Thiel, "Time, Judgment, and Competitive Spirituality," 742.

as "stark", perhaps a more charitable interpretation would be "restrained", for by offering very little direction on how purgatory might be understood to function in alleviating these temporal consequences of sin and affecting conversion for those in its domain, the definition offered by the *Catechism* in effect opens up crucial space for further development of the doctrine. Accordingly, and seemingly in response to Lane's provocative question, there has been recent movement by a growing number of theologians to rehabilitate the doctrine by attempting to reimagine the purification of sin's secondary effects as a process of post-mortem sanctification, in which God's purgative grace is received as a means of personal reformation and relational rehabilitation.[9] Generally speaking, purgatory continues to serve within such an understanding as an opportunity for post-mortem purification for the countless individuals who have sinned during their earthly life and who at the point of death require more time for the necessary resolution of the effects caused by these sins. Instead, it emphasizes that these secondary effects of sin are understood to be expunged though continued exposure to God's divine love, which in turn allows the person to grow in an awareness of their own brokenness, and gain in appreciation of the consequences of those instances in which they themselves failed to be loving, However, it also allows that same person to grow in a capacity to receive God's love, to allow it to transform their entire being, and to be drawn forever closer into God's own being along with the rest of God's transformed creation. Thus, this process of personal reformation could also be understood as one of *personal sanctification*, that is, as a growth in holiness, which recognizes that, as Terence Nichols puts it, "to come fully into the presence of God, we must be loving as God is loving. If we are not, our love needs to be purified of self-centeredness and recentered on God and others."[10]

While such an understanding might be considered as a constructive development over previous understandings of how purgatory was thought to function in its assigned role, this present articulation nevertheless continues to feel somewhat incomplete. It lacks, one could argue, a certain grounding in the very tradition that it is attempting to occupy. While attention has been paid as to why a so-called "sanctification-based" model of purgatory is desirable, and thought has gone into how such a model might function, surprisingly little attention has been paid to how such a shift in understanding is in fact possible, in light of the doctrine's long history and tradition. As such, it is arguable that efforts to substantially ground this

---

9. See, for example, the recent visions of purgatory offered in Ratzinger, *Eschatology*, 224–33; Phan, *Living into Death*, 115–16; Nichols, *Death and the Afterlife*, 171–76; and Kelly, *Eschatology and Hope*, 123–31, to name just some.

10. Nichols, *Death and the Afterlife*, 174.

present understanding within the doctrine's theological tradition remain underdeveloped.

Moreover, it would seem that many of the present models so far proposed also leave room for further development of how God's grace might be thought to operate in purgatory. If, as we have seen, the purifying dynamics of purgatory are perhaps now understood more within the context of growth in relationality and personal virtue, this notion of sanctification has generally been considered with respect to the purification as a form of personal reformation from the various experiences of the secondary effects of an individual's sins. While this effectively captures the eschatological dimension of one of the themes identified by the Second Vatican Council, certain other themes—especially the communal eschatological dynamic—remain relatively unexplored in present reflection of the doctrine. Consequently, little attention has been made beyond the context of personal sin to consider how communal, circumstantial, and/or environmental realities of sin may affect a person's overall relationship with their experience of personal sin, its lingering effects, and its necessary purification.

Thus, while the contemporary approach to purgatory as a post-mortem opportunity for personal sanctification should be considered a positive development in the doctrine's history, its place within contemporary theology has remained truncated by a lack of action in more fully exploring certain questions and implications raised by the eschatological themes identified by the Second Vatican Council, such as: Have we been limited in our understanding of how sin's effects remain present in our lives by focusing almost exclusively upon its personal dimension? And relatedly, how might the communal dimension of sin be resolved eschatologically? And finally, have we been limited in our understanding of how God's grace may operate in purgatory by focusing predominately upon its restitutional and reformational dimension, again, within a personal context? Perhaps undergirding these questions lies an even more fundamental question, which can be broadly expressed by asking, in light of recent theological developments and eschatological emphases signaled by the Second Vatican Council, how might purgatory be envisioned as a specifically *hopeful* reality within an emphatically *hope-filled* eschatology? It would therefore seem that in order to effectively respond to the current doctrinal and popular challenges facing the doctrine of purgatory, the present sanctification-based model remains in need of further development: development "backwards," so as to better harmonize it with its hope-filled origins and subsequent history, and development "forwards," expanding upon certain eschatological themes already present so as to better respond to the hopes, needs, fears, and desires of the present day. Curiously, perhaps, some of the more promising contributions toward furthering such development may be found in the work of certain theologians outside of the Catholic tradition and their recent efforts to situate a sanctification-based understanding of purgatory within a much broader discussion concerning the question of theodicy.

The question of theodicy is presently one of the most pressing issues within contemporary theology, garnering no fewer than four thousand works in the last forty years.[11] The word itself comes from the Greek *theo*, which means "God," and *dike*, which means "justice." Thus, the word is a kind of technical shorthand for "the defence of the justice and righteousness of God in face of the fact of evil."[12] Finding an explanation to justify the goodness and love of God in the face of the existence of evil has been the work of religion for millennia; yet, every solution that has so far attempted to explain the problem of evil has eventually found itself to be the recipient of a variety of criticisms, among the most damaging of which being the existence of destructive, meaningless suffering.[13] It is in response to these challenges that John Hick constructed his now famous "soul-making" theodicy.

John Hick (1922–2012 CE) was a theologian and philosopher who wrote extensively during the latter part of his academic career on the topic of religious pluralism. However, his earlier research was dedicated to the questions of the problem of evil and theodicy, and what form a Christian response to these questions might take. Inspired by the thoughts of Saint Irenaeus of Lyons, Hick interprets Irenaeus's understanding of theological anthropology to posit the idea that God created a spiritually, morally, and intellectually immature humanity, set at an "epistemic distance" from himself.[14] Hick reads in Irenaeus an understanding of humanity according to which it was *not* created in a state of primordial perfection, but rather as metaphorical children, with only a rudimentary and grasping understanding of who God is and how they might relate to God. However, Hick would also read in Irenaeus a clear belief that humanity was created with the ability to evolve in maturity—and come to know God gradually—over time, so as to ensure personal authenticity and relative freedom in action as a person embarks on a process of moral and intellectual development that will ultimately conclude with spiritual union with God. Crucially, Hick goes on to postulate that, in specific instances along this journey, experiences of

---

11. This is according to Tallon, *Poetics of Evil*, 15.
12. Hick, *Evil and the God of Love*, 6.
13. Such criticism can be found in Mackie, "Evil and Omnipotence," 25–37, and more recently in Rowe, "Paradox and Promise," 274–87.
14. Hick, "Irenaean Theodicy," 43.

evil and suffering can, too, contribute to a person's intellectual and spiritual development: a process which Hick refers to as "soul-making."[15]

According to Hick's soul-making theodicy, the role assigned to what he might refer to as the "post-mortem intermediate state" (Hick eschews the term "purgatory," for reasons which will soon be made clear) is not primarily the expiation of sin's ill-effects, but rather as a further opportunity for a person (indeed, Hick believes that this is an opportunity granted to every person) to continue—and ultimately conclude—their own unique journey of spiritual, intellectual, and moral development.[16] Depending upon what may be required for each individual to complete this personal journey, the sanctifying dynamics of Hick's intermediate state therefore encompass not only opportunities for gaining deeper self-awareness and profound self-reformation, or opportunities for further growth in virtues, knowledge, and relationship, but also as an opportunity for constructive meaning-making for persons who have experienced (or indeed who have caused) occasions of suffering during their earthly lives, including instances of destructive suffering in which there can be found no conceivable immediate or proximate causes for spiritual growth, and subsequently were unable to personally develop to the degree to which they might have otherwise been able.

Thus, within a soul-making context, the notion of a post-mortem process of sanctification and personal transcendence of sin's ill-effects is effectively extended to not just to grave or mild sinners, but to victims of life and circumstance as well. Moreover, by including in his consideration the total development of the human person—historical, environmental, emotional, intellectual, and spiritual—Hick's proposed understanding of a soul-making intermediate state may indeed offer an expanded vision of how God's grace may operate within the post-mortem realm, and in turn shed new light onto how the post-mortem dynamics of sanctification may be understood within a Catholic context. Such an understanding is unique in its ability to capture within the province of the intermediate state's transformative function the full complexity of the human personality and how it relates to both God and the created world, as well as for offering the broadest possible means for considering within that context all the events of a person's life that were formative in the construction of their personal identity. And finally, in so doing, it also posits the intermediate state as the next positive—perhaps even desired for—step in a person's journey of ever-deepening relationship with God.

---

15. This is a term that Hick would adapt from a letter by John Keats to his brother and sister-in-law; see Hick, *Evil and the God of Love*, 259.

16. Hick, *Evil and the God of Love*, 336–39.

While Hick's formulation of a soul-making intermediate state can potentially inform a contemporary Catholic understanding of purgatory's eschatological role and function, there remain a number of unavoidable obstacles in such an undertaking. The first is an understanding of the role of tradition in these respective understandings. A key feature of Hick's understanding of the intermediate state was that it was postulated totally outside of the Catholic theological tradition. When offered the opportunity to identify a so-called "patron saint" for his soul-making project, Hick explicitly chose Saint Irenaeus, whose insights into the nature of the human person, suffering, and the afterlife he contrasted favorably over those of Saint Augustine of Hippo (whose insights have principally inspired what Hick views as the overly juridical preoccupation within the Western theological tradition). In so doing, it would seem that Hick, by extension, is also choosing to reject much of the Western theological tradition that Augustine helped to form.[17] Consequently, the eschatological role of the post-mortem intermediate state as envisioned by Hick is considerably different from that found within Catholicism, wherein, as we shall see, it in effect becomes a post-mortem opportunity for every person to grow perfect in virtue, as opposed to being the post-mortem venue for the purification of the secondary effects of sin for those who died in a basic state of right-relationship with God. Ultimately, if we are to take Hick's point and accept the fact that centuries of Catholic theological thought have been broadly situated within this Augustinian theological landscape, it will need to be demonstrated that it is indeed possible for a soul-making understanding of the intermediate state/purgatory to be grounded within the Catholic tradition.

The other obstacle, alluded to above, is Hick's confident assertion that through the intermediate state, every person will be saved. Hick maintains that the integrity of his soul-making theodicy can only remain intact if every instance of evil is decisively responded to by God's divine love;[18] thus, the intermediate state becomes for him a crucial vehicle through which the process of this response takes place, inevitably leading to a situation in which every person in human history becomes saved, through the gradual elimination of every instance of evil and every lingering trace of sin. While the sheer optimism of such a view may indeed seem attractive in some respects, it undeniably extends beyond the parameters of the role assigned to the doctrine of purgatory within the Catholic tradition and would indeed also pose a severe challenge to most traditional Christian conceptions of the afterlife. Thus, this basic conceptual difference must also be addressed

---

17. See Hick, "Irenaean Theodicy," 41.
18. Hick, *Evil and the God of Love*, 339–42; see also, Hick, "Irenaean Theodicy," 51.

before Hick's soul-making insights can be explored within the Catholic context.

However, it will be argued that these obstacles can indeed be addressed, ultimately resulting in an understanding of purgatory that maintains its traditionally understood role within the Catholic eschatological system, yet informed in how it functions in that role through a qualified appropriation of Hick's soul-making insights. This book will therefore contend that the basic concept of soul-making (and how an understanding of purgatory informed by such a perspective) can indeed be accommodated within the existing Catholic teachings on the human person, sin, and especially the afterlife, while continuing to maintain the eschatological role according to which the doctrine has been historically understood. Moreover, it will also contend that present understandings of the doctrine, particularly the theology underpinning how purgatory is understood to function within its assigned role, will be dramatically enriched if allowed to be influenced by certain elements found within a soul-making understanding of the afterlife.

The insights offered by Hick and soul-making may indeed contribute toward the possible answers to the earlier questions posed in the wake of the Second Vatican Council. Specifically, these insights may shed some light on how purgatory's sanctifying purifications and may be considered to encompass not just the purgation of the effects of an person's past wrongs, but also the purgation of past wrongs *done to* a person, a purgation of the person's relationship with others, their community, and various other historical or circumstantial factors that have contributed, either positively or adversely, to their own personal identity and relationship with God. Hick perceptively maintains that these purgations can also take on a more positive, developmental, and person-making aspect; however, this book will additionally suggest the possibility that, according to such an understanding, they can take on the form of healing as well, especially in instances where a person has had experiences of destructive suffering.

Such an expanded understanding of purgatory's transformative dynamics can serve to effectively reemphasize the sanctification model's basic assertion that a person's experience of purgatory fundamentally remains an experience of receiving and being transformed by divine grace. Curiously, as we shall see, it may also be the case that these insights effect a certain reengagement of the doctrine's historical roots and allow it to recapture aspects of its original pastoral intention: as a "place" of hope, where God's love, compassion, and continued providential care for God's creation is clearly demonstrated. In other words, they can help purgatory more fully serve as a confirmation of God's initial creating love for the world, and to convey God's continued care for its inhabitants—especially those in need of further personal development and/or healing. In so doing, it is hoped that these contributions will help to more fully realize the theological and pastoral potential of a sanctification-based understanding of the doctrine within the contemporary Roman Catholic context, and perhaps offer an articulation of the doctrine that Christians from other theological traditions might also find ecumenically intriguing, if not appealing.

As such, Hick's soul-making insights can help purgatory move beyond what may be viewed as certain problematic aspects of its history, which seemingly allowed it to become something that responded to—and perhaps perpetuated—a person's fear of death and judgment by an exacting God of justice, to become, rather, something a person can look forward to as the next positive step of their spiritual journey toward perfect union with a compassionate and merciful God of love. Ultimately, it will be argued that these insights can help to re-situate the doctrine of purgatory within the current eschatology of hope emphasized within contemporary Catholicism. This book, therefore, will seek to argue that John Hick's soul-making understanding of creation, theodicy, and the afterlife can help develop the current Roman Catholic models of purgatory to both better reflect broader trends in contemporary Catholic eschatological reflection and offer a more comprehensive account of how purgatory's transformative sanctifying dynamics are understood to operate. This argument will be developed over the course of six chapters, divided into three principal sections.

The first section will broadly discuss the history of the doctrine of purgatory within the early Catholic theological tradition and will be composed of two chapters. The first chapter will outline the doctrinal origins of purgatory and will trace its historical development up to the mid-twentieth century. Special attention will be given to the popular origins of purgatory as what could crudely be described as a place of hope amongst the early lay faithful, its historical relationship with the doctrines of heaven and hell, and how a model of purgatory emphasizing divine satisfaction quickly gained prominence within both the Catholic hierarchy and popular religious culture, becoming woven into the official Catholic understanding of the doctrine for several centuries.

The second chapter will examine the history of the doctrine since the Second Vatican Council up to the present day. Its doctrinal status after the Council, as well as its fall into popular disregard, will be investigated. Also studied will be recent efforts to reimagine the doctrine by stressing its possible reformational and sanctifying elements over its restitutional, and how these efforts have attempted to affect a shift in how the doctrine is understood. The various strengths and shortcomings of this new understanding will also be outlined, and will conclude with the observation that while a so-called sanctification model of purgatory indeed offers a number of constructive developments over the previous satisfaction model, by continuing to concentrate on the relationship between purgatory and personal sin, these articulations—and their theological and pastoral implications—could still be developed further in light of current eschatological themes, particularly those pertaining to a more communal understanding of sin and salvation, that have emerged within the post-conciliar Catholic Church.

The second section of the book will consist of one chapter. It will identify the need to look toward modern developments in the understanding of what might be called the "post-mortem intermediate state" outside of the Catholic theological tradition and will focus particularly upon the "soul-making" understanding of the intermediate state as articulated by John Hick. Acknowledging its potential to possibly inform Catholic theological reflection on the human person and the afterlife, this chapter will explore the very concept of soul-making, including its theological and historical origins, so as to determine its basic compatibility with the Catholic tradition. In so doing, it will first examine its relationship with the anthropological thought of Irenaeus of Lyons, from whose work Hick takes particular inspiration. Next, it will be studied in relation to the anthropology of Augustine of Hippo, whom Hick understands to be representative of the broader Western theological tradition and whose conclusions he believes are particularly problematic to his soul-making project. This chapter, however, will argue that the theological origins that undergird soul-making may also be relevant within a Catholic context, as it will demonstrate that there exists a great deal of convergence in the thought of Irenaeus and Augustine, and that the concept of soul-making in fact remains basically compatible with the so-called "Augustinian/Western" theological tradition.

The third section will consist of three chapters, and together will determine how the Catholic doctrine of purgatory can be informed by John Hick's soul-making understanding of the intermediate state. The fourth chapter will return to Hick's soul-making theodicy and will explore in greater detail the role and function of the post-mortem intermediate state within his particular understanding. It will be demonstrated that by finding a connection between the intermediate state and theodicy, Hick's understanding of the intermediate state possesses a more sophisticated and nuanced awareness of the extent to which the effects of sin and evil remain present in a person's life, as well as what might be required by the intermediate state to effect their purification. This chapter will go on to identify additional key insights found within Hick's understanding that could be of some benefit to the existing sanctifying model of purgatory presently advocated by some Catholic theologians.

The fifth chapter will identify some of the limitations in Hick's understanding of soul-making, as well as certain stumbling-blocks in adopting Hick's soul-making understanding of an intermediate state within a Catholic context. Of particular interest will be Hick's insistence that a soul-making understanding of the intermediate state necessarily facilitates a universal reconciliation between humanity and God. This question will be further explored, as well as the implications for any appropriation within a Catholic setting. It will be determined that, while a critical issue, the relationship between soul-making and universalism is not necessarily integral, in spite of Hick's insistence, in developing an understanding of purgatory informed by Hick's soul-making insights. This will be the subject of the following chapter; however, before this is carried out, a brief survey of how purgatory has been developed amongst other non-Catholic theologians will be offered, in order to see if there are any other possible contributions that can be identified.

The sixth and final chapter will offer some conclusions regarding how a soul-making understanding of purgatory might operate within a contemporary Catholic eschatological context. It will demonstrate that while purgatory's traditionally assigned role remains firmly fixed within the Catholic tradition, the way in which it can be understood to function in that role can be dramatically enriched through the qualified adoption of a certain number of Hick's soul-making insights. The various pastoral and theological implications of this revised understanding of purgatory will also be explored.

The conclusions reached in this exploration can have far-reaching implications upon contemporary Catholic approaches toward understanding the eschatological character of sin and its lingering effects on the human person, as well as how purgatory could be understood to function as a venue for the resolution of those effects. Generally, they work to bring the doctrine more in line with current theological trends guiding reflection on God, the human person, sin, and eschatology. By broadening dramatically the scope of our understanding of both how sin's effects can touch the human person and how God's grace can respond to and transform these effects, purgatory's sanctifying function is likewise broadened beyond the general context of resolving the effects of personal sin. Instead, by emphasizing the importance of a person's communal, environmental, and relational circumstances in any consideration of their post-mortem journey of purification, an opportunity thus emerges to replace a narrower understanding of how it is thought to function within its established theological role with a fuller understanding of purgatory's sanctifying potential.

Moreover, by providing the grounding upon which a more constructive and compassionate understanding of purgatory's purifications can be emphasized, it becomes far easier to associate such a conception of purgatory with a contemporary, more relational understanding of a loving and merciful God, for whom purgatory becomes an instrument for helping a person become who they were called to be, in perfect communion with God. Also, the suggestion that a soul-making understanding of purgatory can serve as a place for continued soul-making, and even as a place for possible personal healing and growth from experiences of destructive suffering, may carry certain implications regarding pastoral approaches to the question of suffering. For these reasons, it thus becomes possible to more clearly and coherently situate such an understanding of the doctrine as an essential component within what might be characterized as a more hope-filled eschatological system inaugurated by the Second Vatican Council and advanced by numerous contemporary theologians. In addition, it might also help to raise purgatory's broader relevance as an object of faith if the lay faithful are able to understand it as something that can more compassionately and constructively respond to their personal hopes, fears, experiences, and circumstances, as they transition to the afterlife in their ongoing journey toward God.

Finally, it is also likely that such an understanding of purgatory might help to inform any further ecumenical or interreligious dialogue on the subject of the intermediate state. This book will touch upon a number of Christian theologians who find the concept of an intermediate state appealing but remain unable to accept certain elements of its historical development within the Catholic tradition. It is hoped that the understanding of purgatory as presented in these pages might somehow help to contribute toward finding some degree of convergence regarding the role and function of a post-mortem intermediate state within any Christian eschatology of hope.

1

Historical Development of the Doctrine of Purgatory from Its Origins to the Second Vatican Council

CHARTING THE DEVELOPMENT OF the doctrine of purgatory before 1274 CE can be rather difficult, as it only gained official status within the Catholic Church at that time, when it was formally defined at the Second Council of Lyons. Before then, its existence within the church was unofficial and its proper place was always tenuous. Until the time when the doctrine was officially embraced by the Catholic Church, purgatory's place within its overall theological system was never guaranteed, despite its obvious popularity amongst the faithful. Initially ambivalent, the church hierarchy only gradually warmed to the idea of purgatory as popular belief in it continued to grow. And so, without any early formal proclamations or major documents on the subject of its doctrinal status or theological content, the concept of purgatory instead grew largely out of a general religious impulse from the lay faithful, which was then intermittently clarified and systematized by certain individuals over time.[1]

Unlike the case with so many other doctrines, purgatory enjoys no clear revelatory, geographic, or intellectual origin. As noted by Isabel Moreira, "that more is believed than put down in writing may be the albatross of historical inquiry generally, but it is a problem that particularly besets the earliest history of purgatory."[2] What documentary origins there are

---

1. See Le Goff, *Your Money or Your Life*, 75–76.
2. See Moreira, *Heaven's Purge*, 3.

can only be found—usually indirectly or just in passing—in a few sporadic Scripture verses, and in the miscellaneous writings of early church theologians. Never dealt with exclusively, early theological reflection on purgatory occurred rather haphazardly, depending on whether or not it was a subject of interest or personal belief for a particular theologian. And while these theologians may have included popes and famed Doctors of the Church, it was rarely the case that their ideas were ever universally embraced or would go on to become the cause of purgatory's growth in popularity. Thus, for the most part, purgatory's early theological significance was perpetuated simply by the popular piety of the early Christian laity as a grassroots or almost "underground" belief, and it was the hierarchy's job to play catch-up.[3] Yet due to its initial status as a vague folk belief and corresponding lack of official attention from the early church hierarchy, it would seem that early understandings of purgatory remained relatively unsophisticated in the initial stages of its development, and simply lacked the refinement that an article of belief would normally possess at a doctrinal level.

At this period in its development, what was to become purgatory could perhaps more accurately be described, in the words of Moreira, as "a loose system of compatible ideas about prayer, intercession, afterlife belief, and theology concerning infernal realms that somehow coalesced and gelled . . . to become a place, or prolonged stage, that was given existence in the afterlife."[4] Accordingly, due to its lack of early formal systematization, the precise geographic location and theological purpose of purgatory was never initially defined, which in turn allowed the basic religious intentions that were present in its origins to become obscured and even manipulated by the later church hierarchy as it eventually caught up to—and assumed control over—the doctrine. But what were these initial religious intentions? That question will be examined in this chapter, along with an exploration of how these early, rudimentary religious impulses were transformed into a sophisticated and complex doctrine that found itself firmly entrenched in Catholic religious thought and practice well into the twentieth century.

PRE-CHRISTIAN ANTECEDENTS TO PURGATORY

Greco-Roman Background

It is important to state once again: before it was formally defined in the councils of the Catholic Church, the main source and initial perpetuation

---

3. Le Goff, *Birth of Purgatory*, 289.
4. Moreira, *Heaven's Purge*, 6.

of purgatory's popularity was not the theologians but rather the lay faithful. Although its initial conceptions were extremely rudimentary, popular belief in that which became known as purgatory grew because, broadly speaking, it dramatically broadened the spiritual path that led to salvation. In explaining purgatory's ongoing appeal, John Casey notes that throughout its history, "purgatory . . . answered profound needs. If it reduces the terror of judgment that had been centrally important to Christian tradition, this can count as an argument in its favour. For it tempers terror with justice and, indeed mercy. It had always been a hard doctrine to swallow that a man who died with any un-repented sin should suffer for all eternity."[5] Such an understanding, which undoubtedly was a major reason for the doctrine's initial and ultimate success, was achieved through the crystallization of a number of related contemporary concerns, combined with residual pre-Christian beliefs, which will be discussed below.

Belief in what came to be known as purgatory emerged out of the values, hopes, and desires of early Christian society. Yet many of these same values, hopes, and desires of course predated Christianity, especially those concerning death and the afterlife. Thus, what came to be known as purgatory emerged in part from a variety of preexisting beliefs. The most likely explanation for the initial popularity of the doctrine of purgatory was the simple fact that it was, to a degree, the organic Christian continuation of a pre-Christian religiosity. This, among other things, would include an anxiety over the question of salvation for oneself and for one's loved ones, and the belief that the prayers of the living can have an effect on the dead.[6]

The notion that the concepts which have traditionally perpetuated the doctrine of purgatory also precipitated it is not new. This idea has been touched upon by then-Cardinal Joseph Ratzinger, who writes that "the essential elements of the doctrine of purgatory crystallized out of the traditional materials offered by . . . late antique sensibility, Judaism and Christianity. The central feature of it all is the idea of a suffering on the part of the dead was capable of being alleviated by prayer."[7] Other scholars, such Jacques Le Goff and Jerry L. Walls, also emphasize the essential role that popular culture played in the purgatory's origins and subsequent development, with the former pointing out that "what is rooted in tradition is more likely to succeed than what is not. Though new to Christianity, purgatory borrowed much of its baggage from earlier religions."[8] Situated in the imperial Roman

---

5. Casey, *After Lives*, 230.
6. Ratzinger, *Eschatology*, 222–23.
7. Ratzinger, *Eschatology*, 222–23.
8. Le Goff, *Birth of Purgatory*, 11. Walls suggests an even broader range of religions

milieu, the popular culture from which purgatory arose tended toward the urban and heterogeneous. A mixture of Jews and pagans (generally of either Greek or Roman heritage), these first believers brought with them a diverse background of former beliefs, yet nevertheless shared a number of common concerns. Of those is one of the most important ideas that underpins purgatory in particular, and indeed in religion generally speaking: that the dead will in some form be judged for the actions they committed while still alive.

With regard to the early Christians of pagan background, concern for one's personal state after death was a relatively recent phenomenon. Briefly stated, the ancient general belief (which, due to the number of opinions regarding the afterlife available at that time, any statement on Greco-Roman afterlife beliefs must be stated generally) of the Greeks and Romans was that the afterlife would be a remarkably similar experience for just about everyone—a place of sadness, impotence, and death.[9] According to this understanding, there existed in Greek thought, which was largely influenced by Homer's *Odyssey* and *Iliad*, the belief that in every person resides a *psyche*, which is not the person themselves, but rather the animating force or "breath of life" of a person.[10] After death, the *psyche* separates from the person's body and, no longer attached to the person itself, becomes an *eidolon*, a phantom image of who that person used to be. Residing in *Hades*, the dwelling place of the dead, an *eidolon* bears only a slight resemblance to the person when they were physically alive and exists instead as something more akin to an image of the former person reflected in a mirror: capable of being seen, but not grasped.[11]

Thus, after death, the common fate of all individuals was to forever persist in this form of half-existence. Resignation to this form of an afterlife existed until around the middle of the fifth century BCE, at which point a dramatic shift began to take place regarding how the afterlife was viewed. Due to their very loose cohesion, Greek afterlife beliefs were more susceptible to the introduction of new ideas, which could in turn influence how the overall belief system was understood. As noted by Walter Burkert, "The ideas about death and afterlife, just because they were less explicit and less uniform . . . were subject to greater and more radical change."[12] Accordingly, the Greco-Roman world would become heavily influenced by

---

that might have influenced purgatory's origins, noting elements from Indian, Persian, Egyptian, Greek, Roman, Babylonian, and Jewish texts that offer certain parallels to what would become purgatory. See Walls, *Purgatory*, 10.

9. Casey, *After Lives*, 66.
10. Casey, *After Lives*, 69.
11. Burkert, *Greek Religion*, 197. Quoted in Casey, *After Lives*, 69.
12. Burkert, *Greek Religion*, 198–99.

a set of teachings attributed to the legendary poet Orpheus (for the shift introduced by Orphic thought in Greece was also adopted by the Romans, largely informing their own particular understanding of the afterlife),[13] which introduced to new beliefs and practices regarding how the afterlife was to be understood. The distinguishing characteristic of Orphism (the movement that emerged from these teachings) is the idea that while Homeric popular religion believed the soul (*psyche/eidolon*) to be the mere shadow of the former person, Orphism "considered the soul as immortal and the body as its prison," from which the soul would eventually break free upon bodily death.[14] However, in its passage to the afterlife, the soul was no longer predestined to reside in a shadowy resting-place common to all, but rather would be judged depending upon how "righteously or wickedly" it had spent its earthly existence.[15] In order to achieve a happy rest, the Orphic movement demanded "righteousness and moral purity" from the individual, and anyone who was not purified in their earthly life would remain impure in the afterlife.[16]

While originating as a peculiar religious curiosity, the tenets behind Orphism gained coherence and broader acceptance through the writings of Plato (himself possibly influenced by the movement's ideas), whose belief that an individual continued to fully exist in the afterlife through the concept of an immortal soul gradually gained momentum within the pagan world.[17] According to his understanding, influenced as it may have been by Orphism, it was the soul which indeed contained the full contents of "personhood," but was unfortunately being constrained by the various limitations of the physical body. Thus, when a person died, the belief emerged that instead of merely residing—impotently—in a shadowy, half-real realm of the dead, the afterlife came to be understood as the place where, freed from all material limitations, the human person (as a disembodied soul) becomes fully alive. For Plato, the objects of the sensory world to be illusory and incomplete reflections of the corresponding essences (known as "Forms" or "Ideas") that inhabit the spiritual realm. This "Intelligible" world can only be perceived by the pure rational principle of our soul, which alone has the ability to perceive ideal beauty and absolute goodness. This ability is hindered by the body, which through its various desires and weaknesses contaminates the soul and obscures this proper spiritual vision. Thus, it is

13. Cumont, *After Life in Roman Paganism*, 73–74.
14. Nilsson, *Greek Folk Religion*, 116.
15. Casey, *After Lives*, 89.
16. Nilsson, *Greek Folk Religion*, 116.
17. Casey, *After Lives*, 95.

only when the soul is liberated from the body that this true world can possibly become fully realized. The depth and clarity of this contemplative vision depends on the moral development of the person. If the needs of the soul are ignored, the person will receive reformative punishment.[18]

Although there is some debate over Plato's exact understanding of the afterlife, it would seem that he maintained a position that regardless of one's spiritual trajectory (toward either sin or virtue), there existed the possibility of reincarnation, which, through multiple lives, would allow for the opportunity of eventually gaining the clarity and purity that comes with knowledge of true philosophy—the prerequisite for the desired goal of pure contemplation of Ideas. It is only then, when this process of punishment and rebirth is completed, that the soul would finally ascend into the realm of Ideas. However, while the practice of reincarnation would appear to provide numerous opportunities to those who for better or for worse continue to lack the required purity and vision, there continues to remain the possibility of person's sins rendering them irredeemably lost, and so for them, they will remain in *Tartarus* (a place similar to the Christian understanding of hell, where the punishment would continue indefinitely), with no hope of escape.[19]

It is therefore along with the Platonic belief in the immortality of the soul that there also emerged the notion that the actions that a person freely commits during their earthly life will have a direct effect upon the state of their soul in the afterlife. Referencing the Platonic dialogue of *Gorgias*, John Casey describes the way in which Socrates explains the myth of the judgment of the soul after death:

> Here the soul will be stripped of the body and revealed as it really is—its crimes and vices will show themselves in all their deformity, analogous to the deformities of an unhealthy or misused body; the soul that is guilty of perjuries and injustice will be a mass of wounds; luxury, insolence, and incontinence will show as disproportion and ugliness. Judgment will be given in a meadow, whence are two ways, one leading to the Isles of the Blest, and the other to Tartarus.[20]

---

18. Plato makes a number of references to the concept of Forms throughout his works; however, this theory was perhaps most famously explained in his "Allegory of the Cave," found in the *Republic*. See Plato, "Republic," 7:514–20. An explanation of this theory can also be found in Casey, *After Lives*, 95–100.

19. Ramelli, *Apokatastasis*, 389.

20. Casey, *After Lives*, 98.

Thus, within the pagan world, belief in—or at least awareness of—the concept that (a) one's identity can be essentially expressed in one's immaterial, immortal soul, and that (b) one has a certain degree of control as to where one's soul will spend eternity, helped create the space for the eventual emergence of a belief in a post-mortem intermediate state. Although these philosophical concepts would certainly be modified as they become incorporated into Christian belief, we are already able to identify within pre-Christian pagan thought the basic material that will come to undergird the eventual doctrine of purgatory: belief in the immortality of the soul, the idea of individual responsibility and free will, and the corresponding belief in a definitive judgment of how an individual used their own free will. And while it cannot be claimed that late pagan attitudes toward the afterlife directly precipitated an early Christian understanding of a post-mortem intermediate state, it remains nevertheless apparent that they helped to create an environment out of which one could eventually emerge. And that was what happened when Christianity experienced an influx of pagan converts; Greek ways of thinking were allowed to seriously interact with the ideas and religiosity of the other main element operating within early Christianity: Judaism.

Judaism

In his analysis of purgatory, Joseph Ratzinger identifies Judaism as providing the strongest early religious foundations for the doctrine: "The roots of the doctrine of purgatory, like those of the idea of the intermediate state in general, lie deeply embedded in . . . Judaism."[21] Indeed, it is within the Hebrew Scriptures that one can find what is perhaps the clearest example of pre-Christian belief in a post-mortem intermediate state. Likely written by a Jew of the Greek-speaking diaspora sometime in the second century BCE, 2 Maccabees, although considered a deuterocanonical book within the Hebrew Scriptures, nevertheless offers fascinating insight into Jewish afterlife beliefs present at that time. In chapter 12:39–46, one finds Judas Maccabeus and his band of warriors happening upon a group of slain Jewish rebel fighters. These rebels were wearing amulets around their necks, which they supposedly thought would have given them special powers. This superstitious practice was forbidden in Jewish custom. In response to this discovery, Judas and his group perform a sacrifice and then prayed for the souls of the deceased, which was in turn praised as a pious act by the narrator of the story. This passage is significant in that it offers evidence of a certain religious practice clearly present at that time that would go on to become another

---

21. Ratzinger, *Eschatology*, 220.

key premise underpinning belief in what will eventually become purgatory: that prayers and actions of the living do indeed have some beneficial effect upon the lot of the deceased. Moreover, the passage also indicates that the souls of the deceased are situated not in a place where there is finality (i.e., heaven or hell, in which, due to their irrevocable natures, there is no need for the prayers of the living), but rather in a non-definitive liminality where the supplications of the living can actually have some effect on the condition of the deceased; in other words, an intermediate state, where the deceased undergo some sort of (it may be assumed, purgative) change that could somehow reverse or even erase the effects of sins committed while on earth.

Therefore, in the book of 2 Maccabees, one can already find within certain elements of the Jewish tradition at that time a foreshadowing of what would later become the Christian doctrine of purgatory. Again, as was the case in reviewing the religious concepts of the afterlife in Greek thought, it would not be reasonable to suggest that this was the sole precursor to the particularly Christian understanding itself; it would, however, be reasonable to infer from this that the basic understanding of the post-mortem intermediate state held by the author of 2 Maccabees was already present and operating in the background of their religious milieu, and would eventually go on to leave a lasting impression on how the intermediate state would come to be understood by early Christians. Moreover, beneath both these understandings lies the same premise that both Jews and early Christians found so attractive, namely, "that sins could be forgiven after death, and that prayers by the living could help achieve this."[22] Thus, while early Christian belief in an intermediate state was not a direct import from either Hellenistic or Jewish religious thought, strong elements within both cultures nevertheless held beliefs that maintained the existence of an eternal heaven and hell, and were to a greater or lesser degree open to the possibility of some form of an intermediate state.

Noting the influence of pre-Christian religious cultures upon the emergence and development of a particularly Christian understanding of a post-mortem intermediate state, Ratzinger observes that within the early Christian communities, "the idea of purgatory developed in its initial stages . . . with the beliefs of the Christian people, marked as these were by the earlier sensibility

---

22. Walls, *Purgatory*, 12. Jacques Le Goff is in agreement with Walls, and points out this passage's immense importance to the Church in confirming the two premises upon which purgatory was to be built: "in accordance with the Fathers of the Church . . . Christians looked upon this text as confirming two things: that sins can be redeemed after death and that the prayers of the living are an effective way of accomplishing this" (Le Goff, *Birth of Purgatory*, 42).

of the classical world and of Judaism."²³ When Greeks or Jews became Christian, they brought many aspects of their own particular cultures with them, which may or may not have included some vaguely held, not always coherent, and occasionally divergent notions of a post-mortem intermediate state in which sins could still be forgiven, that the soul could receive continued reformation, and that the prayers of the living could still be of some benefit for the deceased. These notions, it must be stressed, although scattered, disorganized, and varying in intensity of belief, would have most likely remained as underdeveloped cultural residuals of the newly converted, who were at that time contending with a flood of new concepts and ideas. The belief in an intermediate state therefore serves as a powerful example of the possible staying power, and indeed influence, of some native ideas in the process of inculturation. For while these cultures tolerated or even condoned certain beliefs or practices pertaining to an intermediate state, the Christian Scriptures, as we will see, provide in and of themselves little direct evidence for its existence. Thus, it appears that the primary source for early conceptions within Christianity of a post-mortem intermediate state originated from—and was initially perpetuated by—pre-Christian cultures, and that certain passages from the Christian Scriptures served primarily to reenforce a preexisting belief in an intermediate state and are not solely responsible in the inauguration of a belief in an intermediate state in and of themselves.

EARLY CHRISTIAN UNDERSTANDING OF PURGATORY

Referencing early archeological evidence regarding the afterlife beliefs of early Christians, Jacques Le Goff reaches the following conclusion:

> From the earliest centuries of the Church, Christians, as funeral inscriptions reveal, hoped that a dead man's fate was not definitively sealed at his demise, and that the prayers and offerings—that is, the intercession—of the living could help dead sinners escape hell or, at least, benefit from less harsh treatment than that meted out to the worst inmates of hell, as they waited for the final sentence at the Last Judgement.... But there was no precise knowledge about any eventual redemption after death, and belief in redemption remained vague, chiefly owing to confusion about the geography of the infernal regions, where no specific receptacle existed for those whose admission to heaven or to hell had been delayed.²⁴

---

23. Ratzinger, *Eschatology*, 224.
24. Le Goff, *Your Money or Your Life*, 75–76.

Although one can identify the sources of the eventual doctrine's inspiration in Hellenistic thought generally and the later Hebrew Scriptures in particular, it will still take some time for these ideas about a post-mortem intermediate state to become woven into anything coherent within the Christian tradition. An important reason for this extended period of incubation is the simple fact that early Christians had little material to work with from within their own emerging tradition that could directly inform their understanding of the afterlife, and in particular, a post-mortem intermediate state. There are no clear references to a post-mortem intermediate state within the Christian Scriptures, and with no direct scriptural references to serve as a catalyst for theological reflection, informed Christian thought on the subject took place only gradually. Instead, what exists are a small number of cryptic passages, which *may* be interpreted as making some sort of reference to such a state. Of these passages, three stand out as the most significant.

In the Gospels, one finds Matt 12:31–32, in which Jesus offers a declaration that apparently includes the suggestion that sins can be remitted in the afterlife: "Therefore I tell you, people will be forgiven for every sin and blasphemy, but blasphemy against the Spirit will not be forgiven. Whoever speaks a word against the Son of Man will be forgiven, but whoever speaks against the Holy Spirit will not be forgiven, either in this age or in the age to come."[25] Another notable Gospel passage is Luke 16:19–26, which, while indicating that sins cannot actually be forgiven in the afterlife and that one's place in the afterlife indeed becomes fixed at one's death, nevertheless seems to leave open the possibility of some form of communication between the dead and the living. This is the story of the rich man and Lazarus, in which the unnamed rich man and Lazarus, a neglected beggar, happen to die simultaneously. While Lazarus ascends into heaven, the neglectful and self-interested rich man descends into "hades." From his place in hades, the rich man looks up to heaven only to see Lazarus standing beside Abraham. Pleading for relief, Abraham rebuffs the rich man, telling him that "between you and us a great chasm has been fixed, so that . . . no one can pass from there to us." The rich man then asks Abraham to send Lazarus back to earth to warn his brothers so that they may avoid the rich man's fate. This request was also denied.

Outside of the Gospels, 1 Cor 15:29 offers one of the more peculiar and mysterious references to a possible post-mortem change that can be experienced by the soul. In his attempt to defend the belief in bodily resurrection to the Corinthian community, Paul writes: "Otherwise, what will those people do who receive baptism on behalf of the dead? If the dead

---

25. For further interpretation of this passage, see Le Goff, *Birth of Purgatory*, 42.

are not raised at all, why are people baptized on their behalf?" By referencing (and not condemning) a practice not mentioned anywhere else in the Pauline corpus, there has been much debate over the true meaning of this passage;[26] but whatever Paul's intended meaning, this passage appears to serve as yet another example of a fluid and developing eschatological understanding within early Christianity, in which a belief seemed to be emerging (at least within certain Christian communities) that allowed for opportunities for further post-mortem activity on the part of the disembodied soul before the general resurrection and the Last Judgment. Earlier in the same epistle, 1 Cor 3:10–15 contains one of the more significant passages regarding a purgative intermediate state within the Christian Scriptures. In it, Paul describes the process that happens to the human soul as it transitions from bodily death to the afterlife: "the work of each builder will become visible, for the Day will disclose it, because it will be revealed with fire, and the fire will test what sort of work each has done. If what has been built on the foundation survives, the builder will receive a reward. If the work is burned up, the builder will suffer loss; the builder will be saved, but only as through fire." This passage indicates that after death, each person must undergo some sort of trial to determine their ultimate fate, which appears to take place during the time of the Last Judgment. If there is no foundation, that person will be consumed; but if only certain parts of the structure (built upon the foundation) are found to be defective, it will be burned off with cleansing fire, thereby saving the individual.

While the above passage does seem to indicate a period of post-mortem purgation, the significance of this does not appear to have been immediately apparent to the very earliest of Christians. For them, upon death, one was destined to spend eternity in either heaven or hell, and too often the criteria to be satisfied in order to get into heaven was so strict that an eternity in hell—even for a baptized Christian—always remained a very distinct possibility, through backsliding into sin. Initially, when the early church thought that the *parousia* was imminent, the notion of remaining morally strong until the end of the world seemed feasible, and consequently there was no immediate need to consider a post-mortem intermediate for those who may have already fallen by the wayside.[27] However, as the *parousia* began to appear less and less immanent—and perhaps might not even

---

26. A succinct history of interpretation of this passage can be found in English, "Mediated, Mediation, Unmediated," 423–26.

27. Le Goff believes that for these earliest of Christians, any awareness of purgatory "remained hidden in the depths of their consciousness" (Le Goff, *Birth of Purgatory*, 13).

occur during the lifetime of the earliest Christians—doubts began to creep in over the possibility of remaining in a state of justification until death.

When the end of the world was thought to be near, the dividing line between heaven and hell, and consequently the saved and un-saved, was as clear as it was welcomed by the embattled Christian community. The saved would just have to persevere for a very short while, and then they would be rewarded, while the unrighteous would also receive what was justly theirs. However, once these apocalyptic expectations waned, and the believers realized that their bodily death might possibly come first, anxieties arose over whether one would be able resist backsliding for the rest of their earthly life, or whether one would have enough time to sufficiently atone for one's sins if backsliding did indeed occur. John E. Thiel refers to this concern as "eschatological anxiety," by which he means "emotional consternation about one's eternal destiny, which, in a Christian context, amounts to worry about the final integrity of one's life, about its ultimate meaningfulness or meaninglessness, about its consummate happiness or desolation. This anxiety emerges in the prospect of a judgment before God in which one's deeds and misdeeds truly matter."[28]

Eventually, the clear distinction between heaven and hell, so welcomed earlier as a means of reinforcing identity, gradually became a chasm that could strike fear into the heart of almost any believer. Remembered once again were the Greek and Hebrew ideas regarding the afterlife and the possibilities they offered in bridging that chasm. Thus, the eventual doctrine of purgatory grew in part out of the general need to resolve fears over the possibility of *Christians* spending eternity in hell by running out of time before they were fully absolved of all their sins; this would include both fears for oneself, as well as for loved ones who already died, perhaps after living only a lukewarm Christian life. As Richard K. Fenn writes:

> Hell is quite simply the place where one has run out of time: time for repentance or contrition, time to acquire merit and to undo the past. In purgatory, however, there is still time in which to redeem the soul: to pay its debts to the living, to make up for lost time on earth, and to pass the tests that separate the soul from its true, eternal essence. Those still in this life can buy time not only for those in purgatory but for themselves, not only by penitent action and humility but by praying for themselves as well as for those whom they have loved.[29]

---

28. Thiel, "Time, Judgment, and Competitive Spirituality," 749.
29. Fenn, *Persistence of Purgatory*, 46.

Presented with such a possibility, Le Goff points out that a certain hope for opportunities of a post-mortem repentance or absolution would begin to finally surface within these early Christian communities: "in order for the idea of purgatory to develop, it was essential that the living be concerned about the fate of their dead, that the living maintain contacts with the dead, not in order to call on them for protection, but rather in order to improve their condition through prayer."[30] When loved ones died, early Christians continued to pray for them. And although it seems unclear as to whether they themselves were fully aware of the reasons why they did so, and how their prayers were actually efficacious, it can nevertheless be assumed that these prayers were not only intended to maintain a connection with the deceased but were also of some help to them in some undefined way. Early evidence for the efficaciousness of these prayers is surprisingly plentiful, primarily through widespread accounts of the dead appearing to earth-bound believers by way of "dreams, visions, and apparitions . . ."[31] Amongst these early Christians—against the best efforts of the local church leadership wary of possible opportunities for superstition, heresy, or even a return to paganism—swirled stories of deceased loved ones demanding prayers or presenting petitions, appearing to the living in order to relieve sufferings or to resolve some sort of unfinished business on earth.[32] While the veracity of these stories obviously cannot be confirmed, they nevertheless are able to point to the fact that by the second century CE, there already was, at a popular level, a widespread practice of praying for the dead, as well as a corresponding belief in a liminal state of existence between bodily death and an eternal afterlife, in which the dead would temporarily reside to receive the benefits of those prayers.

As these beliefs matured, one can now return to 1 Cor 3:10–15 and observe how time allowed such Scripture passages to influence emerging Christian ideas about the afterlife and the intermediate state. As such, that which would come to be known as purgatory came to exist in the minds of early Christians merely as an indefinable intermediary state, where both the faithfully and the more-or-less faithfully departed were cleansed of not-yet fully repented sins through a purgative fire. Thus, as pointed out by Jacques Le Goff, before being thought of as a "place" *as such*, purgatory was "first conceived as a kind of fire, whose location was not easy to specify but which embodied the doctrine from which the later doctrine of purgatory was to

---

30. Le Goff, *Birth of Purgatory*, 46.

31. Fenn, *Persistence of Purgatory*, 4.

32. This distrust in the post-mortem intermediate state on the part of the church leadership would continue for some time despite its apparent popularity amongst the laity; see Le Goff, *Your Money or Your Life*, 76.

develop."³³ Accordingly, purgatorial fire was considered to be like the fires of hell—although purgatorial fire was not eternal, it was every bit as hot.

While the purgatorial image emerging was one of a searing fire, this should not necessarily be interpreted as an overly pessimistic development in early Christian thought on the afterlife, but rather as a basically hopeful reflection on sin and the possibility of salvation. In the face of an aforementioned eschatological anxiety, heaven was no longer the final destination of a very small and select few; by means of a purgative process of transformation within a post-mortem intermediate state, salvation could become a possibility for the average believer. Even for sins not yet fully atoned for, there was now added time to do so, and the speed for this process to occur could be aided by the prayers and actions of the living on earth—a process which became clearer through the simultaneous development of the church's understanding of what would come to be known as "the communion of saints."

While the belief that some form of interaction can indeed occur between the living and the dead has long been present in cultures throughout human history, the communion of saints would become the distinctly Christian belief that while the church exists physically on this planet, it also exists spiritually, both in our reality and in the afterlife, bound together in Jesus Christ. Therefore, while either living or dead, one remains a member of the same church, and the link between the living and the dead within the church is known as the "communion of saints." It is this link which makes interaction between the living and the dead possible. And while the early Christians did not possess an exactly sophisticated understanding of the communion of saints, they nevertheless understood that this interaction was indeed possible, which in part can explain the numerous accounts of visitations from the dead to the living asking for their prayers, and how the prayers and suffrages of the living could alleviate the sufferings of the dead.³⁴

As praying for the dead was a relatively new concept to early Christians (as opposed to praying *to* the dead, which was a common non-Christian practice), it therefore seems unlikely that the first Christians had a particularly complex *Christian* understanding regarding the mechanics of how their intercessory prayers aided the plight of the deceased. Nevertheless, it was their belief that they did, and upon this rests what Le Goff would identify as one of the principal foundations of the eventual doctrine of purgatory: "in order for the idea of purgatory to develop, it was essential that the living be concerned about the fate of their dead, that the living maintain contacts

33. Le Goff, *Birth of Purgatory*, 43.
34. See Le Goff, *Birth of Purgatory*, 48–51.

with the dead, not in order to call on them for protection, but rather in order to improve their condition through prayer."[35]

Seemingly underpinning this development, therefore, was the belief that the God of justice is also a God of mercy, desiring to unite and draw all of creation back to himself. Thus, while actual belief in the theological role and function of the early post-mortem intermediate state remained vague and undefined, and the imagery it consistently conjured was that of a painful, purifying fire, it must still be considered as an object of early Christian proclivity toward optimism and indeed hope for a blessed afterlife. For out of this atmosphere of optimism and hope emerged the doctrine of what would become purgatory. However, this process of emergence would prove to be long and drawn-out, as it would only be during the third century CE that the disparate ideas which underpinned belief in a post-mortem intermediate state—Greek and Jewish thought, certain passages from Christian Scripture, and a paradoxical Christian attitude of anxiety and hope for the afterlife—would begin to be drawn together and systematized by certain early Christian theologians.

EARLY DOCTRINAL FORMULATIONS

As the Christian church continued to grow and expand within the Roman Empire, it began to develop certain regional characteristics. Although one local church would have numerous similarities and differences from the next, almost every local church would come to fall under one of two general cultural spheres of influence: either the Latin-speaking West or the Greek-speaking East. While these local churches, along with the intellectual and social structures of the East, enjoyed a period of relative political stability, the western portion of the Roman Empire would come to experience great upheaval through the arrival of the so-called "barbarians" from outside the boundaries of the Roman Empire and the consequent political social breakdown of its western territories.

Yet in spite of such pressures, there emerged a few individuals within the West who were able to provide significant intellectual contributions to early Christian reflection on the possibility of an intermediate state. One such person was Irenaeus of Lyons (ca. 130–ca. 202 CE). Born in Smyrna in present-day Turkey, Irenaeus's ecclesial career occurred primarily in southern France, where he served as priest and then bishop. It was during that time that Irenaeus, in an attempt to refute the teachings of local gnostics, would go on to write *On the Detection and Overthrow of Knowledge Falsely*

---

35. Le Goff, *Birth of Purgatory*, 46.

So Called, commonly referred to as *Against Heresies* (*Adversus haereses*). This five-volume work serves as one of the first attempts at systematic theology, and would go on to confirm Irenaeus as one of the Christian church's first great theologians.[36] Within this document, Irenaeus offers a brief glimpse into what he understands to happen to the soul after bodily death, noting that just as Christ, after death, "went away in the midst of the shadow of death (Luke 6:40)," so too will the souls of all of his disciples, "upon whose account the Lord underwent these things, shall go away into the invisible place allotted to them by God, and there remain until the resurrection, awaiting that event; then receiving their bodies, and rising in their entirety, that is bodily, just as the Lord arose, they shall come thus into the presence of God."[37]

Notwithstanding Irenaeus's contribution to the Christian theological tradition, it would seem that due to the constant turmoil experienced by the Latin West, the vast majority of Christianity's earliest systematic theologians came out of the much more stable Greek-speaking East, whose approach to theology remained heavily influenced by Hellenistic thought. Of those theologians, two stand out regarding their contribution to the early development of the idea of an intermediate state: Clement of Alexandria, and Origen. Both Clement and Origen lived and worked in the city of Alexandria. And while it is clear that Origen was influenced by Clement's thought, the exact nature of their relationship seems uncertain.[38] Clement of Alexandria (150–215 CE) was one of the first systematic theologians to consider—if not extensively—the nature of the post-mortem intermediary state. He was, at the very least, open to the idea that the soul could indeed be purified after death and was also the first theologian to distinguish two categories of sinners (the incorrigible, who are bound for hell, and the repentant, who are bound for heaven) and two corresponding categories of punishments in the life to come (the temporary and the eternal).[39] Although Clement maintained the existence of an irrevocable hell for certain sinners, he nevertheless set very generous conditions according to which a sinner could repent

36. Benedict XVI, "General Audience," 2007. Pope Francis would go on to declare Irenaeus a Doctor of the Church on January 21, 2022.

37. Irenaeus, *Against Heresies*, 5.31.2. Earlier, in an effort to respond to the concept of reincarnation or reembodiment, Irenaeus mentions that the souls of the deceased will pass not from body to body, "but that they preserve the same form [in their separate state] as the body had to which they were adapted, and that they remember the deeds which they did in this state of existence, and from which they have now ceased, in that narrative which is recorded respecting the rich man and that Lazarus who found repose in the bosom of Abraham" (Irenaeus, *Against Heresies*, 2.34.1).

38. See Trigg, *Origen: The Bible*, 54.

39. Le Goff, *Birth of Purgatory*, 54.

and attain salvation. In the case where a person repents and yet does not have the time to perform the necessary penances, Clement postulated a period after death in which the person would undergo a process of correction in which they would gradually become reconciled to God. This correction manifested itself in the form of an "educational fire that corrected the corrigible and . . . was a fire that did not devour but cleansed like a baptism."[40] In Clement, therefore, one nevertheless finds an early attempt to synthesize the various Christian afterlife beliefs circulating during that time. Although the intermediate state remains geographically undefined in his writings, he acknowledges that there is indeed a place or state (again, it is unspecified, but most likely something akin to a state) in which the individual would experience some sort of purgative educational fire. In so doing, Clement provided a rough outline that allowed the idea of an intermediary state a chance to develop within the orthodox Christian tradition.

Systematic theological reflection on the intermediate state continued in the work of Origen (184–253 CE), a man likely familiar with Clement and one of the early church's more comprehensive theologians. Dedicating his life to finding harmony between Greek philosophy and Christian belief, Origen quickly gained fame for his attempt to organize numerous disparate Christian beliefs into a more coherent theological system; however, he also over time gained notoriety for his views on how the afterlife operated within that system.[41] While not necessarily adhering to a concept that approximated purgatory as such, Origen cautiously maintained an essentially universalist understanding of salvation,[42] and as such considered hell itself to be an ultimately impermanent intermediate state. Briefly stated, Origen's eschatological ideas hinged upon the belief that at the end of time, God will be "all in all," including all of the beings that God chose to create. According to Mark S. M. Scott, Origen argues that "since all creatures share in the incorruptible *intellectualis lux* of the Father, Son, and Holy Spirit, they must also share in God's incorruptibility (Origen, 4.4.9). If any creature were to fade into oblivion because of sin, God's goodness would be diminished."[43]

It is important to note that for Origen, all beings first existed as souls, who were created at once and exercised their free will to enjoy the presence

---

40. Moreira, *Heaven's Purge*, 24.

41. See Greggs, "Exclusivist or Universalist?," 317; see also Scott, "Guiding the Mysteries of Salvation," 362–67, for further analysis on how Origen was understood to transmit his more controversial beliefs.

42. See Greggs, "Exclusivist or Universalist?," 326; Scott, "Guiding the Mysteries of Salvation," 348; and Ramelli, *Apokatastasis*, 140–41.

43. Scott, "Guiding the Mysteries of Salvation," 356.

of the Good, i.e., God.[44] At a certain point, the free will of many souls became slothful and negligent in maintaining their presence with the Good; there thus occurred a "Fall" event which resulted in a number of souls falling away from God, to a greater (i.e., demons) or lesser (i.e., humans) degree. The process of God being "all in all" is thus a process of these fallen souls' journey back toward full communion with God. "If God is really to be in all," writes Ilaria Ramelli, "this implies that evil, which is the opposite of God (*qua* non-Good and non-Being), will be no longer in any being."[45] Thus, due to what Ramelli describes as its "ontological non-subsistence," evil—which God did not create, but rather emerged through the freely made choices of creation—will eventually be reduced back to nothingness as each creature is gradually restored back to God.[46] In describing how all sinners, demons, and even Satan is restored back to goodness, Origen maintains that since evil's very nature is non-being and *not* part of the essence of any creature, it will eventually recede back to nothingness, thereby annihilating the creature's sinful identity and leaving only the redeemed creature to remain: "In this way," writes Ramelli, "what will disappear will be the enemy and death; what will be saved will be God's creature, who by then will be no longer opposed to God, nor will be 'death' any more."[47]

This process of restoration will take place in hell, which in Origen's mind took on many of the same characteristics that would traditionally be ascribed to purgatory, including the notion that all of hell's inhabitants will encounter excruciating fire. However, the flames of Origen's hell were only temporary; moreover, they also served a non-literal, constructive purpose: namely, the purgative cleansing of every existing soul. As Origen himself writes:

> Now I think that another species of punishment may be understood, because, just as when the limbs of the body are loosened and torn away from their mutual connections we feel a torment of intense pain produced, so also when the soul is found outside the order and connection and harmony in which it was created by God for good action and useful experience, and not to harmonize with itself in the connection of its rational movements, it must be supposed to bear the chastisement and torment of its own instability and disorder. But when the soul, thus dissolved and rent asunder, has been tried by the application of rational

44. Origen, *On First Principles*, 2.9.1.

45. Ramelli, *Apokatastasis*, 143. This belief is inspired by 1 Cor 15:24–28, and is further explained in Origen, *On First Principles*, 3.6.2–3.

46. Ramelli, *Apokatastasis*, 144

47. Ramelli, *Apokatastasis*, 146.

fire, it is undoubtedly reinforced in the consolidation and re-establishment of its structure.[48]

According to Origen, hell's fires take on a basically "rational" or instructive character, through which an individual may come to recognize and be wholly confirmed in their desire union with the Good, i.e., God. Any post-mortem "punishments" experienced would therefore not be for their own sake, but would rather be carried out with the intention of restoring the soul to full participation with God.[49] Within *De Principiis*, Origen further develops this more humane and compassionate understanding of God, wherein God is famously referred to as a sort of divine "Physician of our souls," who, "desiring to wash away the ills of our souls, which they had contracted through a variety of sins and crimes," carefully applies a purgative fire so that each soul can once again become healthy.[50] What is key in Origen's description is his clear rejection of any notion that hell's fires ought to be understood as retributive divine punishment. Instead, as the lengthy but very insightful passage below indicates: his understanding of sin's consequence as profound self-isolation and torment in desperate need of alleviation and correction suggests an interpretation more in line with present understandings of how hell might be experienced:

> If then, such be the quality of the body which will arise from the dead, let us now see what the threat of *eternal fire* signifies. . . . It seems to be indicated . . . that every sinner kindles for himself the flame of his own fire, and is not plunged into some fire which has already been kindled by another or existed before himself. . . . And I think that just as in the body an excess of nourishment and a detrimental kind and quantity of foods gives rise to fevers, and the fevers are also diverse either in kind or duration, according to the degree in which accumulated intemperateness supplies material and fuel for the fevers . . . so also, when the soul has gathered together a multitude of evil works and an excess of sins in itself, at a suitable time all that assembly of evils boils up to punishment and is set aflame to chastisements; at which time, the intellect itself, or the conscience, bringing to memory by divine power all those things, the impressions and forms of which it had stamped on itself when sinning, will see exposed before its eyes a history, as it were, of its evil deeds, of every single act it had done, whether foul or shameful, and had

---

48. Origen, *On First Principles*, 2.10.5.

49. Greggs, "Exclusivist or Universalist?," 318. See also Scott, "Guiding the Mysteries of Salvation," 358–59.

50. Origen, *On First Principles*, 2.10.6.

> even impiously committed; then the conscience itself is agitated and pierced by its own stings and becomes its own accuser and witness ... From which it is understood that, in what concerns the substance of the soul, certain torments are produced from the hurtful affections of the sins themselves.[51]

For Origen, the process of a person receiving their corresponding punishments in hell, while certainly intense and inevitably painful, are not administered for the sake of retribution or justice, but rather as the corresponding divine action required for sincere self-reformation for the purpose of eventual reunion with God. It is fundamentally a process of purification which guarantees the soul's eventual salvation.[52] Origen would go on to characterize this experience as a process of "improvement and correction" that will be experienced by every rational being:

> Into this condition [that of possessing a spiritual body], then, it must be supposed that this entire bodily substance of ours will be brought when all things will be restored, when they shall be one, and when *God shall be all in all*. It must be understood, however, that this shall happen not suddenly, but gradually and by degrees, during the passing of infinite and immeasurable ages, with the improvement and correction being accomplished slowly and by degrees, some hastening on in advance and tending towards perfection by a quicker route, and others following behind at a close distance, with others far behind: and so, through the many and innumerable ranks of those making progress and being reconciled, from enmity, to God, until *the last enemy*, which is called *death*, is reached, so that it too may be *destroyed* and no longer be an enemy.[53]

Thus, every soul in hell is to be cleansed according to this method, which culminates in their final ascent into heaven. Such purgation will continue until the entire contents of hell have been cleansed and evil will no longer exist in any form whatsoever. By maintaining such an opinion, Origen's work would remain controversial with later Christian generations; but nevertheless, one encounters in his understanding of the afterlife the same popular themes present in pre-Christian thought, as well as in the thought of Clement of Alexandria: hope in a merciful God and belief that the "punishments" God metes out in order to purify a person's sins are not retributive in character but rather "educational," intended to reform the

---

51. Origen, *On First Principles*, 2.10.4.
52. Greggs, "Exclusivist or Universalist?," 322.
53. Origen, *On First Principles*, 3.6.6.

person through a process of sanctification, that is, continued spiritual and moral development.[54] Although these ideas were often ignored during the course of the doctrine's development, traces of their presence can be identified within purgatory's spiritual and theological origins. In summarizing Origen's contributions toward purgatory's theological development, Jacques Le Goff offers the following assessment: "If Origen glimpsed the future of purgatory, still his idea of purgatory was so overshadowed by his eschatology and by his idea of hell as a temporary abode that ultimately it vanishes from view. Nevertheless, it was Origen who clearly stated for the first time the idea that the soul can be purified in the other world after death."[55] Thus, while Origen admittedly never dealt with purgatory *as such* in his career, he indirectly helped the development of the doctrine by identifying basic themes by which it would be associated, as well as through his simple insistence on post-mortem purification, as heterodox as it may have been.

At this point it seems important to underline the fact that the would-be doctrine of purgatory, from its early pre-Christian Jewish and Greek origins, has so far been considered largely within the Greek intellectual tradition. But it is during the fourth and fifth centuries that belief in the post-mortem intermediary state shed its initial Eastern Greek flavor, and gradually developed the theological characteristics of the Latin West, which in turn reflected a preexisting legal culture that had come to dominate Western intellectual thought. No theologian was more instrumental in infusing these principles into the doctrine than Augustine of Hippo (354–430 CE). Described as the "true father of purgatory," Augustine was responsible more than anyone else in giving the doctrine its distinctly Roman character, thereby paving the way for its eventual acceptance within the institutional Roman Catholic Church.[56]

A LATIN UNDERSTANDING

Along with his theological predecessors, Augustine cautiously affirms that after death and before the general resurrection, the soul can indeed continue to exist in a purgative intermediate state. However, unlike Origen, Augustine strongly believes in the permanency of hell, thereby maintaining the geographic uniqueness of the intermediate state. And while Augustine clearly understood this state as fundamentally an expression God's mercy, his description of it diverges from its more traditionally Greek understanding

---

54. Le Goff, *Birth of Purgatory*, 52.
55. Le Goff, *Birth of Purgatory*, 56–57.
56. Le Goff, *Birth of Purgatory*, 61.

and uses language that instead emphasizes its function and processes as an extension of God's justice.

As a post-mortem opportunity to find a final positive resolution for those who were neither totally good, nor totally wicked, and who at first glance would appear destined for neither paradise or hell, Augustine appears to have understood the intermediate state as a solution to the theological tension between emphasizing the divine attributes of justice and mercy. This distinction, between a greater and lesser sinner, marks an important point in how the intermediate state was to be understood, which R. R. Atwell succinctly states in his summary of Augustine's position:

> Given the fact that God in His sovereign will draws to Himself those whom He wills, and the fact that the death of an individual sets an irrevocable seal upon his destiny as worked out in his lifetime, Augustine nevertheless entertained the proposition that within the broad differentiation of "saved" and "reprobate" there are those who, while not meriting eternal damnation, yet require purification of their sins to make them fit to stand in the presence of the Holy God at the Last Day.[57]

By rejecting the possibility of a post-mortem conversion, and by taking Clement's notion of the saved repentant sinner and making the further distinction between the greater and lesser sinner, Augustine categorized the inhabitants of the intermediate state by a criteria more complex than merely "justified" and "damned," a shared common fate in which everyone who was fortunate enough to be justified would spend an unspecified period of time experiencing fiery punishments due to the residual effects of past sins. Instead, now within the realm of those who are bound for heaven (he did not posit any gradients of those bound for hell), space was left for nuance. There was an acknowledgment that a sliding scale of sanctity existed amongst the justified, and that certain individuals might indeed require a longer period of purgation than others, depending upon the type and severity of their sins. Thus, for Augustine, this was the purpose of the intermediate state: an opportunity for continued purification for reconciled sinners through what would come to be called "temporal punishments," that is, spiritual purgations that are consequently necessary to purify the lingering, negative effects of their sins, thereby saving the person from the eternal fires of hell. Emphasizing that this purification is only for those who have repented and received penance while on earth, the connection between—and an increasingly legalistic concept of—purgatory and penitence was stated more clearly

---

57. Atwell, "From Augustine to Gregory the Great," 176.

than ever before by Augustine.[58] For sins that were pardoned, a penance was assigned that would help to satisfy any injustice committed against God, as well as to help to fortify the soul as it recovers from the sin's ill-effects. If, according to Augustine, there was still some residual ill-effects not covered by the penance, or if a person was assigned a penance but could not complete it in due time, that penance would be brought to completion in this intermediate state.

In the West, the view emerged that when an individual died, it was almost always the case that there still existed some sort of lingering debt that could only be lifted through God's mercy. However, according to Isabel Moreira, it ought to be noted that within Augustine's understanding of the intermediate state, that mercy was principally experienced in the form of severe correction, which perhaps could be characterized as retribution, with reformation being only a secondary effect: "At death the soul was no longer corrigible by voluntary efforts at purification, because it was no longer under the sinners' control. Whereas in life the sinner might feel contrition, do penance and other forms of reparation, . . . once the sinner had passed into the afterlife, the soul's 'body' was its only vehicle for correction. Enslaved by sin in life, in death, the sinner's correction, like that of a slave, would proceed only through the most severe punishment."[59]

At this stage of its understanding, the fires of the intermediate state were not at all conceptually different from the fires of hell. Although such similarities may have led to some confusion regarding the exact identity of the intermediate state (that is, whether or not it is actually a subsection of hell, located geographically close to hell, closer to heaven, etc.), its particular place in the afterlife was preserved by the following distinction: if assuming that the individual is destined for heaven, the fiery punishments of the intermediate state will be temporary, effectively cleansing the soul from any remaining stains of the already-forgiven sin from the already-justified person; yet if that person died in a state of sin in which no penance was sought or assigned, then the punishments experienced will be eternal. Therefore, by maintaining that it is still indeed possible for the not-very-good and the not-very-evil to receive salvation, Augustine's understanding of purgatory does in fact uphold its originally intended function as a post-mortem realm of God's mercy.[60] Yet this mercy is infused with a strong legalistic sense of justice and the need to satisfy the ongoing effects of past wrongs. Cautiously accepting the image of purifying fires found in 1 Corinthians as the form of

---

58. Le Goff, *Birth of Purgatory*, 69–70.
59. Moreira, *Heaven's Purge*, 41.
60. See Atwell, "From Augustine to Gregory the Great," 177.

the punishment in the intermediate state, Augustine states that "for some the result of that test will be that the structure erected by them on Christ, the foundation, will prove to be such as will not be burnt up and destroyed by the fire. For others there will be a different result; the fire will set on fire their superstructure, and this will mean loss for them; but they will be saved, because they have retained Christ as their firmly laid foundation, with a love exceeding their other lovers."[61] These purifying fires, Augustine indicates, will be primarily disciplinary, or retributive, in their effects:

> On our part we acknowledge that even in this mortal life there are indeed some purificatory punishments; but penalties inflicted on those whose life is not improved thereby or is even made worse, are not purificatory. Punishments are a means of purification only to those who are disciplined and corrected by them. All other punishments, whether temporal or eternal, are imposed on every person in accordance with the treatment he is to receive from God's providence; they are imposed either in retribution for sins, whether past sins or sins in which a person so chastised is still living, or else they serve to exercise and to display the virtues of the good."[62]

In addition to providing clarity regarding the nature of the population of the intermediate state, Augustine's other great contribution to the development of the doctrine is his description of the benefits of intercessory prayer and actions on the part of the living to alleviate the duration and intensity of the punishments inflicted upon the souls of the dead. In his *Enchiridion*, he explains in greater depth that which has been generally accepted—if not deeply interrogated—during the few preceding centuries:

> The souls of the dead are benefited by the piety of their living friends, who offer the sacrifice of the Mediator, or give alms in the church on their behalf. But these services are of advantage only to those who during their lives have earned such merit, that services of this kind can help them. For there is a manner of life which is neither so good as not to require these services after death, nor so bad that such services are of no avail after death; there is, on the other hand, a kind of life so good as not to require them; and again, one so bad that when life is over they render no help. Therefore, it is in this life that all the merit or demerit is acquired, which can either relieve or aggravate a man's sufferings after this life. No one, then, need hope that after he is

---

61. Augustine, *City of God*, 21, ch. 26.
62 Augustine, *City of God*, 21, ch. 13.

dead he shall obtain merit with God which he has neglected to secure here.[63]

This passage is significant in that (a) it specifically identifies the condition of individuals who actually populate the intermediate state (which has already been discussed above), and (b) by appealing to a merit-based system, lays the groundwork for the eventual explanation for how it is that the living can help the dead. Without saying so in so many words, Augustine is acknowledging the basic elements of what, as we have already seen, will become the Catholic Church's eventual understanding of the afterlife: that as members of the same church united in Jesus Christ, the living and the dead remain intimately connected to one another through a particular communion, known as the communion of saints. As already mentioned, such an understanding allowed that a certain amount of interaction between the living and the dead is still possible, and that the prayers of the living, by directing the intentions of their meritorious agency toward the deceased, could somehow alleviate the suffering of those in purgatory. However, as Augustine's insights into the afterlife received an increasingly legalistic and merit-based interpretation, the notion arose that the way in which the prayers of the living actually alleviated the sufferings of the dead was through a "paying off" of the amount of residual spiritual debt that the dead accumulated throughout their own sin history.[64] Accordingly, once this notion of indebtedness began to be considered by the members of the church in relation to the special bond that they believed existed between the living and the dead, the consequences, as Jerry Walls points out, become obvious: "But if what needs to be resolved is an objective debt, it is altogether intelligible that fellow members of the same mystical body should share and relieve the burden of debt incurred by their errant siblings in the faith."[65] With sins accordingly understood as debt deserving of recompense, and prayers/suffrages/alms as merit that might lessen the demand for recompense, the belief emerged that the merit accumulated by the living can be applied to the meagre merit that the not-so-good but not-so-bad deceased failed to accrue during their earthly life. When applied, the merits of the living would aid the dead in that they would lessen the time that the dead must experience the punishing purgatorial fire, which purges the person of the debt that they owed to God.

Over time, as the Catholic Church developed an increasingly sophisticated and elevated ecclesiology, the belief arose that as the Body of Christ,

---

63. Augustine, *Enchiridion of Faith, Hope, and Love*, CX.
64. See Fenn, *Persistence of Purgatory*, 44.
65. Walls, *Purgatory*, 68.

the boundaries of the institutional church extended from our present reality to the spiritual realms. This would allow it to claim jurisdiction over the souls on earth as the "Church Militant" (the church as it exists in the temporal realm). For that reason, all were bound to its authority and care. However, since the souls in purgatory are still temporally bound, the argument would be made at that time that they too should be considered to be within the realm of the Church Militant, and thus, the church ought to have at least partial jurisdiction over them.[66] Therefore, according to the church's self-understood role as the storehouse of merit accumulated through Christ's sacrifice on the cross (as well as from all of the good works performed by the saints) and distributor of that merit to its members according to its understanding that it has been given the authority to "bind and loose" by Christ,[67] it believed it had the ability to apply its spiritual reserves to help lessen the duration and intensity of the suffering of the temporal "punishments" of the forgiven sins of those members who have passed, according to its function as intervenor for—and intermediary of—the various prayers and suffrages offered on behalf of the dead.

Augustine's insights into the afterlife will prove highly influential in purgatory's process of doctrinal formalization within the Catholic Church. As R. R. Atwell succinctly points out, Augustine's thought helped to form "the continuing presence of two formative factors in Western theology: on the one hand, the progressive and increasingly systematic ordering of the penitential system within the Catholic Church, one that differentiated mortal from venial sins (and whose categories could easily be translated to the afterlife); and on the other hand, a perennial concern with merit."[68] By beginning the process of seriously theologizing the purpose and function of the post-mortem intermediate state, Augustine's designation as the father of purgatory is certainly justified. But it is also at this point that one can see the beginnings of a gradual movement away from its popular folk-based origins that were rooted in an inarticulate yet clearly present hope (in God's mercy, the concerned intercessions of loved ones, etc.), to an institutionalized doctrine predicated upon an emphasizing of God's divine justice, and the need to make satisfaction in order for penance and post-mortem purification to be efficacious. As both respected bishop and renowned theologian, Augustine, more than anyone else, helped to steer belief in the post-mortem intermediate state away from its Jewish and Greek origins to its eventual

66. Le Goff, *Birth of Purgatory*, 12. Eventually a new and distinct ecclesial category, "Church Penitent," would arise to encompass those who are in purgatory.

67. See Matt 16:13–19.

68. Atwell, "From Augustine to Gregory the Great," 177.

Latin resting place. By incorporating this belief into the Western church's increasingly sophisticated and elaborate penitential system, Augustine remains largely responsible for initially framing the theme and context from which the formal Catholic doctrine of purgatory would eventually emerge.

The move toward institutionalization would continue through the writings of Pope Gregory the Great (540–604 CE), whom Le Goff considers to be the last founder of purgatory.[69] Essentially holding to Augustine's understanding of the post-mortem intermediate state, Gregory continued purgatory's march toward full formalization, and in this process, his contribution to the development of the doctrine was twofold: firstly, he more boldly stated and elaborated upon Augustine's conclusions, focusing especially on how sin, in all of its nuances (including, in the words of Le Goff, "'slight, petty, and minor' sins . . ."), is to be understood, and eventually expiated.[70] Secondly, Gregory also expanded the doctrine's mass appeal by allowing for the concrete theological insights of Augustine to interact with the common supernaturalism and popular piety of the day, thereby ensuring its relevance and continued growth within the religiosity of the lay faithful.[71]

Both Gregory and Augustine focus their particular understandings of the intermediate state around their respective understandings of sin. However, despite the conceptual clarity that he added to considerations of the intermediate state, Augustine's understanding still required further nuance. While he makes the distinction between the greater and lesser sinner, Augustine says very little about what constitutes a greater or lesser sin—the formal distinction between a "mortal" sin and a "venial" sin had yet to be made.[72] This is achieved in the writings of Gregory, where attention is paid to the various distinctions that can exist in sin. With the notion of mortal sin already very much understood, Gregory emphasizes occasions of "slight, petty, minor" sins, and how those, too, can affect the intensity and duration of the time spent in the intermediate state. Noting how these sins might not necessarily condemn a person to hell and yet still demand some sort of restitution on the part of the perpetrator, Gregory introduces the category of "venial sins," a distinction that is still operational within the Catholic Church today.

The concept of venial sin helped to add increased depth and complexity in determining whether or not a person is a greater or lesser sinner. And this, by extension, added greater depth and complexity in determining the

---

69. After Clement, Origen, and Augustine (Le Goff, *Birth of Purgatory*, 88).
70. Le Goff, *Birth of Purgatory*, 91.
71. Atwell, "From Augustine to Gregory the Great," 186.
72. Le Goff, *Birth of Purgatory*, 84.

length that a person was to stay in the intermediate state, as well as the intensity of their required punishment. Such a concentration of energy and thought on the relationship between sin and the afterlife indeed worked to accelerate the spiritual and conceptual union between the intermediate state and personal sin, as it continued is transition from a vague subject of hopes and dreams to a concrete place that can be understood, and in a sense, even controlled. For indeed, the consequence of this transition is a substantial increase in authority for the church, as it will reserve the right to discern and classify any sin committed and assign a corresponding punishment accordingly. Thus, by placing purgatory under further church control, Gregory drastically accelerated the process of transforming a general anxiety of the afterlife into a sort of spiritual leverage that could be utilized by the institutional church. As Le Goff writes: "To imagine the other world was to wield a political weapon. But the only weapon available to Gregory was that of hell, and this ultimate weapon could be used only in extreme cases. Purgatory made it possible to shape the threat to fit the case."[73]

While working to integrate intermediate state into the emerging penitential system on the one hand, Gregory also whole-heartedly embraced certain popular supernatural aspects of the emerging doctrine on the other. As R. R. Atwell notes:

> Augustine was not a superstitious man but Pope Gregory most certainly was. He lived and breathed a different air from that of Augustine, a supernatural air in a world where visions and miracles were commonplace, where the souls of the dead begged the living for their intercession, where demonic intervention was a fact of life to be contended with, but where mercifully the saints, ever-watchful, ever-present, were attentive to the pleas of the faithful for their assistance.[74]

Thus, in addition to further developing the theology of Augustine, Gregory also seemingly condoned an understanding of the intermediate state closely associated with various folk beliefs, stories, and superstitions. And while these extrinsic elements were not necessarily considered by later theological formulators in the doctrine's process toward formalization, they nevertheless contributed to the way in which the doctrine came to be broadly understood by the lay faithful, who still most likely clung on to certain supernatural elements of their pre-Christian past.[75]

---

73. Le Goff, *Birth of Purgatory*, 95.
74. Atwell, "From Augustine to Gregory the Great," 185.
75. Le Goff, *Your Money or Your Life*, 65–66.

For these Christians, belief in an intermediate state still offered hope regarding their ultimate fate as well as the fate of their loved ones, and evidence for this hope could be found in increasingly more sophisticated and persuasive explanations on the reality of the intermediate state, as well as the countless tales of interaction between the living and the dead. But it was an intermediate state that, while seemingly responding to a general anxiety over the afterlife and a hope for one's loved ones, was also stealthily becoming a purgatory that was inextricably linked to the central authority of the hierarchical church and its control over the emerging institution of sin and penance. And ultimately it was this understanding, a mixture of high speculative theology combined with broad and spurious folk beliefs, that would become both gradually accepted by the church hierarchy and also ingrained upon the religious consciousness of the lay faithful for centuries to come.

The final theologian who must be recognized for his contribution to the development of the doctrine was the Venerable Bede (672–735 CE), who built upon the work of his theological predecessors in entrenching the doctrine in mainstream orthodox theology. As Isabel Moreira writes, Bede's principal contribution was "to frame purgatory as an orthodox response to heresy."[76] Moreira claims that although a distinctly Latin understanding of purgatory was obviously by now present in the West (through the work of Augustine and Gregory), Eastern Hellenistic ideas nevertheless continued to linger; particularly the beliefs in post-mortem conversion and universal salvation, beliefs which Bede was determined to refute—and did so by emphasizing the eternity of hell.

Particularly distasteful to Bede was the idea of universal salvation. However, he also recognized the inherent attractiveness of the idea and so in response chose to emphasize the existence of a temporally bound post-mortem intermediate state as an eschatological alternative that maintained the integrity of an eternal hell and yet also reflected the hopes and desires of the faithful: "Repudiation of universal salvation," Isabel Moreira writes, "provided purgatory with a theological justification. Bede . . . saw purgatory as a positive response to, and clarification of, Origen's unacceptable but possibly appealing theological idea."[77]

Bede had a clear idea of who would actually populate this intermediate state, namely, those who were free from mortal sin yet perhaps were not as careful and as conscientious in their faith as they ought to have been: "[Those] to be examined and tried, which, putting off confession and amendment of the crimes they did commit, have recourse at length to

---

76. Moreira, *Heaven's Purge*, 159.
77. Moreira, *Heaven's Purge*, 165.

repentance in the very instant of death, and so depart out of the body; and yet, because they have made confession and repented even in death . . . come all to the kingdom of heaven at the day of judgment."[78] To help the deceased in this process, the layperson is advised that prayers, almsgiving, fasting, and the celebration of masses "of those that yet liveth help to deliver many even before the day of judgment."[79] Yet despite Bede's technical understanding of who might end up in what would come to be known as purgatory, and of what might be done to expedite the duration of their stay, he also offers a more optimistic vision of the purgatorial experience itself, which might resemble that of peaceful souls in a field, where one might "seest this fair company of youth all joyful and bright, is the very same place where their souls are received, which depart out of the body in the doing of good works; yet are not of such perfection that they deserve to be brought straightways to the kingdom of heaven: but for all that, in the day of judgment they shall all have access to the sight of Christ and the joys of the heavenly kingdom."[80]

In a general assessment on how the rise of the belief in purgatory effected theological reflection on the afterlife, Jacques Le Goff offers the following observation: "Purgatory was not consciously or explicitly discovered in order to depopulate hell. But this is what tended to occur in practice."[81] While Bede did indeed help craft an understanding of purgatory that served as an orthodox compromise to Origenist universalism, it is clear that Bede's primary intention was never to "depopulate" hell, but rather to preserve its original integrity as an irrevocable place of punishment for the eternally damned. However, to do so, it seems that hell by consequence had to surrender its claim on the world's "lesser sinners" to the temporary punishments of purgatory. Thus, the general message that Bede was trying to convey was that there was still an eternal hell, but the more likely path for the average Christian was that which led one to heaven, after an extended period of purgative suffering (which of course could be lessened through earthly penance and the meritorious actions on the part of the living).

While its actual formal articulation was still centuries away, the "idea" of purgatory had at this point in history now gained all of the components required for it to effectively grow into a coherent, independent doctrine. Clement and Origen provided the first attempts at theologically explaining the already-existing idea of a post-mortem intermediate state, while Augustine and Gregory worked to systematize the nascent theory and helped send

---

78. Bede, *Ecclesiastical History*, 263.
79. Bede, *Ecclesiastical History*, 263.
80. Bede, *Ecclesiastical History*, 264–65.
81. Le Goff, *Your Money or Your Life*, 78.

it on its eventual path to full incorporation in the institutional church by harmonizing it with the church's emerging understanding of sin and more formalized penitential system. Finally, Bede helped belief in an intermediate state to grow in both popularity amongst the public and in acceptance by the church hierarchy by proposing it as a means by which the particularly heretical demands of universalism could be mollified through an accommodation of the undoubtedly appealing spirit of hope that continued to lay behind the doctrine to the rigorous demands of theological orthodoxy. It is this final point that Moreira persuasively explains in a lengthy but crucial passage toward the end of her book, *Heaven's Purge*:

> Purgatory was successful as an idea in these early centuries because it accomplished a number of things: it impressed upon lukewarm Christians the need for ongoing penance; it suggested coherence at the point at which the scriptures and religious practice converged, as in the prayers for the dead; and it drew ordinary Christians within the eschatological net of salvation. Yet, I think we come closest to understanding purgatory's success and longevity when we ask . . . when did purgatory achieve theological viability? The answer . . . is the point at which Origen's universalism was repudiated in favour of an expanded access to salvation as was endorsed in the work of Bede. Purgatory's future was assured once it was supposed that a broad segment of the Christian population could be saved by means of exposure to purgatory's fires, even if they repented only at the very moment of death, and even if they were compelled to rely on the piety and resources of their "friends."[82]

The above passage conveys what has always been the average Christian's hope behind purgatory's existence, as well as the chief motivation behind its continued perpetuation. Such an understanding was made possible through the cumulative efforts of successive theologians, and perhaps reached its fullest expression in the work of Bede. And although it would still take several hundred years for purgatory to be either classified as a specific place or achieve any sort of formal doctrinal status, it was by now apparent that—through the efforts of various Western theologians and through simple public demand—full formalization was inevitable. References to purgatory became increasingly commonplace as it gradually integrated into the Western theological *milieu*. Thus, during the period of time that runs roughly from the eighth to the twelfth century, very little progress was made in the theological construction and development of the doctrine

---

82. Moreira, *Heaven's Purge*, 211.

of purgatory. But there was very little need for further theological innovation, as all the necessary components required to allow the commonly held belief in a post-mortem intermediate state to transition into the formal Catholic doctrine of purgatory had now been set firmly in place. As Jacques La Goff states, "The fire remained, and while there was nothing new in the theological aspect of the subject, there were visions of the other world and imaginary voyages in the hereafter aplenty, along with developments in the area of liturgy that helped to prepare the way for the notion of purgatorial fire and to cement relations between the living and the dead."[83]

FULL FORMALIZATION

By the seventh to eighth century that the Western church's understanding of the intermediate state reached maturity and became entrenched within the collective consciousness of the general Christian public. However, while the doctrine's extended incubation took place over centuries, concrete moves toward actual doctrinal formalization only began to occur during the twelfth century. It was at this point that the word "purgatory" was used for the first time as a proper noun, thereby bringing an end to the confusion over purgatory's geographic location within the afterlife and allowing for a common understanding to gain widespread adoption (previously, the word "purgatory" was only used as an adjective to qualify the sort of fires that one would experience in the intermediate state. But by "becoming" a proper noun, instead of simply referring to the sort of fire that one will experience in an un-defined state, purgatory increasingly came to be understood as its own distinct place, wherein these post-mortem purifications would take place).[84] Shortly thereafter, the famous literary text *St. Patrick's Purgatory* emerged, which tells the fantastical tale of a brave knight's descent and return from purgatory's torturous depths.[85] But while this, like the folk-tales before it, appealed to popular imagination, the imagery that was conjured was incredibly violent and fearful, as the fiery punishments of purgatory took on more literal and visceral forms. Moreover, the actions that both warranted these punishments and determined their duration were finally

---

83. Le Goff, *Birth of Purgatory*, 96.

84. Fenn, *Persistence of Purgatory*, 5. This conclusion is supported by Le Goff, who identifies the theologian Peter Comestor as the likely source of the change, who, at some point during the decade of 1170, began to use the neologism *purgatorium* in his writings (Le Goff, *Birth of Purgatory*, 157).

85. It is notable to mention that St. Patrick's Purgatory is an actual ancient pilgrimage site on Station Island, County Donegal, Ireland, and is known to have a cave that was thought to be the physical entrance to purgatory.

specified as well, following Gregory the Great's distinction between venial and mortal sin.

According to its earliest understanding, the time one might spend in purgatory was indefinite and undefined, regardless of the sin committed. And while it came to be acknowledged that one would experience a period of cleansing for the residual effects of one's sins, with more time required for greater sins and less time for smaller ones, the length of that period was never formally declared. However, that would change as the understanding of sin within the Catholic tradition became ever-more complex and systematized, and its pastoral response to sin became more uniformly consistent. Instead of relying upon the often arbitrary and uninformed discretion of the local priest in assigning the penance for the sacrament of reconciliation, manuals which organized categories of sin and normalized their corresponding penances became increasingly popular. Although the initial intention behind this movement was indeed pastoral (acknowledging that some sins were more severe than others, and by making sure that penance assigned would not be too severe or lenient for the corresponding sin committed), it was nevertheless a product of its time; for, as Jacques Le Goff observes, "the lay world was one of savage violence. In the face of this violence, the Church, with the help of kings and emperors, tried to impose order . . . A code of pre-established penance was applied to sins, a code inspired by the punishments decreed by barbarian law. A person did not improve his character, rather he redeemed his errors."[86]

Consequently, it was not long until a certain formalized legalism began to creep into its practice. Instead of paying attention to the situational and personal contexts of the confession and proceeding accordingly, the confessor would simply listen for the sin committed, consult his handbook and assign the corresponding penance, without exceptions or any consideration for individual circumstances. Thus, as the Latin West became increasingly preoccupied with notions of personal sin, and developed increasingly litigious methods of understanding its reality, it should come as no surprise that the way in which the authorities and theologians of the Catholic Church came to understand purgatory in the twelfth century has been described as an "accountancy of the hereafter,"[87] in which the time of an individual's purgatorial "sentence" could now be calculated through a careful addition of an individual's sins:

> The idea of a "term of sentence" is part of a broader mental outlook, which sprang originally from a concern for justice and

---

86. Le Goff, *Your Money or Your Life*, 68.
87. Le Goff, *Birth of Purgatory*, 229.

eventually led to the institution of a complex system of bookkeeping associated with the world to come. The fundamental idea, handed down from the earliest Fathers, from Augustine . . . was this: that punishment, and specifically, in this instance, the time spent in purgatory, should be proportioned to the seriousness of sin.[88]

It is in the above statement that one now has the answer to the question over why it took until the twelfth century for the doctrine of purgatory to finally achieve its formal status within the church: the doctrine of purgatory could only find security once it was able to fit into the "broader mental outlook" of the Catholic Church at that time. Far from the vague and divergent understandings that were present in early Christianity, long periods of theological reflection and clarification from within an emerging ecclesial atmosphere of logical rigorism allowed for a precise and coherent doctrine of purgatory to finally be formulated according to certain themes that were valued by the medieval church. However, this clarification was achieved only through great turmoil, as belief in the post-mortem intermediate state experienced numerous upheavals to get to the point of becoming the actual doctrine of purgatory. And even though these same theological innovations made the idea of purgatory itself more appealing and intellectually coherent amongst the members of the clerical elite, they would, on the other hand, force the doctrine of purgatory to be understood by the average person as something more fear-inducing, wherein its torturous punishments were meted out according to strict categories of judicial procedure, administered by the church.

Nevertheless, belief in its existence endured, most likely due to the undeniable (if increasingly manipulated) hope that purgatory provided for the average layperson as they considered their own salvation, as well as the salvation of their friends and loved ones, against the backdrop of an increasingly legalistic, all-pervading, and anxiety-inducing understanding of personal sin and its effects. Thus, on the eve of its formal reception as a doctrine of the church, the idea of purgatory was stronger than ever, but now rested firmly in the control of the institutional church. No longer a vague and undefined realm of hope and divine mercy, purgatory now existed as a specifically defined place of justice, where divine debts were satisfied—either through punishment meted out upon the deceased, or through prayers and suffrages on behalf of the living.

Through the work of the theologians and the strength of public belief and devotion, purgatory-the-noun was finally embraced by the church

88. Le Goff, *Birth of Purgatory*, 228.

hierarchy in the thirteenth century. It was officially described as a place for post-mortem purification in the First Council of Lyons in 1245, and was then formally defined at the Second Council of Lyons in 1274, at which point it became an official doctrine of the Catholic Church:

> Those who after baptism lapse into sin must not be rebaptized but must obtain pardon for their sins through true penance.... If, being truly repentant, they die in charity before having satisfied by worthy fruits of penance for their sins of commission and omission, their souls are cleansed after death by purgatorial and purifying penalties ... and to alleviate such penalties the acts of intercession of the living faithful benefit them, namely, the sacrifices of the Mass, prayers, alms, and other works of piety that the faithful are wont to do for the other faithful according to the Church's institutions.[89]

As Le Goff points out, "Latin theological reflection on the subject of purgatory was essentially complete by 1274, the year in which purgatory was officially consecrated by the Second Council of Lyons."[90] At this point, ongoing formal theological discussion on purgatory was essentially just a reiteration and elaboration—if perhaps in more forceful language—on what already existed; this would include treatises written by individual theologians as well as pronouncements by subsequent church councils, including the Council of Florence and the Council of Trent. The Council of Florence (1431–1449 CE), notable for its attempts to formally heal the schism between the Eastern and Western churches, nevertheless offered a clear definition of purgatory that essentially repeats the declaration from the Second Council of Lyons.[91] Perhaps unsurprisingly, while the Council proceedings contributed toward a clarified understanding of the doctrine, they failed in their ecumenical objectives. Pressured by political powers in Constantinople desiring an amicable outcome, and an insistence by the Latin party that purgatory's theological role and function be clearly defined, the Greek parties acquiesced to a definition that it would seem they did not fully support (perhaps exacerbated, as Joseph Gill points out, by the fact that the Greeks themselves did not possess a universally defined understanding of purgatory within their own theological tradition),[92] and this discrepancy, among a number of other theological and political reasons, led to the definition established in Florence to ultimately not be fully received within the Eastern churches.

---

89. Denzinger, *Enchiridion*, no. 855–56.
90. Le Goff, *Birth of Purgatory*, 239.
91. Denzinger, *Enchiridion*, no. 1,304.
92. Gill, *Council of Florence*, 272.

In spite of its ecumenical implications, the Western church would remain firm in its defined understanding of purgatory. This resolution would endure, even during the tumult of the Protestant Reformation, during which the doctrine would be attacked by the reformers on the grounds that it was not biblically based, that it was theologically erroneous, and that it was mired in ecclesiastical corruption. In response to these—and many other—criticisms, the Catholic hierarchy convened the Council of Trent (1545–1563 CE), which robustly defended its theology of purgatory as well as its various attending spiritual practices. However, after reiterating a belief in purgatory, in which the souls there receive purifying punishments, which can be alleviated by the suffrages of the faithful and by the grace of Christ's sacrifice on the cross perpetuated through celebrations of the Catholic mass, the Council members offer the following comment, which is very telling in its inclusion:

> Therefore, this holy council commands the bishops to strive diligently that the sound doctrine of purgatory, handed down by the holy Fathers and the sacred councils, be believed by the faithful and that it be adhered to, taught, and preached everywhere.
> But let the more difficult and subtle questions that do not make for edification and for the most part, are not conducive to an increase of piety be excluded from the popular sermons to uneducated people. Likewise they should not permit opinions that are doubtful and tainted with error to be spread and exposed. As for those things that belong to the realm of curiosity or superstition or smack of dishonorable gain, they should forbid them as scandalous and injurious to the faithful . . . .[93]

Not wanting to give the reformers further grounds for attacking the doctrine, the Council of Trent sought to uphold purgatory's theological legitimacy, but also eliminate the abusive and superstitious practices that had come to be associated with it. While many of these practices, the selling of indulgences, for example, were indeed curbed through the Council's intervention, purgatory would continue to remain an object of attack for later reformers and a source of eschatological anxiety for the Catholic faithful. For although the Council would explicitly warn against overly speculative imaginings of purgatory, it would seem that this warning may have come too late. More so than though any theological treatise or statute, the public perception of purgatory had largely already been formed through centuries of legends, artwork, and poetry—all of which would appeal more to their imagination rather than their sense of understanding. The role played by the

---

93. Denzinger, *Enchiridion*, no. 1,820.

imagination in purgatory's historical development cannot be underestimated. And in that regard, few appeals to the imagination were more important than *Purgatorio*, written by Dante Alighieri (1265–1321 CE), in forming within the faithful an idea of what sort of experience might be waiting for them in the afterlife.

APPEAL TO IMAGINATION

As the doctrine of purgatory became more theologically sophisticated, it also became increasingly incomprehensible to the average layperson. Confident that purgatory exists, but uncertain regarding its actual operation, the laity of Catholic Europe had to rely upon whatever they were told by their clergy, as well as certain stories—often fantastical—that appealed directly to their imagination (hence the decree that was issued from Trent). While stories pertaining to the afterlife have existed since the origins of Christianity (and obviously well before it), certainly the most famous and by far the most important was *The Divine Comedy*, which was completed by Dante in 1320 CE. An explicitly fictional work of poetry, the three books of *The Divine Comedy* (*Inferno*, *Purgatorio*, and *Paradiso*) presented an accessible impression of the afterlife and was particularly influential in how purgatory would be perceived by the public. Using vivid (and often violent) imagery and familiar historical/literary characters, Dante created a purgatory that would have been both intelligible and relatable for the average person in fourteenth century Italy.

Dante's purgatory remained faithful to the essence of the defined doctrine, yet in this fidelity, the author paints a picture of a post-mortem intermediate state that manages to touch upon almost every aspect of the doctrine that has so far been introduced to the Christian imagination.[94] For example, the person indeed suffers gruesome punishments that specifically correspond to the sins that they have committed, yet, crucially, these sufferings are nevertheless "shot through with hope and charity—confident hope of eventual salvation, and love of God."[95] In *Purgatorio*, Dante travels through a realm that, perhaps at face value, *appears* quite similar to hell. In both places, the reader encounters persons who are having to endure various forms of punishment that is being inflicted upon them. Yet if the reader allows themselves to not be distracted by the physical—sometimes visceral—novelty of these punishments, they will find a profound distinction that Dante is drawing between a person's experience of hell and a person's

---

94. Casey, *After Lives*, 234.
95. Casey, *After Lives*, 240.

experience of purgatory. The key difference between the two is that the punishments of hell are experienced as an expression of—or perhaps one could say, the corresponding fruit of—a person's own sin, while those in purgatory are experiencing punishment as a means of cleansing the very roots of sin that continue to dwell within them. Accordingly, while the punishments of Dante's hell exist to serve as the due reward for the particular sins of each person there, the punishments of Dante's purgatory exist to serve as the remedy necessary to properly correct and heal the person's soul from the particular effects of sin that have accrued to it over the course of the person's life.

Dante makes this distinction very clear through a host of examples found within the first two books of *The Divine Comedy*, of which two can be raised as particularly illustrative. For punishments corresponding to the sin of wrath, those in hell are doomed to a fractious and unrelenting reality of perpetually fighting amongst themselves, forever mired in the slime and muck of the Marsh of the Styx, while those in purgatory roam about a smoke-filled realm, praying to God for mercy and peace by chanting in unison the *Agnus Dei* (with the graces of unity, mercy, and peace serving as the remedy to the discord and violence commonly associated with wrath).[96] For punishments corresponding to the sin of lust, on the other hand, those in hell experience it as a perpetual torrent of tornado-like winds, an expression of their earthly impulsiveness and superficiality in loving, while those in purgatory experience their corresponding punishment as a fire, cleansing them from the disordered passions that dominated their lives as they sing the hymn *Virum non cognosco*, in emulation of the Virgin Mary, who serves as a positive model of virtue as they continue their process of purification.[97]

Although the punishments found in *Purgatorio* all possess a certain physical character, they also, as the above examples illustrate, all contain a medicinal or pedagogical dynamic, ultimately serving to correct and restore the soul. Moreover, as alluded to above, Dante also offers within his vision of purgatory particular exemplary models, appropriate to each sin, that appear to help the penitents also grow in the virtues as they continue their process of cleansing. With this in mind, it would seem that Dante's purgatory ultimately serves to reaffirm a basically hopeful vision of the intermediate state, in which the punishments rendered were not intended simply for their own sake, or to satisfy God's sense of justice, but rather to benefit the soul of the penitent. Indeed, *Purgatorio* is peppered throughout with

---

96. Dante, *Inferno*, Canto 7:103–31, and *Purgatorio*, Canto 16:1–24, respectively. The note on the significance of the *Agnus Dei* can be found in Ciardi's translation, *Divine Comedy*, 424.

97. Dante, *Inferno*, Canto 5:25–48, and *Purgatorio*, Canto 25:109–40, respectively.

passages pertaining to a post-mortem hope, grounded in a strong sense of God's mercy and compassion that seemingly becomes all the clearer as the penitent soul moves through purgatory. For as Dante continues his journey, he finds that the experience of purgatory's punishments lessen in intensity as the person climbs its seven circles (one for each deadly sin, ranged above each other in the form of a mountain), when finally, they reach the top and experience a final purification by wading across the mythical River Lethe. Then, as described beautifully by Dante, the person emerges from the river "remade, as new trees are renewed when they bring forth new boughs, I was pure and prepared to climb unto the stars."[98]

Especially emphasized the importance of the act of repentance, and of how repentance—even for the briefest moment—is sufficient for salvation. One notable example regarding the power of repentance is the instance where Dante meets Bonconte of Montefeltro, a rakish soldier who lived a violent life right up to the moment of death. Yet as he lay dying, his last act on earth was to pray to the Virgin Mary for help which, according to Dante, as enough to secure his salvation: "There with a final moan which was the name of Mary, speech went from me. I fell, and there my body lay alone . . . God's angel took me up, and Hell's cried out: 'Why do you steal my game? If his immortal part is your catch, brother, for one squeezed tear that makes me turn it loose . . . .'"[99] Another example is an intriguing interaction Dante has with Manfred of Sicily, who died excommunicated from the Catholic Church. With excommunication came a denial of the sacraments, including confession. Yet, instead of finding this person in the pit of hell (where he should have been, given his situation) Manfred was instead found in purgatory's antechamber. Destined for heaven, he declares that "no man may be so cursed by priest or pope but what the Eternal Love may still return while any thread of green lives on in hope."[100]

By choosing to offer such radical illustrations of God's mercy and compassion (themes, as we have seen, that have taken on a lesser prominence since the hierarchical church's adoption of a more formalized approach to sin and the afterlife), Dante's prose appears to emphasize a certain direct spiritual relationship between the person and God—a relationship that is not entirely governed by the strictures of the institutional Catholic Church. And by taking the opportunity to illustrate such relationships, in which the

---

98. Dante, *Purgatorio* (Mandelbaum), Canto 33:144–45.

99. Dante, *Purgatorio*, Canto 5:106–13. Again, in a later passage that underlines the optimism that is at the heart of this work, an angel of God tells Dante that "they are from Peter, and he bade me be more eager to let in than to keep out whoever cast himself prostrate before me" (Dante, *Purgatorio*, Canto 9:127–29).

100. Dante, *Purgatorio*, Canto 3:133–35.

generosity of God's grace to such persons is underlined, Dante's vision of purgatory perhaps serves to offer a subtle critique of the presumed authority of the institutional church at that time, and as such his depiction of purgatory could almost be seen as something of a reaction to the institutionalization of the doctrine by the church hierarchy. As already mentioned, purgatory would have been codified and largely understood according to abstract juridical categories, which of course would be arbitrated and mediated through the efforts of the church itself. And once endowed with such power, the church hierarchy inevitably began to take certain liberties regarding its understood responsibilities. As the above example points out, this would include a progressive politicization of the church's self-understood role as "gatekeeper" to the afterlife, in which it would use its authority to effectively deny certain persons the possibility of entry into heaven if they were thought to have spoken or acted against the institutional church. Although some of Dante's subtle criticisms were later acted upon in a decidedly more decisive fashion by later Protestant reformers,[101] the doctrine of purgatory, as it was essentially understood during his time, survived the various Protestant upheavals (who all but did away with the doctrine within their own theological and spiritual traditions) and remained fundamentally unaltered through the next several centuries. During this great period of time, the tenets of the doctrine, in response to strident Protestant criticism and other world events that the Catholic hierarchy viewed as a threat to the church's spiritual and temporal authority, were reiterated with greater—if increasingly polemical—clarity with regard to its initial propositions as Catholic apologists sought to defend its legitimacy and further integrate it into the larger Catholic theological system.[102]

In response, the Catholic faithful continued to participate in the various religious practices associated with the doctrine: mass intentions were petitioned for (or bought), alms were given, indulgences were acquired, prayers were offered, acts of piety were recorded. Yet, as we have seen, these actions were now motivated more by fear of God's judgement and a desire to mitigate the punishments that would follow than they were out of joyful hope of God's mercy in the afterlife. And so, with the Catholic Church unwilling to acquiesce and change its formal understanding of the doctrine, and with the public too anxious to not do all that it possibly could to escape further post-mortem suffering, this pattern of belief and practice would continue in Catholicism, with more or less the same intensity, well into the

---

101. The relationship between Protestantism and purgatory will be explored in greater detail in chapter 5 of this book.

102. Le Goff, *Birth of Purgatory*, 169.

twentieth century. Indeed, even on the eve of the Second Vatican Council, purgatory remained essentially unchanged—either doctrinally or culturally—from its medieval understanding.[103]

However, after the reforms of Vatican II, it has been observed that the doctrine's popularity began to wane, to the point that since the Council, active belief in purgatory has effectively vanished.[104] Although the reasons for this are highly speculative, and very little can actually be substantiated, the Catholic scholar John Thiel nevertheless offers the following hypothesis:

> The diminishment of the sense of personal sin has led to the virtual disappearance of the sacrament of penance in popular Catholic practice, a change in religious behaviour that reflects the loss of a belief in the rigor of divine judgment. And since purgatory is about judgment, it is hardly surprising that the doctrine of purgatory has largely disappeared from Catholic belief and practice.[105]

This appears to be an accurate analysis, in that since Vatican II, both the theological emphasis and public opinion within Catholicism has shifted away from the previously formal, impersonal, and juridical understanding of sin and penance to a more personal, contextually aware, and pastoral understanding. And while purgatory found its theological home in the Catholic Church by conforming to the broader ecclesial themes of divine judgment and punishment, it continues, as we shall see, to search for its proper place within the present theological system.

---

103. See Jugie, *Purgatory*, 6–8, which heavily emphasizes themes of justice, divine satisfaction, and expiation for sins. This was a popular book on purgatory and was in print up until the Second Vatican Council. As such, it offers an important perspective of how the doctrine of purgatory was theologically and popularly understood on the eve of Vatican II. As Jugie's understanding illustrates, it seems clear that the themes present during the process of purgatory's formal acceptance within the Catholic Church, detailed within this chapter, endured well into the twentieth century.

104. Thiel, "Time, Judgment, and Competitive Spirituality," 743.

105. Thiel, "Time, Judgment, and Competitive Spirituality," 741–72.

2

Doctrinal and Popular Status of Purgatory Since the Second Vatican Council

WHEN THE SECOND VATICAN Council was convened by Pope John XXIII on October 11, 1962, an invited spirit of change swept through many aspects of the Catholic Church's teachings and identity. And while purgatory was left largely untouched—at least doctrinally—by these changes, it would nevertheless experience two important developments in the Council's aftermath: firstly, its general slide into disregard and spiritual irrelevance amongst a great number of the lay faithful,[1] and secondly, for those who still maintain its relevance (let alone existence) within the body of Catholic teachings on the afterlife, a gradual understanding of its role and function along more existential and personalist lines, as opposed to strictly material, retributive, and legalistic.[2] And while this contemporary reexamination of the doctrine has yielded very valuable conceptual insights that have undoubtedly left it more theologically palatable and could work toward to the renewal of its pastoral relevance, the doctrine of purgatory nevertheless continues to occupy a marginal position within the realm of contemporary theology, and as such, contributions toward its ongoing development remain few and far between, and have yet to capture widespread attention.

However, it is perhaps due to purgatory's lack of ongoing attention that there remain certain theological and pastoral implications that have yet to be explored and could further develop the contributions that have already been made. Thus, by reviewing the history of the doctrine of purgatory

1. See Thiel, "Time, Judgment, and Competitive Spirituality," 780.
2. See Pasulka, *Heaven Can Wait*, 5.

since the Second Vatican Council, and by observing its status leading up to and following the Council itself, as well as its treatment by certain contemporary theologians and members of the church hierarchy, we will be able to identify both certain constructive insights that have contributed toward the doctrine's present understanding, as well as the limitations of those insights, which in turn can point to ways in which those insights can be further developed.

THE DOCTRINE OF PURGATORY AROUND THE TIME OF THE SECOND VATICAN COUNCIL

The doctrinal content of purgatory remained largely untouched throughout the course of the Second Vatican Council. But that is not to say that it remained unaffected by the changes the Council brought about, as the various cultural, spiritual, ecclesiological, and theological reforms inaugurated by the Council undoubtedly had a residual effect upon how purgatory was theologically and popularly understood. And it is from these reforms that the current understanding of the doctrine would emerge: one that maintains essentially the same doctrinal framework that has existed since its initial formalization, yet whose theological and pastoral focus has shifted from an emphasis upon divine satisfaction to personal sanctification.

Yet before the Council was opened, the theological and pastoral interpretation of purgatory's doctrinal elements continued to correspond to its traditional understanding since the Second Council of Lyons, that is, as a temporal, post-mortem realm of existence where one achieved perfection by satisfying the residual effects of a person's earlier sins. A material understanding of purgatory as a geographic place of literal purgative fire, was still largely held. And although signs of a shifting understanding away from materiality were already present,[3] the nature, function, and mechanics of purgatory remained relatively unchanged within the overall (popular and theological) Catholic understanding of eschatology well into the twentieth century. It continued to exist as an unquestioned component of the Four Last Things (Death, Judgment, Hell, and Heaven) within the traditional Catholic understanding of eschatology. This understanding was very linear in character, with each eschatological event happening clearly and in proper order. There also existed throughout a startling attitude of certainty, and treatments on the subject contained a strong catechetical character. This was an eschatology that remained stubbornly within the realm of dogmatics,

---

3. See Pasulka, *Heaven Can Wait*, 5. Pasulka states that this material understanding of purgatory persisted into the nineteenth century.

was confidently detailed in its assertions, and was so preoccupied with the almost-mechanical nature of the afterlife, that eschatology was consequently thought to have "little critical and transforming effect upon the state of the present world."[4]

Catholic eschatology persisted in stark contrast to a mainline Protestant emphasis upon progress, historical-cultural development, and the optimistic belief that activity could indeed build up the kingdom of God within one's earthly life.[5] These two understandings of the eschaton persisted totally exclusive of one another well into the twentieth century, with Catholicism concerned primarily with that which would happen to an individual upon their death, and the more liberal strands of Protestantism concerned primarily with the communal effects of the *eschaton* that are present and can be experienced in the here and now. However, with the advent of the Second Vatican Council, the Catholic approach to eschatology experienced a dramatic paradigm shift when it was finally allowed to engage contemporary philosophical and Protestant theological currents, as well as many other external forces and pressures operating within the modern world. This is in keeping with what is perhaps one of the Second Vatican Council's most important overall theological achievements: allowing modern scientific, intellectual and social disciplines to inform Catholic theological reflection, thereby allowing its theological culture to transition from a "classical culture to an historical consciousness, that is to say a shift from fixed essences, timeless truths and immutable substances to an open, malleable and historical culture."[6] The documents issued by the Second Vatican Council marked a decisive turn toward modernity within the Catholic Church, and this turn would affect every aspect of the its identity, doctrines, and teachings, including, as already indicated, its understanding of eschatology and eschatology's constituent parts.

According to Dermot Lane, "a credible eschatology . . . must be able to chart a course that contains some degree of continuity between past, present and future while at the same time leaving room for the important elements of change and transformation."[7] Historically, the Catholic Church's official attitude toward change and transformation has been decidedly suspicious. However, through the renewal brought about by the Second Vatican Council, the Catholic Church became open to engaging the forces of modernity, recognizing and acknowledging the "sign of the times," and allowing them

---

4. Novello, "Eschatology Since Vatican II," 410.
5. Novello, "Eschatology Since Vatican II," 411.
6. Lane, *Keeping Hope Alive*, 5.
7. Lane, *Keeping Hope Alive*, 13.

to enter into dialogue with the Catholic Church's understanding of itself, and its role in the world.[8] This fundamental openness to the ever-changing operations of the world is precisely what was signaled in the first paragraph of one of the Second Vatican Council's most important documents, *Gaudium et spes* (*the Pastoral Constitution of the Church in the Modern World*), which states:

> The joy and the hope, the grief and anguish of the men of our time, especially those who are poor or afflicted in any way, are the joy and hope, the grief and anguish of the followers of Christ as well. Nothing genuinely human fails to find an echo in their hearts. For theirs is a community composed of men, of men who, united in Christ and guided by the Holy Spirit, press onwards towards the kingdom of the Father and are bearers of a message of salvation intended for all men. That is why Christians cherish a feeling of deep solidarity with the human race and its history.[9]

Lane suggests that the Catholicism's new-found consideration of historical consciousness signaled not only an awareness of the interconnectedness between the Catholic Church and the world, but also an awareness of her "responsibility to shape and structure the world that we inhabit." Through the reforms of the Second Vatican Council, the Catholic Church effectively expanded the horizons of its concern beyond its institutional boundaries to that of the entire world. It began to take into account an awareness of the various factors, both positive and negative, effecting the world today, and with that awareness was also an acknowledgment that the interconnectedness of these factors indeed leaves no individual—whether they are a member of the Catholic Church or not—unaffected. Consequently, when particular doctrines or teachings were considered, this same broad awareness was brought to bear upon their renewal within the tradition, with eschatology being no exception.

Regarding the inclusion of eschatological considerations within the Council documents themselves, it might initially appear as though forces of modernity that were sweeping through the Council were not allowed to fully engage Catholicism's specific eschatological doctrines, including purgatory. Direct commentary was rare and explicit declarations were virtually non-existent. Indeed, purgatory is only referenced once, and only obliquely, in one of the documents:

---

8. This phrase, often associated with the Second Vatican Council, can be first found in John XXIII, *Humanae Salutis*, #4.

9. Second Vatican Council, *Gaudium et spes*, #1.

Until the Lord shall come in His majesty, and all the angels with Him and death being destroyed, all things are subject to Him, some of His disciples are exiles on earth, some having died are purified, and others are in glory beholding "clearly God Himself triune and one, as He is"; but all in various ways and degrees are in communion in the same charity of God and neighbor and all sing the same hymn of glory to our God. For all who are in Christ, having His Spirit, form one Church and cleave together in Him. Therefore the union of the wayfarers with the brethren who have gone to sleep in the peace of Christ is not in the least weakened or interrupted, but on the contrary, according to the perpetual faith of the Church, is strengthened by communication of spiritual goods.[10]

Instead of offering a series of detailed pronouncements on a theology of the end times and the afterlife, the Council limited its statements on eschatology to a few, seemingly general, paragraphs in *Lumen gentium* (*the Dogmatic Constitution of the Church*), one of the other key documents to emerge from the Second Vatican. Council.[11] Throughout the document, or anywhere else in the other documents issued by the Council, no major doctrinal reforms were enacted regarding how either eschatology or, specifically, purgatory were to be understood. Additionally, the formal documents issued after the Council that concerned or mentioned purgatory only served to clarify some of the doctrine's already-existing finer theological points.[12] Thus, during and immediately after the Council there were ultimately no radical additions, subtractions, or alterations to purgatory at a doctrinal level, leaving its earlier theological understanding essentially intact.

However, while eschatology and, specifically, purgatory did not experience any explicit doctrinal change, it would be a mistake to assume, notwithstanding the brief attention paid toward it in the conciliar documents, that eschatological consideration as a whole was left unaffected by the proceedings of the Council. On the contrary, just as the renewal brought about by the Council allowed the church to engage the spirit of modernity, that same spirit was also allowed to inform the theological consideration of any number of its particular teachings, including eschatology. Thus, what is so striking about *Lumen gentium*'s treatment of eschatology is not so much its commentary on eschatology's doctrinal aspects, but rather its decision to

10. Second Vatican Council, *Lumen gentium*, #49.
11. Second Vatican Council, *Lumen gentium*, #48–51.
12. See, for example, Pope Paul VI's 1967 Apostolic Constitution, *Indulgentiarum Doctrina*, which reformed the use of indulgences within the Catholic Church, but did not abolish the practice altogether.

emphasize not the person's experience of the *eschata* through their own personal death and judgment, but rather the whole of humanity's experience of the *eschaton* over and above personal experience, through an understanding that the *eschaton* is already active in the world and that the process of transformation has already begun, even as the world continues to wait for its final consummation:

> The promised and hoped for restoration, therefore, has already begun in Christ. It is carried forward in the sending of the Holy Spirit and through him continues in the Church in which, through our faith, we learn the meaning of our earthly life, while we bring to term, with hope of future good, the task allotted to us in the world by the Father, and so work out our salvation. Already the final age of the world is with us and the renewal of the world is irrevocably under way.[13]

Throughout, its declarations suggest a broader context in which eschatological reflection ought to be framed. While eschatology was previously understood to be primarily concerned with the events experienced by an individual after their death, its scope of concern expanded along with the acknowledgment that to a certain degree, individual destiny is indeed bound up with the destiny of the whole human race.[14] Its concern, therefore, is broadened from merely what happens at the end of a person's life (and with it a personal hope for a blessed afterlife), to a concern that reflects humanity's place and responsibility within the world, and with it a living hope held by all Christians in the here and now for the coming transformation of the world.[15] Hence, instead of concentrating upon the personal dynamics of how the eschaton is to be experienced, the Council chose to place subtle emphasis upon what was perhaps the original focus of eschatology: the hopeful waiting of the church for the final transformation of all creation at the end of time:

> We have been warned, of course that it profits us nothing if we gain the whole world and lose or forfeit ourselves. Far from diminishing our concern to develop this earth, the expectation of a new earth should spur us on, for it is here that the body of a new human family grows, foreshadowing in some way the age which is to come. That is why, although we must be careful to distinguish earthly progress clearly from the increase of the kingdom of Christ, such progress is of vital concern to the

---

13. Second Vatican Council, *Lumen gentium*, #48.
14. Lane, *Keeping Hope Alive*, 7–8.
15. Novello, "Eschatology Since Vatican II," 412.

kingdom of God, insofar as it can contribute to the better ordering of human society.¹⁶

With such a focus, the Council members attempted to recover the more traditionally communal spirit of eschatology, present during the time of the earliest church when all its members expected the transforming promise of the *parousia* to occur within their lifetimes. And in recapturing this early eschatological spirit, the renewal brought about by the Council would in turn open up the possibility of allowing a number of particular eschatological components, including purgatory, to be reframed through that lens. Within *Lumen gentium*'s section on eschatology, entitled *Chapter VII: The Eschatological Nature of the Pilgrim Church and Its Union with the Church in Heaven*, the opening paragraph begins with a brief meditation on the Second Coming of Jesus—as well as on the final consummation of all things;¹⁷ but following that affirmation, the rest of the chapter clearly refrains from further speculation on what is to happen at the end of time. Instead, the document then shifts its focus to the traditional teaching of the church as the Mystical Body of Christ (which both confirms and builds upon Pope Pius XII's encyclical, *Mystici Corporis Christi*, in which he declares that the church is a living entity, both a physical and spiritual reality, founded, headed and sustained by Christ—in and through whom all members are joined to one another as parts of [Christ's] spiritual body),¹⁸ and how, through the bonds of communion within that body, the church both awaits for the eschatological event of the *parousia*, and has already begun to experience its arrival.¹⁹

16. Second Vatican Council, *Gaudium et spes,* #39. Quoted in Phan, *Living into Death*, 160–61. For an elaboration upon such an understanding of hope, see Phan, *Living into Death*, 135–37.

17. See Second Vatican Council, *Lumen gentium*, #48.

18. See Pius XII, *Mystici Corporis Christi*, #57.

19. Second Vatican Council, *Lumen gentium*, #49–51. In a very helpful explanation of this particular part of the document, especially regarding the tension between the "already" and the "not yet" within its description of eschatology, Benoît-Dominique de La Soujeole writes that *Lumen gentium* successfully "situates the true nature of the Christian life on earth: Eternal life has *already* begun. After death, at the definitive entry into God's glory, it is not another life that will begin; rather, we will find the fulfillment of the life given to us to live here on earth . . ." He goes on to write that "there is, on the one hand, hope (in French, *espoir*), which is the waiting for a good thing to come (for example, a student's expectation of school vacation). On the other hand, there is hope (in French, *espérance*), which is waiting for the accomplishment of something that one already possesses (for example, when one says in French that a woman has '*espérances*,' this means that she is pregnant; her child already exists in her womb, but she is waiting for its birth at the end of her pregnancy). Christian life possesses a hope (*espoir*) of knowing the return of Christ, but that which will come on the last day is not a

It is here in these sections that purgatory is referenced, although not by name: "In full consciousness of this communion of the whole Mystical Body of Jesus Christ, the Church in its pilgrim members, form the very earliest days of the Christian religion, has honoured with great respect the memory of the dead; and, 'because it is a holy and a wholesome thought to pray for the dead that they may be loosed from their sins' (2 Macc. 12:46) she offers her suffrages for them."[20] In the next section, the document continues to affirm the spiritual bonds linking the living with the dead in purgatory, as well as the tradition within which this teaching (otherwise known as the "communion of saints") is situated, declaring that

> this sacred council accepts loyally the venerable faith of our ancestors in the living communion with exists between us and our brothers who are in the glory of heaven or who are yet being purified after their death. . . . At the same time, in keeping with its pastoral preoccupations, this council urges all concerned to remove or correct any abuses, excesses or defects which may have crept in here or there, and so to restore all things that Christ and God be more fully praised.[21]

Thus framed, purgatory's eschatological significance in this document is not explained through reference to it as the next eschatological stage on the path of the individual believer; rather, its communal character is emphasized by describing its role within the Mystical Body of Christ. It is where the person remains connected to the living, receives their prayers, and continues to grow in sanctity through the grace of God, as they await both the completion of their personal path toward perfection, as well as the final purification of all things that will be brought about by the eschaton.

Therefore, through the renewal brought about by the Second Vatican Council, it is possible to observe that, while continuing to maintain its historical doctrinal integrity, the broader Catholic understanding of eschatology experienced two important and not unrelated developments: firstly, as indicated above, contemporary eschatological reflections began to take into account decidedly more organic and communal considerations, and secondly, a more robust optimism and insistent understanding of hope became one of the principle themes that would guide further eschatological thought. Eschatological

---

completely new coming because Christ is already in the womb of the Church, directing it from the inside to the consummation of history: *espérance*." Thus, "eternal life, which has already begun and enhances the value of our time on earth [is also] our eternity that plays out today in time" (de La Soujeole, "Universal Call to Holiness," 44).

20. Second Vatican Council, *Lumen gentium*, #50.
21. Second Vatican Council, *Lumen gentium*, #51.

consideration was no longer an insular and self-referential affair, where the person worked out their own destiny, as an accountant would a balance sheet, with a certain amount of fear and trepidation. Gone also was the strident insistence upon the details of its processes and mechanics.[22] The following observation by Henry Novello offers a succinct summary of its effects:

> The Council did not, of course, abandon the traditional teachings concerning the last things, but it did clearly move away from an exclusive focus on the destiny of the individual—a preoccupation with the salvation of "my soul"—when it sought to acknowledge the universal dimensions of the Christ event and the meaning and value of this earthly life, so that individual destiny and hope is portrayed as bound up with the destiny and hope for the whole of humanity and the entire universe.[23]

By reemphasizing a more collective and dynamic understanding of eschatology, it can be argued that the Second Vatican Council allowed for an opportunity—even if the Council chose to not comprehensively do so itself—to reframe its constituent doctrines according to themes that more accurately responded to and reflected the perennial hopes and desires of the lay faithful. Instead of imposing upon the consciousness of the broader church an understanding of eschatology in which it was treated as a terrifying and inevitable force that demanded reckoning from each and every person, the eschatological emphasis that emerged from the Council—which would go on to become the theological and pastoral emphasis that would take root within the broader Catholic theological context thereafter—was one in which the eschaton is something to be hoped for, an event that would transform the brokenness of the world and all who inhabit it. Again, in the words of Henry Novello:

> Those engaged with reflection on eschatology today generally consider it desirable and necessary to address the issue of how Christian hope relates to the specific hopes of humanity in general. For if Christian hope is not related at the outset to human hope in general, then it will fail to speak to the ordinary as well as ultimate concerns of human existence and will become something quite otherworldly, irrelevant to the here and now, and possibly a form of escape from the ugliness of present reality.[24]

---

22. Novello, "Eschatology Since Vatican II," 417.
23. Novello, "Eschatology Since Vatican II," 415.
24. Novello, "Eschatology Since Vatican II," 414.

The reforms of the Second Vatican Council allowed the subject of eschatology to transition away from a strictly doctrinal consideration and permit it to interact with the various forces of modernity that were already at work in the Council. This would include an awareness of world events and their impact upon all of society, contemporary theological understandings about God and humanity, and, most importantly, the spirit of hope that is present throughout. In this respect, the Second Vatican Council did much to recover the ancient eschatological spirit of the early Christian church, from which what would become the doctrine of purgatory initially emerged. It is therefore ironic that within the theological and spiritual atmosphere of the post-conciliar Roman Catholic Church that same spirit may have also worked to unintentionally undermine the very relevance of purgatory itself.

RAMIFICATIONS OF THE SECOND VATICAN COUNCIL FOR THE DOCTRINE OF PURGATORY

Returning to the passage from *Gaudium et spes* mentioned earlier, one can clearly see an acknowledgment from the Council members that God's grace is not understood to be circumscribed by the boundaries of the institutional Christian church but rather is present in all aspects of creation. Commenting on such a shift in the heretofore restrictive Catholic understanding of salvation, John E. Thiel writes that "the post-conciliar emphasis on the availability of God's grace had a host of effects on Catholic belief and practice. It depeccativized the world. It dulled the pointed sense of God's judgment that believers felt upon their lives. It calmed the eschatological anxiety that had filled Catholic lives throughout the earlier tradition."[25]

While this emphasis upon the availability of God's grace was allowed to permeate the Catholic understanding of eschatology, issues regarding consistency arose when the subject for consideration shifted from a subject as broad as eschatology to a subject as specific as purgatory; for while the Council allowed eschatology, in the general sense, to be considered according to the spirits of modernity and hope that emerged from its proceedings, and while purgatory itself was even allowed to be described using language that emphasized its more communal aspects, the actual doctrine itself remained untouched. According to Henry Novello: "The Magisterium has continued to strongly defend the traditional teaching on the last things, which is referred to as the 'eschatology of souls.' While eschatology since Vatican II has incorporated the language of hope, the teachings on the immortality of the soul, an interim state, purgatory as having a duration, suffrages for the dead,

---

25. Thiel, *Icons of Hope*, 100.

and the existence of hell, continue to be upheld against many challenges to this traditional framework of thought."[26]

Thus, while general eschatological consideration was allowed to be carried through the twentieth century upon the spirits of modernity and hope that have become the hallmarks of Vatican II, the Catholic Church's particular teaching on the doctrine of purgatory was not itself fully explored in light of those same spirits. As already stated, the overall theological change in climate regarding eschatology did not result in any doctrinal changes to purgatory; moreover, even within the already-existing doctrinal framework, the theological signals indicated by the Council were not followed up by a thorough examination of the doctrine. As a consequence, a tonal dissonance began to emerge between Catholicism's overall post-conciliar eschatological outlook and its particular understanding of purgatory, which remained locked within pre-conciliar theological concepts. Over time, it would appear that the continuation of this dissonance has ultimately resulted in a lack of relevancy regarding the doctrine of purgatory for most Catholics who have to a greater or lesser extent chosen to move along with the spirit of the Council.

This is essentially the theory proposed by Thiel, who describes this disconnect as one between a "Matthean" and "Pauline" style of faith. According to Thiel, a spiritually competitive "Matthean" style of faith was the predominant religious and spiritual culture that existed within the Catholic Church before the Second Vatican Council. This culture can be understood as being dominated by a sort of spiritual "merit system," and is evidenced in such passages as Matt 11:21–23 and Matt 25:31–41, which all place primacy upon a person's "deeds" as they stand before God in judgment.[27] It holds above all else the individual's response to Christ's sacrifice on the cross, and espouses that the ultimate fate of their Christian life will be judged according to the authenticity of that response, evidenced by deeds and actions:

> Here, the grace of God that breaks into the world in the life, death, and resurrection of Jesus expects the proof of discipleship in deeds that imitate the Saviour's life and by which the believer will be judged.... God's judgment presupposed human

26. Novello, "Eschatology Since Vatican II," 415. Recent documents that have endorsed a traditional understanding of eschatology include Pope Paul VI's 1967 Apostolic Constitution, *Indulgentiarum Doctrina*; the Congregation for the Doctrine of the Faith's "Letter on Certain Questions Concerning Eschatology," 1979; the International Theological Commission's "Some Current Questions in Eschatology," 1992; and the 1994 edition of Catholic Church, *Catechism of the Catholic Church*, 998–1050. These will be discussed at greater length later in this chapter.

27. Thiel, *Icons of Hope*, 66–67.

> responsibility not only for sin but also for virtue.... Moreover, judgment in this style of faith highlights the believer's active decision before the alternatives of moral achievement or moral failure, and ultimately before the eschatological destinies of heavenly glory or internal condemnation.[28]

Thiel goes on to write that, within this model, "Jesus calls believers to a discipleship of deeds measured by the sacrifice of the cross, a standard that Jesus had defined in his own saving death and that each martyr profoundly imitated in the act of becoming a saint."[29] If Jesus was the ultimate standard against whom an individual's actions were judged, than the martyr, saint, or ascetic were the proximate standards. And more often than not, when held against these standards, the achievements (or lack thereof) of the average believer inevitably left them spiritually wanting. Concern over this discrepancy was what led to the aforementioned "eschatological anxiety," defined by Thiel as the "emotional consternation about one's eternal destiny, which, in a Christian context, amounts to worry about the final integrity of one's life, about its ultimate meaningfulness or meaninglessness, about its consummate happiness or desolation," from which purgatory emerged as an opportunity for the average believer to "catch up" in the merit necessary to be judged approvingly in the eyes of God.[30]

It was within this competitive spiritual culture that a corresponding understanding of eschatology coalesced, and the belief in a post-mortem intermediate state was formally codified, as discussed in the previous chapter. However, through the renewal brought about by the Second Vatican Council, a new culture emerged, which Thiel refers to as the spiritually noncompetitive "Pauline" style of faith. If the Matthean style of faith is characterized by the belief that there is a standard of holiness that must be achieved, and that one's personal actions will be judged against it alongside others, who may also have lived a more virtuous life, the Pauline style of faith is marked primarily by an understanding that, due to the universality of sin, its inevitable—if not enduring—presence in every person's life makes it impossible for any individual to favorably measure themselves against any conceivable standard of faith. As Thiel points out, the Pauline style of faith is characterized by the basic recognition that "all human deeds are wanting. Sin seeps so deeply into every natural act that there is no natural virtue."[31]

---

28. Thiel, *Icons of Hope*, 66.
29. Thiel, *Icons of Hope*, 67.
30. Thiel, *Icons of Hope*, 67.
31. Thiel, *Icons of Hope*, 67.

Thus, while "the Matthean style of faith presupposes the believer's active responsibility before real alternatives in eternal destiny," believers according to the Pauline style of faith "understand their acts of discipleship to be energized by the grace of Christ."[32] By affirming the equalizing force of God's grace upon a universally fallen humanity, the notion of a competitive spirituality vanishes, as any sense of personal merit derived from certain deeds becomes supplanted by a basic trust in the grace of God. And it is though this grace that the institutional structures that facilitated the awarding of merit within a hierarchical understanding of discipleship are undermined. Indeed, after earlier noting *Lumen gentium*'s exhortations on the universal call to holiness and the common priesthood of all the faithful as a challenge for all members of the Catholic Church "to reimagine the meaning of the traditional notion of the hierarchy of discipleship in a way that accentuated the baptismal vocation of all believers,"[33] Thiel goes on to claim: "Without competition among believers for a favourable divine judgment, all the dynamics of the hierarchy of discipleship dissolve away, and with them some of the typical forms of belief and practice that have flourished through Catholic history."[34]

A strong sense of the universality of God's grace will seriously test any hierarchical understanding of how that grace can be received. This was one of the principal challenges experienced and addressed by the Second Vatican Council as it guided the Catholic Church from a predominantly Matthean to a predominantly Pauline religious and spiritual culture, and its ongoing response to this challenge continues to have ramifications upon how it understands itself in the world today. Yet these ramifications extended beyond identity and organization. Indeed, that challenge would also extend to specific teachings, such as those on eschatology which, as we have already seen, has led to an understanding of the afterlife that has situated the significance of individual action and judgment within the context of a communal eschatological experience shared by all. And in particular, it extended toward the doctrine of purgatory, which, as we have seen, was itself largely codified according to the Matthean style of faith. Thus, as both the availability of God's grace and the social dimensions of salvation were once again given prominence within contemporary eschatological consideration, the particular salvific value of purgatory as a place where one can spiritually make amends through intense punishments that have been judged appropriate according to the detailed accounting of personal virtue and sin

---

32. Thiel, *Icons of Hope*, 67.
33. Thiel, *Icons of Hope*, 100.
34. Thiel, *Icons of Hope*, 103.

as found within a Tridentine system of merit rapidly became anachronistic within the larger contemporary eschatological system.

Thiel thus concludes that unless deliberate effort is made to harmonize the doctrine of purgatory with a Pauline style of faith, its descent into irrelevancy becomes the inevitable outcome. Thiel has pointed out that when present, the Pauline style of faith (elements of which he claims can also be found in the emergence of the Protestant theological tradition) has led to a virtual disappearance of belief in purgatory: "If Reformation sensibilities teach the formal lesson that purgatory disappears where strong grace prevails, then perhaps we have some direction for understanding the remarkable loss of belief in purgatory since Vatican II."[35] History seems to have demonstrated the factual merits of Thiel's theory, as almost no mainstream Protestant church formally holds to the doctrine of purgatory.[36] Yet, as Thiel mentions above, this has increasingly been the case within Catholicism as well, resulting in a certain confusion over the doctrine's theological content and status, as well as its decline in popularity amongst the lay faithful.[37]

After this brief survey of how the doctrine of purgatory both entered into and emerged from the Second Vatican Council, it can be concluded that the doctrine began its decline in spiritual relevance amongst the lay faithful once the noncompetitive Pauline faith came to replace the competitive Matthean faith as the predominant spiritual culture within the Catholic Church. And while purgatory was briefly mentioned in light of the theological cultural shift brought about by the Council, such a shift was not reflected in any doctrinal reforms or theological documents that followed. Thus, while the theological culture of the Catholic Church continued along according to the religious and spiritual culture conditioned by a Pauline style of faith, the spiritual and theological content of the doctrine of purgatory remained unaffected by these developments, thus creating a disconnect between itself and the religious sensibilities of the contemporary lay faithful. To a certain extent, this disconnect continues into the present day, where only recently Catholic theologians have begun to reexamine the doctrine and offer fresh perspectives regarding its role and function in an attempt to recover some of the theological and spiritual significance that it previously held.

---

35. Thiel, *Icons of Hope*, 99.

36. Although there are notable exceptions. These will be discussed at greater length in chapter 5 of this book.

37. Thiel, *Icons of Hope*, 100–101. See also Pasulka, *Heaven Can Wait*, 3; Egan, "In Purgatory," 882–83.

CONTEMPORARY CATHOLIC EXPRESSIONS OF THE DOCTRINE OF PURGATORY

In its brief section on purgatory, the *Catechism of the Catholic Church* offers this sparse description: "All who die in God's grace and friendship, but still imperfectly purified, are indeed assured of their eternal salvation; but after death they undergo purification, so as to achieve the holiness necessary to enter the joy of heaven. The Church gives the name of *Purgatory* to this final purification of the elect, which is entirely different from the punishment of the damned."[38] Gone are any allusions to such concepts as debt, merit, and satisfaction. The word "punishment" is never used. Instead, the editors settled upon "purification" as the term used to describe the process of purgatory. How is it that a doctrine that was once never short on details regarding its particularities has now been reduced to a few lines on a single page of the *Catechism*? And within those lines, what sort of understanding (or understandings) of purgatory has been drawn out and offered for consideration? By examining the recent history of the doctrine, it will become clear that in spite of a continuing general ambivalence, confusion, and even hostility toward the doctrine, efforts have been made by certain groups and individuals to reexamine purgatory's theological and pastoral role and function in light of the theological trends that had emerged from the Second Vatican Council; however, as we shall see, it remains unclear as to whether these attempts have succeeded, or are succeeding, in making the doctrine more compatible with Catholicism's emerging Pauline spiritual culture.

Documents Issued from the Vatican

Amidst the great upheaval that followed in the wake of the Second Vatican Council, the fact of purgatory's precipitous decline in significance regarding its role and function within the spiritual lives of the lay faithful has been largely overlooked. Often overshadowed by the more dramatic changes effected by the Council, purgatory's decline has been largely unheralded, apparently being borne out through a quiet—almost indifferent—rejection, resulting in its present obscure existence, and more often than not viewed by large segments of the lay faithful with a certain confusion regarding its present place within Catholic theology, if not their personal spiritual lives.

As already mentioned, the reason for the disconnect between this particular doctrine and its place within the spiritual lives of contemporary Catholics can be attributed to a remaining incongruity between the

---

38. Catholic Church, *Catechism of the Catholic Church*, #1020–31.

particular teachings of the doctrine itself and the overall theological atmosphere that emerged from the Council. An early example of how the doctrine of purgatory was formally taught within the post-conciliar Catholic Church is Pope Paul VI's Apostolic Constitution, *Indulgentiarum Doctrina*. Returning to the notion of the Catholic Church's self-understanding as the storehouse of merit accumulated through Christ's sacrifice on the cross (as well as from all of the good works performed by the saints) and distributor of that merit according to its understanding that it has been given the power to "bind and loose" sins and their effects by Christ, this document offers direction on how these powers are to be exercised. Accordingly, the application of these spiritual reserves to help lessen the duration and intensity of the suffering associated with the purification of a forgiven sin's secondary effects—to take place either in this life or in purgatory—is known as an *indulgence*, which a person can obtain on one's own behalf through pious acts and works, or, through the spiritual bonds found in the communion of saints, on behalf of a deceased acquaintance.

After operating for many centuries within Catholicism's complex merit system, indulgences attracted the ire of the church Reformers, who took issue with the Catholic Church's presumed authority to intervene on such matters.[39] Moreover, abuses over their outright sale, and doubts over their assumption that purgatorial temporality could be measured in exact time (purgatorial remittances, for example, were offered in years and months) served to undermine the spiritual legitimacy of indulgences. In response to some of these lingering concerns, *Indulgentiarum Doctrina* was promulgated in 1967 and was intended to reform the way in which indulgences, and, indirectly, penances were to be understood. Following *Lumen gentium*'s example, *Indulgentiarum Doctrina* also offers less pointed speculation regarding the mechanics of the afterlife, and a more robust emphasis of the doctrine's communal dynamics; however, it would appear that the document did not affect a serious reexamination of purgatory's role and function. While *Indulgentiarum Doctrina* officially redefined the way in which indulgences were understood to be effective in light of a less literal understanding of how time was conceived to pass in purgatory,[40] the language employed to describe the

---

39. Beer, "What Price Indulgences?," 528.

40. See Paul VI, *Indulgentiarum Doctrina*, #12. This understanding of purgatorial time was later confirmed and elaborated upon by Pope Benedict XVI, who writes that "it is clear that we cannot calculate the 'duration' of this transforming burning [of purgatory] in terms of the chronological measurements of the world. The transforming 'moment' of this encounter eludes earthly time-reckoning—it is the heart's time, it is the time of 'passage' to communion with God in the body of Christ" (Benedict XVI, *Spe Salvi*, #47).

overall purpose for an indulgence remained the same: "The remission of the temporal punishment due for sins already forgiven insofar as their guilt is concerned . . . ."[41] Indeed, terms found very often in pre-conciliar teachings on purgatory, such as "justice," "expiation," and "punishment" remain peppered throughout the document,[42] inviting the conclusion that purgatory's main function seemingly remained as primarily a place of punishment for any lingering consequences of a person's sinful actions.

Yet it would seem that as the post-conciliar church continued to progress through the twentieth century, statements and documents upholding such an understanding were no longer issued, leaving the doctrine of purgatory, as it has been traditionally understood, to be either rejected or ignored by large segments of the lay faithful. Such attitudes would continue to grow, often leading to confusion regarding to what was actually taught concerning death and the afterlife.[43] This in turn prompted a number of reports that have attempted to clarify the question, with the most significant being the Congregation for the Doctrine of the Faith's (the Vatican department responsible for upholding Roman Catholic doctrine) "Letter on Certain Questions Concerning Eschatology," issued in 1979, and the International Theological Commission's "Some Current Questions in Eschatology" in 1992.

Acknowledging concern over the present state of eschatological awareness amongst the Catholic faithful, the Congregation's "Letter" laments that due to "the unintentional effect on people's minds of theological controversies given wide publicity today, the precise subject and the significance of which is beyond the discernment of the majority of the faithful," it has indeed become commonplace to encounter "discussions about the existence of the soul and the meaning of life after death, and the question is put of what happens between the death of the Christian and the general resurrection. All this disturbs the faithful, since they no longer find the vocabulary they are used to and their familiar ideas."[44] In response, the document would go on to affirm prayers, funeral rites, and religious acts offered for the dead,

---

41. Paul VI, *Indulgentiarum Doctrina*, #8.

42. See Paul VI, *Indulgentiarum Doctrina*, #3.

43. Wryly commenting on the state of confusion regarding official Catholic teaching on the doctrine, famed theologian Karl Rahner, writing in the style of two theologians in conversation, offers the following fictitious exchange: "A short time ago, one theologian said to another, 'The pope insisted again yesterday on the traditional doctrine of purgatory.' The other replied, 'I've nothing against that. But if I only knew what exactly I am supposed to believe in this respect! Do you know? Can you look into the pope's mind to see what he was thinking? I can't . . .'" (Rahner, "Purgatory," 181).

44. Congregation for the Doctrine of the Faith, "Letter on Certain Questions."

declaring them *loci theologici* (that is, as sources for theological knowledge), perhaps its greater significance lies in its brief definition of purgatory as "the possibility of a purification for the elect before they see God, a purification altogether different from the punishment of the damned."[45] This definition, markedly similar to that found in the *Catechism of the Catholic Church*, succeeds at maintaining purgatory's essential role, while nevertheless refraining from employing traditional a vocabulary of satisfaction and expiation. Moreover, it explicitly states that the purgatorial state is entirely different than the state of the damned; a distinction that historically was not always clear in the often-terrifying descriptions of the purgatorial experience that would usually tend toward the infernal.

The above definition, on the other hand, is undeniably minimal and refrains from indulging in detail. Indeed, any impulse to do so is strongly warned against later on in the document: "When dealing with man's situation after death, one must especially beware of arbitrary imaginative representations: excess of this kind is a major cause of the difficulties that Christian faith often encounters."[46] Thus, while suggesting no major doctrinal change to the doctrine of purgatory, this document's significance lies in the fact that it offered the beginnings of a shift in understanding how purgatory might be understood to function in its traditionally defined role, one that seemed to highlight a function beyond mere divine satisfaction.

This same approach toward the doctrine continued in 1992's "Some Current Questions in Eschatology." While it would comprehensively uphold the traditional Catholic teachings on the question of eschatology and all of its constituent components, and with regard to the doctrine of purgatory would once again reiterate the Catholic Church's traditional teachings on its basic role, it also notably refrains from ascribing a detailed explanation regarding how purgatory functions in that role:

> The Church also holds that any stain is an impediment when it comes to our intimate meeting with God and Christ. This principle is not concerned only with stains which break or destroy friendship with God and which, therefore, should they persist in death, make a meeting with God definitively impossible (grave sins), but also with those which darken such a friendship and require a prior purification, so as to make possible such meeting with God and Christ. To this class belong the so-called 'daily sins,' which we call venial, and also those remains of sin which

---

45. Congregation for the Doctrine of the Faith, "Letter on Certain Questions."
46. Congregation for the Doctrine of the Faith, "Letter on Certain Questions."

persist in the justified when guilt has been remitted and its attendant eternal punishment.[47]

The traditional theological purpose of the doctrine is once again made clear; yet much like the previous document, it would seem that "Some Questions in Current Eschatology" continues to distance the intention behind that purpose away from the previous overly juridical understanding of God and sin. Instead, what is offered is a more relational understanding of the residual effects of sin and yet another admonition against a too close association between the purgatorial process and the punishment of the damned. As the document states, "It is categorically important to avoid any too close assimilation of the purificatory process which precedes our meeting with God with the process of damnation, as if all that lay between them was the opposition of eternal and temporal. . . . In fact, a state whose centre is love, and another, whose centre is hate, cannot be compared. The justified are alive in the love of Christ. Death strengthens the consciousness of such a love."[48]

Although remaining doctrinally unchanged, these above two documents seem to confirm an official change in attitude toward understanding purgatory's function, in describing (at least tacitly) the process that takes place as one of purification instead of punishment and divine satisfaction. However, this is never explicitly stated; again, while these documents do indeed offer some clear direction on certain issues, they also arguably reflect the post-conciliar hierarchy's restraint with regard to offering detailed pronouncements on particular eschatological questions. And in so doing, a certain theological space has been opened, allowing individual theologians to reflect upon some of the details and offer their own perspectives. While some perhaps believe that this space—and the parameters provided—continue to remain too constrictive,[49] it nevertheless has allowed for a relatively minor renewed theological interest in the doctrine of purgatory throughout the latter half of the twentieth century. This interest has been shown by certain theologians, both Protestant and Catholic, and even recent popes, who have offered their own opinions on the meaning, function, and process of purgatory.

---

47. International Theological Commission, "Some Current Questions," 8.1.
48. International Theological Commission, "Some Current Questions," 8.2.
49. See, for example, Phan, "Contemporary Context and Issues," 532–36.

Papal Pronouncements

Although the occasions when Pope John Paul II offered personal commentary on the doctrine of purgatory were rather rare, the opinions that he voiced were nevertheless influential. He chose to frame his understanding of purgatory upon the integrity of the human person and its union with God, wherein purgatory is to serve as a place where that integrity can be restored if found wanting.[50] However, what was perhaps most striking about his observations was his statement that purgatory should no longer be understood as an actual place, but rather as a spiritual state of being:

> Every trace of attachment to evil must be eliminated, every imperfection of the soul corrected. Purification must be complete, and indeed this is precisely what is meant by the Church's teaching on purgatory. The term does not indicate a place, but a condition of existence. Those who, after death, exist in a state of purification, are already in the love of Christ who removes from them the remnants of imperfection.[51]

With this statement, John Paul II indirectly called into serious question the materialistic conception of purgatory, an integral component of its previous, pre-conciliar understanding. He would also go on to stress the communal themes highlighted by the Second Vatican Council, in which purgatory's place within the Mystical Body of Christ was emphasized, as well as the beneficial qualities of intercessory prayer from other members within that body.[52] In so doing, John Paul II seemingly endorsed the theological tone with regard to purgatory set by Vatican II, which only served to further marginalize its pre-conciliar understanding.

Perhaps the pope who worked the most toward finding a thoroughly post-conciliar understanding of the doctrine of purgatory was Pope Benedict XVI. Throughout his theological career, Benedict has often written on purgatory and its place within the tradition of the contemporary Catholic Church. Upon reading his reflections on the doctrine, what is perhaps most striking of Benedict is his understanding of who might actually be populating the intermediate state: "For the great majority of people—we may suppose—there remains in the depths of their being an ultimate interior openness to truth, to love, to God. In the concrete choices of life, however, it is covered over by ever new compromises with evil—much filth covers purity, but the thirst for purity remains, and it still constantly reemerges

---

50. John Paul II, "General Audience," #2.
51. John Paul II, "General Audience," #4.
52. John Paul II, "General Audience," #6.

from all that is base and remains present in the soul."[53] Such a generous understanding could not have been possible in the pre-conciliar conception of purgatory, one in which simple church membership was the first requirement for salvation. But in spite of such innovation, Benedict remains at pains to find harmony between securely establishing a place for the doctrine within a contemporary Catholic theology of the afterlife and maintaining fidelity to its longstanding theological tradition. As such, within his writings, one consistently finds two important and interconnected thoughts: an understanding of purgatory as a balance between divine justice and mercy, as well as an insistence upon the interconnectedness of humanity and its relationship to the intermediate state.

Benedict is in basic agreement with the "opinion" (a word that carries with it an implicit acknowledgment for the need for restraint regarding eschatological speculation) that purgatory is essentially an eschatological encounter with Christ himself, as Judge and Savior, whose gaze is experienced as a "fire which both burns and saves," which in turn melts away "all falsehood" that has been built up around each individual.[54] Elaborating further, Benedict writes that God's judgment can at the same time be thought of as hope, "both because it is justice and because it is grace. If it were merely grace, making all earthly things cease to matter, God would still owe us an answer to the question about justice—the crucial question that we ask of history and of God. If it were merely justice, in the end it could bring only fear to us as well."[55] By "grace," Benedict understands purgatory as an example of God's universal desire to save (as evidenced by the passages above), in which an individual will experience the "purification and healing" that will "mature the soul for communion with God."[56] But by "justice," Benedict refrains from using the concepts that marked the pre-conciliar understanding of purgatory. In this case, justice is not understood as either exacting compensation or meting out an equivalent punishment from an individual for past committed sins; instead, he understands it to mean the corresponding consequences for certain actions and attitudes that are in need of transformation. Throughout,

---

53. Benedict XVI, *Spe Salvi*, #46. Earlier in his career, writing as Cardinal Ratzinger, the same point was made, with emphasis placed upon the person's fundamental decision (or not) toward God, and how that decision might not be immediately evident in every person: "What actually saves is the full assent of faith. But in most of us, that basic option is buried under a great deal of wood, hay and straw. Only with difficulty can it peer out from behind the latticework of an egoism we are powerless to pull down with our own hands" (Ratzinger, *Eschatology*, 231).

54. Benedict XVI, *Spe Salvi*, #47.

55. Benedict XVI, *Spe Salvi*, #47.

56. Benedict XVI, *Spe Salvi*, #45.

the notions of transformation and purification pervade Benedict's thoughts, and in such an understanding, justice becomes the catalyst for purification, not something operating opposed or mutually exclusive to it: "The encounter with [Christ] is the decisive act of judgment. Before his gaze all falsehood melts away. This encounter with him, as it burns us, transforms and frees us, allowing us to become truly ourselves."[57]

Influenced perhaps by the relational eschatological emphasis found in the conciliar documents, Benedict's understanding of justice is also tempered by a strong sense of human interconnectedness, through which we are judged not strictly as individuals, but as a part of a broader societal whole, fully present in human history. Despite the best efforts of the Second Vatican Council, Pope Benedict laments a creeping individualism that continues to infiltrate modern religious thought.[58] Yet if a person is to receive the fairest possible judgment, he believes that the widest possible perspective must be cast, which will necessarily take into account the full effect that they have had upon their broader community, indeed, the entire Body of Christ—something which cannot be fully appreciated until the end of history:

> The being of man is not, in fact, that of a closed monad. It is related to others by love or hate, and, in these ways, has its colonies within them. My own being I present in others as guilt or as grace. We are not just ourselves; or, more correctly, we are ourselves only as being in others, with others and through others. Whether others curse us or bless us, forgive us and turn our guilt into love—this is part of our own destiny. The fact that the saints will judge means that encounter with Christ is encounter with his whole body. I come face to face with my own guilt vis-a-vis the suffering members of that body as well as with the forgiving love which the body derives from Christ its Head.[59]

Indeed, then-Cardinal Ratzinger almost appears to be at pains to emphasize how the communal dynamics that emerged as a central theme from the Second Vatican Council can be found to be present in purgatory's dynamics of purification. Thus, it is perhaps in the written corpus of Pope Benedict XVI that one finds perhaps the most comprehensive comments offered from either the Vatican or the papacy on purgatory's role and function within the eschatological understanding of the post-conciliar Catholic Church. Within Benedict's own understanding of the doctrine, the reader finds an emerging conception of purgatory that honors

---

57. Benedict XVI, *Spe Salvi*, #47.
58. Benedict XVI, *Spe Salvi*, #42.
59. Ratzinger, *Eschatology*, 232.

the renewed corporate emphasis placed upon it by the Second Vatican Council. Accordingly, it also appears that the doctrine may finally be in a position to engage the currents of contemporary theology; yet it remains to be seen what fruit this may bear, for by continuing to employ certain language and elements present in its traditional understanding, and allowing for ambiguity and nuance in other instances, these more recent documents may have, if anything, contributed to the overall sense of confusion around the status of this doctrine.[60] On the other hand, it has already been mentioned that these more recent developments have also allowed a small number of contemporary theologians to follow the recent signals made by the Vatican and the papacy to further explore the theological implications of these said developments. Digging into Catholicism's more mystical tradition, new understandings of purgatory appear to be emerging—understandings which seem more intent to emphasize its purifying dynamics as something akin to a process of personal sanctification.

Contemporary Theological Perspectives

In their more recent statements regarding the doctrine of purgatory, both the Vatican and the papacy have reaffirmed its place within the Catholic Church's theological tradition, yet at the same time have also fostered an understanding that has been couched less in the excessive legalism and speculation of the past. Instead, by offering some clear theological guidelines, and at the same time actually offering less speculation upon the manner by which purgatory must be understood, a certain opening has emerged, in which theologians have become able to offer their own thoughts regarding the role and mechanics of purgatory, which has ranged from cautious skepticism to enthusiastic innovation.

Perhaps the most famous skeptic has been Karl Rahner, whose perspective on purgatory changed throughout his theological career. Reflecting on the doctrine, Rahner writes that "it is by no means certain that the doctrine about the intermediate state is anything more than an intellectual framework, or way of thinking. So whatever it has to tell us . . . does not necessarily have to be part of Christian eschatology itself."[61] Initially, Rahner

---

60. This point has indirectly been made by Rahner, who invites the reader to reflect upon "the ideas of purgatory formerly implied in declarations about the extent of 'temporal punishment' remitted by indulgences: the kind of declarations which the Church today somewhat shamefacedly almost completely avoids" (Rahner, "Purgatory," 181–82).

61. Rahner, "Intermediate State," 115.

subscribed to a theory that he referred to as the "pancosmicity" of the soul. This theory rests upon the key concept that the soul, by its very existence informs material reality: "for the soul's own substantial existence is, so to speak, grafted upon the material reality, so that the act of informing matter is not really distinct from the existence of the soul."[62] Although matter is often associated with just the human body, Rahner relies upon Thomistic metaphysics to propose a broader understanding:

> The human spiritual soul has a transcendental (that is, already given with the very essence of the soul) relationship to matter, a relationship which endures even after death. One has only to accept this doctrine in full and to interpret "matter" in a more exact, ontological sense (rather than merely as indicating the concrete, measurable shape of the body), to recognize that the view here proposed is already contained in the strictly Thomistic and traditional doctrine.[63]

Thus, while the human soul does possess an essential relationship to the material body, it is through that relationship that the soul is essentially open to the world and in intimate communication with it.[64] Yet Rahner would then go on to question whether a post-mortem soul that is "separated" from the body is also separated from the material world, rendering it a-cosmic, or whether, no longer encumbered by material constraints after death, the soul can somehow relate even more intimately with the material whole, so as to become "pancosmic" (*allkosmisch*).[65] Rahner would at that time side with the latter theory, offering the following conclusion:

> Such a relationship of the soul to the world . . . might imply that the soul, by surrendering her limited bodily structure in death, becomes open towards the "all" and, in some way, a co-determining factor of the universe precisely in its character as the ground for the personal life of other spiritual-corporeal beings. We know as a doctrine of faith that the moral quality of each individual human life, when consummated before God, becomes "co-responsible" for his attitude towards the world and towards all other individuals; in a somewhat similar sense, the individual person, once rendered all-cosmic through death and no longer restricted by the limits of our present life, might come to have,

---

62. Rahner, *On the Theology of Death*, 28.
63. Rahner, *On the Theology of Death*, 28–29.
64. Rahner, *On the Theology of Death*, 30.
65. Phan, *Eternity in Time*, 85.

through the actions performed in this world, a real ontological influence on the whole universe.[66]

While this was Rahner's initial understanding of the intermediate state, he would later come to the conclusion that "no one is in danger of defending a heresy if he maintains the view that the single and total perfecting of man in 'body' and 'soul' takes place immediately after death; that the resurrection of the flesh and the general judgement take place 'parallel' to the temporal history of the world; and that both coincide with the sum of the particular judgments of individual men and women."[67] In other words, the particular judgment of an individual and the last judgment are to happen concomitantly, thereby rendering the idea that there is a period of time in-between (an intermediate state) superfluous. Commenting sympathetically upon Rahner's latter perspective, Peter Phan writes: "What is being taught as Christian truths is the perfecting or condemnation of the soul immediately after death and the glorification of the body. Hence, if there is a way of maintaining these truths in their fulness without thereby postulating the doctrine of the intermediate state . . . then clearly this doctrine is nothing more than an amalgam; in other words, it is something said but not meant."[68]

While Rahner may have been among the most notable skeptics over the theological status of the doctrine, there also arose a number of advocates. And among those defenders, one constant theme has emerged: an eschewing of the strident pre-conciliar language of punishment and satisfaction. Referring to the controversy that has emerged, Dermot A. Lane offers his own summation of the critical issues and poses the following question:

> For many the doctrine of Purgatory has lost credibility. The language of "punishment due to sin" and making satisfaction for sin, and of souls suffering for a period of time, sounds to many quite anachronistic. . . . Above all, the image of God portrayed by this language seems to contradict the revelation of the love of God in the life, death and resurrection of Jesus. In a word, the question must be asked: Is the doctrine of Purgatory worth retrieving or can it not be quietly forgotten about?[69]

In response, Lane answers that purgatory is indeed worth retrieving, and he, along with a number of other theologians, have endeavored to take advantage of the opportunity created by recent Vatican and papal documents and

---

66. Rahner, *On the Theology of Death*, 31.
67. Rahner, "Intermediate State," 115.
68. Phan, *Eternity in Time*, 117.
69. Lane, *Keeping Hope Alive*, 146.

begun to frame purgatory according to concepts such as relationship, purification, moral growth, and, ultimately, sanctification. Thus, Lane declares that "purgatory, therefore, is about finalising a process, or better, completing the divine-human relationship already decisively initiated by God in this life through grace and only gradually accepted from a human point of view in this life."[70] This sentiment is echoed by Harvey D. Egan, who writes that "abandoning a legalistic view of purgatory as a place of torture located between heaven and earth in favour of understanding purgatory as an encounter with Jesus Christ, or God, or the Holy Spirit and the mystical body and the cosmos that purifies and transforms the multidimensional social person that we are has many advantages."[71]

While the understanding espoused in the above statements is certainly a departure from the formal pronouncements issued from within the pre-conciliar tradition, it is not entirely novel in its claims. Indeed, as many modern theologians have pointed out in their own respective arguments for a sanctification-based conception of purgatory, one of the first postulators for an understanding of purgatory was Saint Catherine of Genoa (1447–1510 CE), who, in her brief treatise on the subject, strongly argued (against the prevailing theological current of the time) that the main purpose of purgatory was to sanctify—and not punish—the person, through which they may achieve the perfection necessary for entry into heaven. Catherine was first and foremost a mystic, and her vision of purgatory was undeniably formed by her own personal experience of God's love.[72] Choosing to ignore the infernal imagery associated with purgatory that would have been common during her life, Catherine instead writes that "there is no joy save that in paradise to be compared to the joy of the souls in purgatory. This joy increases day by day because of the way in which the love of God corresponds to that of the soul, since the impediment to that love is worn away daily. This impediment is the rust of sin."[73]

Yet Catherine is quick to point out that this process will not be an altogether pleasant experience; pain is inevitable. But the more one remains exposed to God's love, all resistance toward God is eventually broken down; and in this case, the pain one experiences does not derive from the pain inflicted by the suffering itself, but rather from an increased awareness of self and the lingering resistances that continue to hold one back from the

70. Lane, *Keeping Hope Alive*, 147.

71. Egan, "In Purgatory," 888.

72. Egan, "In Purgatory," 876.

73. Catherine of Genoa, *Purgation and Purgatory*, 72. Commenting upon this passage, Harvey Egan declares it "one of the most creative insights in the Christian tradition concerning purgatory" (Egan, "In Purgatory," 877).

total love of God. Thus, while a person's joy may increase, so too does their sorrow, for, according to Catherine, "when a soul is close to its first creation, pure and unstained, the instinct for beatitude asserts itself with such impetus and fiery charity that any impediment becomes unbearable. The more the soul is aware of that impediment, the greater its suffering."[74]

In Catherine of Genoa, one finds an understanding of purgatory that was clearly original in her time,[75] but an understanding that remained essentially forgotten or ignored until only recently. With purgatory's theological and cultural tradition established by the time of her writing, Catherine's insights would have challenged that tradition, and for that reason were largely ignored, if not outright rejected. Yet it would be these very insights that will go on to serve as a template for later twentieth century interpretations of the doctrine. Her basic insight that purgatory is where a person grows in perfect holiness as the residue of their sins is burned away by God's merciful, sanctifying, love does not reinvent purgatory's eschatological role, but decisively recasts the emphasized intentionality behind its established purpose. In other words, she re-imagines how purgatory is thought to function within its eschatological role, and this has effectively become the underlying premise for almost all modern theological reflection on the doctrine. Through the contribution of Catherine, the purgatorial pain previously understood as simply the consequential punishment for sin now finds a grounding within the tradition by modern theologians who understand it as something more of a by-product that arises through the washing away of the residue of sin in the process of sanctification. In the following comments offered by Dermot Lane on purgatorial pain, one can find strong parallels between his and Catherine's (as well as Pope Benedict XVI's) respective opinions:

> The temporal punishment due to sin, insofar as one can talk like this, derives not from God but from sin itself; it is a consequence flowing from the reality of sin. In turning back to God after sin, there will remain within the human personality some of the after-effects of sin: the inner contradiction embedded in the different layers of human personality between being turned once again to God, and self-centred connections and traces of selfishness that remain after conversion. The fundamental decision for God is something that takes time to unfold, permeate and transform the whole personality.[76]

74. Catherine of Genoa, *Purgation and Purgatory*, 73.
75. Benedict XVI, "General Audience," 2011.
76. Lane, *Keeping Hope Alive*, 147. See also, Egan, "In Purgatory," 884; John Paul II, "General Audience," #4; and also Pope Benedict, who writes that through God's gaze, "the touch of his heart has us through an undeniably painful transformation 'as through

As purgatory's theological understanding began to find new grounding within the tradition, certain aspects of the doctrine were correspondingly re-visited as well. Already mentioned were the reforms of *Indulgentiarum Doctrina*, through which the prayers and suffrages of the faithful were no longer understood to merely remove literal time from a person's purgatorial "sentence"; however, as purgatory's understanding evolved throughout the latter half of the twentieth century, a subsequent understanding regarding the way in which prayers and suffrages of the faithful were thought to be meritorious was disassociated from the idea of a reduction of punishment and came to be understood according to the new rubric of sanctification, thus further contributing to the coherent reengagement of the doctrine—a reengagement, it must be stressed, that includes contributions from the writings of the recent popes, which serve as a strong example for the degree to which certain individuals have been able to creatively reflect upon the developments found within the more recent church documents. From these writings, the following description eloquently offered by Pope Benedict XVI must especially be noted, both for its understanding on the utility of the prayers for the dead, but also as an overall statement on how the doctrine is theologically understood in the present day:

> Our lives are involved with one another; through innumerable interactions they are linked together. No one lives alone. No one sins alone. No one is saved alone. The lives of others continually spill into mine: in what I think, say, do and achieve. And conversely, my life spills over into that of others: for better and for worse . . . So my prayer for another is not something extraneous to that person, something external, not even after death. In the interconnectedness of Being, my gratitude to the other—my prayer for him—can play a small part in his purification. And for that there is no need to convert earthly time into God's time: in the communion of souls simple terrestrial time is superseded. It is never too late to touch the heart of another, nor is it ever in vain.[77]

---

fire'. But it is a blessed pain, in which the holy power of his love sears through us like a flame, enabling us to come totally ourselves and thus totally of God" (Benedict XVI, *Spe Salvi*, #47). Note how in the above passage Lane maintains the basic concept of Pope Benedict's understanding of purgatory, that is, as a place where an individual's "basic decision" toward God is revealed and perfected.

77. Benedict XVI, *Spe Salvi*, #48. See also these remarks from Pope John Paul II: "Just as in their earthly life believers are united in the one Mystical Body, so after death those who live in a state of purification experience the same ecclesial solidarity which works through prayer, prayers for suffrage and love for their other brothers and sisters in the faith. Purification is lived in the essential bond created between those who live in this world and those who enjoy eternal beatitude" (John Paul II, "General Audience," #5).

CONCLUSION—PRESENT STATUS AND MOVING FORWARD

Encapsulated in the description offered above are all of the themes of the modern understanding of purgatory accepted today within the Catholic Church. This is an understanding that is premised upon the concept of the Mystical Body of Christ, offered by Pope Pius XII in *Mystici Corporis Christi*; it strongly emphasizes a dynamic communal awareness espoused by the Second Vatican Council, and it also presumes Catherine of Genoa's more mystical conception of purgatory as a transforming encounter with God's love, toward which the prayers and suffrages of the faithful within the Body of Christ can contribute. Although purgatory's theological role remained essentially unchanged at the doctrinal level, a shift in how the residual effects of sin were understood to be purified has led to the emergence of an understanding of purgatory as a post-mortem opportunity for further sanctification that has gone on to take root within present theological reflection upon the subject. And herein lies the great irony, for while the post-conciliar history of purgatory has made considerable gains in bringing the doctrine back to its theological origins: as a place of eschatological optimism and hope that effectively broadens the path of the faithful to salvation, it continues to lack one essential element: broad assent by the faithful themselves.

Although purgatory has experienced a belated theological recovery, it has yet to regain the popular status it enjoyed before the Second Vatican Council. One reason for this must certainly stem from the fact that there continues to remain, in spite of the efforts of recent church officials and documents, much confusion regarding its actual place and role within the Catholic understanding of the afterlife, with "most contemporary Christians—both those who accept and those who reject purgatory," continuing to imagine it "as a demi-hell established by divine justice, a place between heaven and hell, where those who have died are punished for a length of time proportionate to the number and quality of the sins for which they have made insufficient reparation."[78] For this lingering confusion, it would seem that the church hierarchy bears some responsibility, for while taking pains to define certain theological essentials and parameters with regard to the doctrine, it neglected to offer a clear vision of its theological and pastoral purpose capable of capturing the imagination of the faithful. For in spite of the doctrine's theological evolution, it by consequence continues to be popularly conceived according to its decidedly unpopular pre-conciliar understanding, and for that same reason, remains largely neglected—despite the efforts of a dedicated few.

---

78. Egan, "In Purgatory," 882.

Clearly, therefore, while much advancement has been made, it appears to have not gone far enough to affect the doctrine's renewed relevance in the spiritual lives of the lay faithful. Effective instruction remains essential to be sure, but perhaps another reason for the faithful's continuing ambivalence might indeed go beyond a mere question of communication. Even with the theological advancements that have been made, there perhaps remains some work still to do in contributing to the doctrine's theological vision and bridging the gap of relevancy between it and the lay faithful.

In this pursuit, it seems that Dermot Lane offers a clue: "Any formulation of the eschatological question must take account of the presence of new pressures on eschatology. These include the existence of so much mass death in the Third World, the permanency of the nuclear threat, the ongoing ecological crisis, and a new awareness of the finiteness of our small blue planet."[79] If a sense of a competitive eschatological anxiety, as earlier formulated by Thiel, has dissipated since Vatican II, that is not to say that all forms of anxiety have disappeared along with it. Indeed, as Lane alludes to above, serious questions concerning personal security, human freedom, divine omniscience, and the problem of evil continue to preoccupy the minds of many of the faithful; and with our present ability to communicate and receive information, these pressures are perhaps more acutely felt now than ever before. These are the questions that have been traditionally explored within the theological category of *theodicy*—the attempt to affirm the goodness of God in the face of obvious evil. And just as any credible eschatology must address theodicy to some degree in its attempt to explain God's final victory over evil and consummation of all things, it therefore follows that as a constituent component of the Catholic eschatological system, any proposed vision of purgatory should also provide an account of theodicy in its formulations. Yet despite its more recent advances, the questions posed by theodicy remain largely unanswered in the Catholic vision of the doctrine, and it is precisely these questions that must be answered in order to persuasively argue for purgatory's relevance once again in the lives of the faithful.

The rest of this book will go about this task; yet in order to find some direction in how to proceed, one must surprisingly turn to proposed visions of purgatory that rest outside of the Catholic vision. For in the doctrine's most recent history it has been members of Protestant Christianity that have offered the most innovative and compelling visions of how its role and function might be understood. And while certain aspects of these visions may be theologically problematic from a Catholic perspective, they can nevertheless serve to inform further Catholic reflection.

---

79. Lane, *Keeping Hope Alive*, 7.

3

"Soul-Making" and the Western Theological Tradition

IN UNDERSTANDING HOW PURGATORY functions in its theological role of purifying the residual effects of sin, we have seen the prevailing understanding experience a shift away from a model that interprets those residuals as lingering injustices against God's divine majesty toward a model that interprets those residuals as something akin to wounds to a person's character and relationships, requiring divine mercy and grace to effect in personal growth through a process of sanctification. However, in spite of its present general theological understanding, the fruits of that shift have yet to make much headway in the ongoing reception of the doctrine by the lay faithful.[1] And although we have also seen new approaches to the doctrine undertaken since the Second Vatican Council, these have been limited both in number and effect; as such, serious ongoing reflection regarding the role and function of purgatory have remained largely absent from more recent theological discourse, and any momentum toward any sort of popular relevancy that had been gained in the last number of years has seemingly stalled.

The current dilemma that faces the health and vitality of the doctrine is twofold: (a) its lack of relevance in the lived spirituality of the contemporary lay faithful, and (b) its general creative stagnation amongst theologians and within the church hierarchy. However, there are reasons to believe that these challenges are not insurmountable. Compelling theological reflection yielding new insights on the role and function of purgatory has been taking place—and in fact continues to take place; however, its primary innovators,

1. Thiel, *Icons of Hope*, 100–101.

perhaps surprisingly, have not been operating out of the Roman Catholic theological tradition. Indeed, recent contributions toward more contemporary expressions of how a post-mortem intermediate state between bodily death and final beatitude might possibly be understood have been offered by a growing number of non-Catholic Christians.[2] They have done so by exploring its potential relevance to other theological questions, questions that perhaps have attracted more widespread and mainstream theological attention. In particular, the question of how—and in what ways—a post-mortem intermediate state is able to relate to contemporary discussions pertaining to the problem of theodicy sits on the cutting edge of work being done in this field. And although it must be said that purgatory has been understood as a part amongst other parts in these various responses to the question of theodicy, the role and function that purgatory serves in these responses has nevertheless been essential.

WHAT IS THEODICY?

Since its historical origins, theistic religion has attempted to explain how a supposedly loving and personal God could possibly allow for the continual existence of evil and suffering in the created world. The theological dilemma of maintaining the basic goodness of God in light of the depth and scope of human suffering and misery has been one of the enduring challenges of western religious faith, and the quest for a satisfactory explanation to this dilemma is what has come to be referred to as "theodicy." Over the centuries, numerous theodicies have been proposed, each uniquely tackling this problem by offering a particular explanation of how both the reality of evil and a benevolent God can simultaneously exist in the same universe. Of particular interest here is the understanding of theodicy as posited by John Hick, which has famously been described as a "soul-making" model of theodicy.

Although popularized by Hick as a theological term, the term "soul-making" was originally used by the poet John Keats in a letter to his brother and sister-in-law. In it, Keats writes, "The common cognomen of this world among the misguided and superstitions is 'a vale of tears' from which we are to be redeemed by a certain arbitrary interposition of God and taken to heaven—What a little circumscribed straightened notion! Call the world if

---

2. See, for example, Committee on Christian Faith of the United Church of Canada, *Life and Death*; Lewis, *Letters to Malcolm*, 107–11; Brown, "No Heaven without Purgatory," 447–56; Adams, *Horrendous Evils*, 161–68; Barnard, "Purgatory and the Dilemma of Sanctification," 311–30; and Walls. *Purgatory*, 142–52.

you Please 'The vale of Soul-making.'"³ Concisely, "soul-making" is the belief that the human person was created by God with the intention of achieving perfection through a process of moral and spiritual growth within creation, and that creation itself was designed for the purpose of abetting this growth. As such, God did not create the earth to be a static paradise, but rather as a dynamic environment that granted humanity the freedom to act, the freedom to learn, and hopefully, the freedom to attain moral, spiritual, and intellectual advancement. However, such freedom had its consequences: the possibility for sin, evil, and suffering to enter into the world through its misuse. And although Hick's vision of theodicy maintained that this would inevitably happen, it did not signal a decisive downfall of humanity, nor did it permanently halt its potential for growth; rather, it was included in God's plan of salvation and was used as a constructive means to further these divine ends. Within this context of soul-making, Hick compares the story of humanity's relationship with God to that of an infant with their parent/guardian: the child is nurtured and cared for, but allowed distance and time to mature into their own person; and while sometimes this path to maturity is not without its pitfalls and setbacks, these moments are forgiven by the parent, who will often use them as an opportunity to contribute to the child's overall maturity of character.⁴ Hick, accordingly understands the existence of evil (or at least its possibility) to have been present at the point of creation so as to enable the prospect of an authentic soul-making journey; moreover, he also makes the key point that certain instances of suffering and evil can indeed play a constructive role in a life of soul-making, and attempts to explain how and why God allows for its existence along such lines.

While Hick cites "justice" and "righteousness" as the traditional key characteristics of God that theodicy seeks to defend, it is clear that in his own understanding "love" becomes the principal characteristic of God to be defended, and by which every other divine characteristic is to be understood.⁵ Indeed, Hick's notion of limitless divine love will serve as the key hermeneutic lens through which he will develop his theodicy. It is what drives an understanding of soul-making that he believes both guarantees God's boundless love and also preserve authentic human freedom. It is also out of this understanding of God's love for creation that Hick critically posits a belief in what might be termed a "post-mortem intermediary state," that is, an opportunity after bodily death for a person to continue—and

3. Keats, *Letters of John Keats*, 334–35. Quoted in Hick, *Evil and the God of Love*, 259. Later in that same letter, Keats would write, "Do you not see . . . how necessary a World of Pains and troubles is to school an Intelligence and make it a Soul?"
4. Hick, *Evil and the God of Love*, 259.
5. See Hick, "Irenaean Theodicy," 63–68.

indeed conclude—their own personal development on the path toward perfection, given the apparent fact that so many persons do not fully—or even partially—experience soul-making's redemptive ideal in this lifetime.[6] Although there exist strong parallels between both concepts, Hick generally refrains from using the word "purgatory" to describe his own understanding of this post-mortem intermediate state, instead preferring, with reference to Charles A. Briggs, the term "progressive sanctification after death,"[7] or "intermediate state,"[8] or a "continued process of person-making in other environments beyond this world."[9]

Yet however Hick chooses to term such a post-mortem space, its defining characteristic has consistently been one of continued development, a process sustained and animated by God's grace, would include not just opportunities for further moral and spiritual growth, or opportunities for awareness of—and reformation for—past wrongs committed, but also, crucially, opportunities to find some sort of personally fulfilling resolution for any of the aforementioned pitfalls and setbacks—in other words, encounters with evil and suffering—experienced during the person's earthly life that still in some way remain unresolved. By framing his vision of a post-mortem intermediate state within a general theodical vision that emphasizes the soul-making quality of the human person, Hick has pioneered an understanding of a post-mortem intermediate state that is predicated upon the notion of a continued post-mortem process of sanctification that began during a person's earthly life and as such has gone on to become influential with a certain number of Christian theologians, from both the Catholic and Protestant traditions. Moreover, it can be argued that his insights can possibly provide much-needed breadth and depth to the sanctification-based understanding of the doctrine of purgatory within the Catholic context as well.

Although working outside the Catholic tradition himself, Hick's own vision of a post-mortem intermediate state captures many of the same theological themes that have guided purgatory's development toward a sanctification-based understanding during the latter-half of the twentieth century. Yet there may also exist the potential for Hick's vision to more directly enrich the doctrine's present sanctification-based themes by demonstrating how they might be further strengthened when they are integrated with soul-making's key anthropological, theodical, and eschatological insights. By looking at the doctrine through these lenses, Hick asks crucial questions

6. See Hick, "Irenaean Theodicy," 51–52, and *Evil and the God of Love*, 345–49.
7. Hick, *Evil and the God of Love*, 347.
8. Hick, *Evil and the God of Love*, 348.
9. Hick, "Irenaean Theodicy," 66.

regarding what a specific sanctification-based understanding of purgatory might actually entail when intentionally postulated as *an essential component* within a larger eschatological system. In our project of exploring how a belief in purgatory can continue to remain relevant in a contemporary Catholic understanding of the afterlife, it is the purpose of the following two sections to examine Hick's vision and explore in what ways it may be incorporated into a distinctly Catholic understanding of the doctrine. Yet before this can be done, it is important to understand the path that Hick took within the Christian theological tradition to arrive at such a vision, and to determine whether or not such a path is appropriate here.

IRENAEUS AND AUGUSTINE

In developing his soul-making theodicy, Hick largely drew inspiration from the writings of Irenaeus of Lyons. While his opinions on the possibility of an intermediate state have already been noted,[10] of particular interest to Hick was Irenaeus's anthropological understanding, that is, how the human person was created by God, and how sin and evil would arise in humanity, which he considered to be foundational to his own soul-making theodicy.

In order to assess not just the coherency of any theodical tradition, but also the possibility for further theological developments within that tradition, it is imperative to have a clear understanding of creation and human origins, as such an understanding will necessarily include both an account of the origins of evil and explain the nature of its relationship with humanity. In Irenaeus, Hick found an anthropology that struck him as naturally conducive to a soul-making understanding of theodicy and human development. It is perhaps important to briefly note that Hick did not believe that Irenaeus had developed his own explicit theodicy, only to be later rediscovered by himself; rather, he believed that Irenaeus built "a framework of thought within which a theodicy became possible which does not depend upon the idea of the fall, and which is consonant with modern knowledge concerning the origins of the human race."[11] When relating Irenaeus's understanding of humanity's origins to its ongoing existence, Hick declares that Irenaeus "sees our world of mingled good and evil as a divinely appointed environment for man's development towards the perfection that represents the fulfillment of God's good purpose for him," within which the human person was created by God imperfect and immature with the

---

10. See chapter 1 of this book.

11. Hick, "Irenaean Theodicy," 41. For this reason, Hick deems Irenaeus the "patron saint" of his own theological project.

purpose of navigating this world in order to gain moral and spiritual growth in order to finally be brought into the perfection intended by God.[12]

Believing this fundamental anthropological insight—and the particular tradition that it inhabits—to have been overlooked for far too long, Hick would go on to build his own notion of soul-making upon this Irenaean anthropological foundation, which he would further develop by contrasting it with what he considered to be the less-constructive understanding found within the dominant "Augustinian" anthropological tradition, which he claims can be traced back to the thought of Augustine of Hippo. Hick characterizes this principally as the belief that humanity was "created finitely perfect and then incomprehensibly destroyed [its] own perfection and plunged into sin and misery."[13] Criticizing Augustine for an approach to anthropology that he believed to be generally unfavorable to any understanding of theodicy that seeks to acknowledge the possible constructive, soul-making qualities of evil and suffering, Hick would go on to conclude that Augustine—and the overall theological tradition that his ideas would eventually inhabit—has had a negative influence over the historical culture of the Christian church (Hick would describe Augustine's ideas on theological anthropology and theodicy as the "majority report," maintaining that the Augustinian tradition has "dominated Western Christendom, both Catholic and Protestant"),[14] particularly with regard to its understanding of the human person, and subsequent relationship with sin.

But is such an interpretation entirely fair? Does the entire notion of soul-making—and the encouraging implications it may hold regarding our future discussion of sanctification-based understanding of purgatory—rest solely on Hick's particular interpretation of a so-called "Irenaean" understanding of the human person and its origins? And if so, what is to be done with the significant theological corpus within the Christian church's tradition that takes inspiration from Augustine and *his* much more widely held understanding of the human person and its origins? It must be remembered

---

12. Hick, *Evil and the God of Love*, 214–15.

13. Hick, *Evil and the God of Love*, 214. Indeed, it was this notion of humanity's supposed prelapsarian "perfection" that would remain one of Hick's principal criticisms of Augustine's understanding of human origins (Hick, *Evil and the God of Love*, 69).

14. See Hick, *Evil and the God of Love*, 253. This opinion of Hick is shared by numerous theologians. See also Lane, *Keeping Hope Alive*, 162; Swinburne, *Providence and the Problem of Evil*, 38–41; Drever, "Redeeming Creation," 135. Finally, see Daryl P. Domning and Monika K. Hellwig, who make a point to contrast Augustine's supposedly more pessimistic understanding of human origins and nature with the decidedly more optimistic view of Irenaeus, "who after all stood closer to the Apostles in the chain of doctrinal transmission" (Domning and Hellwig, *Original Selfishness*, 156).

that, as demonstrated earlier,[15] Augustine's historical influence extends to the doctrine of purgatory, whose particular understanding of the human person and its ongoing relationship with sin have often been interpreted to supposedly support a satisfaction-based understanding of the doctrine. Must Augustine's contributions to theological anthropology and, subsequently, the doctrine of purgatory, be rejected outright as Hick suggests in order to systematically develop a more intentional and robust sanctification-based understanding of the doctrine? Must the doctrine be stripped entirely of its Augustinian heritage in order for it to be effectively reconstructed in a more Irenaean image, or can less drastic actions be taken to achieve the same effect? And if so, would it not be the case that such an exclusivist retrieval from Christianity's theological tradition might make it difficult to subsequently establish the very theological foundation needed upon which to incorporate Hick's important soul-making insights into a confessional Catholic understanding of purgatory?

By studying both Irenaeus and Augustine's respective understandings of human origins, and humanity's subsequent fall, it should become clear that this supposed issue may not be as problematic as Hick's especially dichotomous interpretation makes it out to be. For while there exist some important qualities unique to Irenaeus regarding language, emphasis and tone, there in fact exist a number of fundamental parallels between both individuals. By looking first at Irenaeus's anthropological insights, followed by those of Augustine, it should become apparent that Augustine need not be Irenaeus's theological foil, and one need not entirely exclude the ideas of Augustine in order to reap the benefits of Hick's soul-making insights into how purgatory's role and function might be understood within a theological context outside of his own. For by demonstrating that the so-called "Augustinian tradition" may also inform the development of a sanctification-based understanding of purgatory, it would show that an enhanced, sanctification-based understanding of purgatory can indeed be supported by a broader range of sources within the Christian theological tradition, and not just from an isolated element. Thus, by drawing from a greater breadth of the tradition, and by not necessarily privileging one voice within it over and against the other, the overall argument for an augmented sanctification-based, soul-making understanding of purgatory will only be strengthened.

---

15. Please see chapter 1 of this book for a more detailed description of Augustine's specific contributions to the theological development of the doctrine of purgatory.

IRENAEUS OF LYONS

According to Christopher Bounds, creation's "perfection" is the key concept that guides Irenaeus's entire theological enterprise:

> Perfection is an all-encompassing soteriological rubric by which Irenaeus describes the creation of humanity, the Fall of Adam and Eve, Christ's redemptive work, the reception of the Holy Spirit, and humanity's final union with God. God has worked in the past and continues to labor in the present to bring His crowning achievement to perfection. As such, Irenaeus's conception of perfection encompasses the entirety of human history and is the focal idea around which his theological system coalesces.[16]

For Irenaeus, God predestined creation for perfection, of which humanity would hold the highest place. While accepting the historical reality of Adam as the first human person, Irenaeus understood Adam's significance at not only an individual level, but also, significantly, at a symbolic level as representative for all of humanity. Thus, while Irenaeus would write that Adam and Eve resembled God in both "formation" and "inspiration,"[17] which could also be understood as "image" and "likeness," he would have also maintained that God created all of humanity in God's own image and likeness for the purpose of growing and sharing in God's perfection.[18]

According to Irenaeus, Adam was created in possession of a certain "similitude" to God by virtue of his ability for rational free thought and action; moreover, if Adam used his powers of rational thought and personal freedom properly, that is, in obedience to God, he would then grow to the point where he would eventually attain the "likeness of God," which Mary Ann Donovan describes as the "incorruptibility that will be bestowed on human flesh when the divine economy reaches its fulfilment."[19] Irenaeus thus considered humanity to have existed in a prelapsarian state of ontological wholeness; yet because of its mutable created nature, humanity also lacked the same sort of perfection that could only be found in an uncreated, unchanging being, and therefore possessed further potential for continued growth in communion with God. Created things, writes Irenaeus, "must be inferior to Him who created them, from the very fact of their later origin; for it was not possible for things recently created to have been uncreated.

---

16. Bounds, "Irenaeus and the Doctrine of Perfection," 167.
17. Irenaeus, *On the Apostolic Preaching*, 46–47.
18. Bounds, "Irenaeus and the Doctrine of Perfection," 167.
19. Donovan, *One Right Reading?*, 136.

But inasmuch as they are not uncreated, for this very reason do they come short of the perfect."[20] Yet Irenaeus did not consider this lack of perfection to be understood as some sort of failing; rather, he interpreted it as an innocence that should be expected of something so newly created. Indeed, it was this emphasis upon the overall innocence of prelapsarian humanity, as well as the language he would employ in describing that innocence, that was perhaps most unique to Irenaeus, and would become significant in later theological interpretations of his thought:

> But created things must be inferior to Him who created them, from the very fact of their later origin; for it was not possible for things recently created to have been uncreated. But inasmuch as they are not uncreated, for this very reason do they come short of the perfect. *Because, as these things are of later date, so they are infantile; so are they unaccustomed to, and unexercised in, perfect discipline.*[21]

This point above is further elaborated upon by Donovan: "Some object that God could have saved an immense amount of bother by making all creatures perfect from the beginning. Irenaeus holds that they do not realize that the very meaning of 'creature' excludes this possibility. By definition a creature receives its beginning of existence from another, and so is inferior to its maker. The newly created (in a view quite typical of Irenaeus) are like little infants who are not used to exercising perfect conduct."[22] Indeed, Irenaeus understood these earliest humans to be, in a sense, like metaphorical children: created with a certain ontological wholeness, but also with the expectation to grow in spiritual and moral wisdom. And as spiritual "infants," they possessed a certain immaturity intrinsic to their created nature. They were created with the intention of growing in understanding of who they were, and of their special relationship with their Creator—and for that reason, their awareness of the fact that they were created in the image and likeness of God was obscured, to a certain extent, by their intellectual and spiritual immaturity. Donovan describes this state as something akin to the "innocence of childhood," and can be evidenced through Irenaeus's description of Adam as "a little one," and as "a child," in possession of an undeveloped sense of judgment.[23]

Yet while Irenaeus believed that humanity, as created beings, possessed an initial fragility and immaturity so as to render it incapable of

---

20. Irenaeus, *Against Heresies*, 4.38.1.
21. Irenaeus, *Against Heresies*, 4.38.1 (my emphasis).
22. Donovan, *One Right Reading?*, 132.
23. Donovan, *One Right Reading?*, 132.

immediately attaining a likeness of God, he maintained that humanity was also created with the ability for spiritual, intellectual, and moral growth in a manner commensurate with its developing maturity, thereby allowing it, with time, to transcend its initial immaturity so as to eventually attain actual likeness of God. Irenaeus further elaborates upon this point through the use of a rather striking metaphor: "For as it certainly is in the power of a mother to give strong food to her infant [but she does not do so], as the child is not yet able to receive more substantial nourishment; so also it was possible for God Himself to have made man perfect from the first, but man could not receive this [perfection], being as yet an infant."[24] Irenaeus envisioned the human being engaging in a process of becoming perfect, drawing incrementally closer to the uncreated and perfect God without ever forfeiting their identity as a human being. And for Irenaeus, it is in this way that a human being can become "like God," stating that "God . . . who both formed this world, fashioned man, and bestowed the faculty of increase on his own creation, and called him upwards from lesser things to those greater ones which are in His own presence, just as He brings an infant which has been conceived in the womb into the light of the sun."[25] This insight would later be expanded upon by Denis Minns, who describes Irenaeus's understanding of human moral, cognitive, and spiritual evolution as a distinct process of *Becoming*:

> [Irenaeus's] God cannot be reproached for not doing in the beginning what He does in the end. For the perfection of humankind is not a static thing, something that can be achieved once and for all. Humankind can never cease being created and therefore never cease to be in a process of Becoming, becoming more and more like the uncreated. Even if Adam had been created with the perfection he will attain in the Kingdom, he would still have continued to develop in the image and likeness of God.[26]

This idea of growth is perhaps one of the strongest characteristics of Irenaean anthropology, with Gustaf Wingren declaring that growth is not just a possibility for humanity but rather its necessary characteristic, and without it, humanity would cease to be what it naturally is.[27] However, humanity's capacity for constructive moral and spiritual growth would soon be seriously threatened through its own actions, leading to "the Fall."

---

24. Irenaeus, *Against Heresies*, 4.38.1.
25. Irenaeus, *Against Heresies*, 2.28.1.
26. Minns, *Irenaeus*, 74–75.
27. Wingren, *Man and the Incarnation*, 210.

Humanity's Fall

In the passage below, Christopher Bounds offers a very concise summary of an Irenaean interpretation of the events of humanity's fall:

> Irenaeus teaches that, before humanity's first parents could mature fully into the image and likeness of God, before they could realize ultimate perfection in the Garden of Eden, the Devil deceived them into defying God's law not to eat from the tree of knowledge. Their "fall" led to consequences far beyond their lives and initiated a history of human misery, sin, enslavement to the Devil and death. In this condition, humanity was powerless to change, impotent to bring about God's purpose for their lives—the perfection of the divine image and likeness.[28]

Yet within Irenaeus's thinking, it was also understood that humanity's initial disobedience was tempered by its aforementioned immaturity—precisely the sort of immaturity that one would expect from a child or adolescent. Minns would remark upon this Irenaean insight by adding that from its origins, the possibility for sin always existed for humanity, as the freedom to do so constituted an essential part of human nature according to the ends for which humanity was created by God; accordingly, such an abuse of its nascent freedom was foreseen, if not intended:

> Irenaeus does not allow the possibility that all human beings might, from the beginning, freely and always have chosen the good instead of evil. As he sees it, the only possibilities are a world in which human beings are free to choose between good and evil, and, because of their moral immaturity, do sometimes choose evil, or a world in which human beings have not power of choice between good and evil but are determined by a natural necessity to do good. Of these alternatives it is far better that human beings should achieve the good by freely choosing it and striving after it, rather than receiving it effortlessly and by necessity of nature.[29]

Thus we find in Irenaeus's understanding of the Fall a clumsy circumvention (on the part of humanity) of God's caring prohibition and an attempt

---

28. Bounds, "Irenaeus and the Doctrine of Perfection," 169.

29. Minns, *Irenaeus*, 90. This uniquely "Irenaean" understanding of human origins has been commentated upon by a number of theologians. See, for example, Steenberg, *Irenaeus on Creation*, 175; Holsinger-Friesen, *Irenaeus and Genesis*, 127; Hick, *Evil and the God of Love*, 250. Hick's understanding of Irenaeus's contributions to the field of theological anthropology and theodicy will be discussed further at greater length in the following chapter.

to achieve a level of power and maturity that it clearly was not yet ready to possess.[30] Nevertheless, in spite of such qualifications, the Fall resulted in humanity forfeiting the potential gifted to it by God.[31] It subsequently found itself being dragged along a downward spiral of depravity, leaving it unable to save itself, even if it wanted to. Yet despite its postlapsarian helplessness, humanity continued to retain its defining characteristic: the possibility for growth that is intrinsic to its creatureliness. Because of the Fall, God had to intervene to reorient process away from its death spiral and redirect it back on a path toward its initial potential. However, also due to the Fall, this action had to be adapted according to the circumstances, carried out more gradually still, in such a way that was commensurate with humanity's further diminished ability and capacity to receive the grace that God was offering. This is essentially the story of salvation history as presented in the Hebrew Bible, where through a series of covenants, God gradually leads humanity back toward the path of constructive growth and fellowship, therein becoming "the means by which the image and likeness to God in humanity could be renewed and perfected."[32] For Irenaeus, this will of course culminate in the incarnation of Jesus Christ, when humanity was finally ready to experience and receive the decisive event in its journey of redemption.

Humanity's Recapitulation in Christ

God's gradual plan for humanity culminates with the entry of Jesus Christ into the world. Particular to Irenaeus is his emphasis upon the idea that humanity's restoration is brought about in Christ's work of recapitulation.[33] Just as humanity was abruptly placed on a downward trajectory through Adam's sin of disobedience, that trajectory could only be corrected and reversed through a perfect act of obedience. Christ, through his life, death, and resurrection, fulfilled precisely that role. For Irenaeus, Christ serves as a recapitulation of Adam, in that just as Adam was for him synonymous with humanity, so too is Christ. And while Adam represented the humanity of the old creation, dominated by death, Christ signified the new creation, destined for union with God. Thus, through the incarnation, the Son "assumed the old creation of Adam, infused it with God's undefeated life, and

---

30. See Wingren, *Man and the Incarnation*, 42.
31. See Steenberg, *Irenaeus on Creation*, 168.
32. Bounds, "Irenaeus and the Doctrine of Perfection," 169; see also Minns, *Irenaeus*, 85.
33. Wingren, *Man and the Incarnation*, 80.

thereby renewed it."[34] Every aspect of life was renewed through Christ. As he passed through each stage of human existence, he charged it with his own perfect humanity, thereby restoring it to perfect communion with God. As Irenaeus himself writes:

> For he [Christ] came to save all through means of himself—all, I say, who through him are born again to God—infants, and children, and boys, and youths, and old men. He therefore passed through every age . . . that he might be a perfect master for all, not merely as respects the setting forth of the truth, but also as regards age, sanctifying at the same time the aged also, and becoming to them likewise. Then, at last, he came on to death itself, that he might be "the first-born of the dead, that in all things he might be preeminent," the Prince of Life, existing before all, and going before all.[35]

Christ restores humanity's image and likeness to God by virtue of his existence as a human person who crucially retained that same image and likeness throughout his life, thereby breaking the bond of humanity to Satan and death. As Gustaf Wingren explains, Satan's mastery over humanity would be destroyed if a human could be found who was capable of withstanding—and defying—Satan's control. With humanity itself too weak to achieve this, God came down to humanity's level, became human, and as a human, defeated Satan by withstanding his torments and temptations. With his own powerlessness exposed, Satan himself is driven out from humanity as Christ decisively reclaims it for God.[36]

Thus, while Satan took humanity as his captive, it was indeed humanity itself (through the salvific actions of Christ) that defeated Satan. According to Wingren, the "eternally valid decision for the whole of humanity is made in the death of Jesus with its unbroken obedience which destroys sin and consequently also destroys death, and is thus already the basis of the Resurrection. At the Cross man's destiny is decided."[37] Wingren emphasizes the enormity of the challenge experienced by Christ while on earth:

> God is in the Incarnate, and it is for this reason that Christ defeats Satan and has power to create. But God is in a man, who is tempted in the wilderness and trembles in Gethsemane. The agony which He has to endure was not easier than ours because

34. Wingren, *Man and the Incarnation*, 96.

35. Irenaeus, *Against Heresies*, 2.22.4. Quoted in Bounds, "Irenaeus and the Doctrine of Perfection," 169–70.

36. Wingren, *Man and the Incarnation*, 103.

37. Wingren, *Man and the Incarnation*, 122.

> of His Godhood, but more terrible than any other man has suffered. If we are going to understand Irenaeus we must see this clearly, otherwise we may conceive of Christ's victory as being purely a logical consequence of His divine nature, when in actual fact it was achieved only in the hardest conflict.[38]

Wingren makes this point to indicate that it was not by a simple divine act that humanity was saved, but rather through a hard-fought struggle, won by humanity itself. In Christ's obedience, humanity, too, finally regains its capacity for obedience to God, thereby reversing that first act of disobedience perpetrated by humanity. In so doing, its previous destiny, death, is replaced with the possibility of achieving its original destiny: union with God.

God's original creation is resuscitated by the defeat of its enemy and is once again able to develop in this state toward the perfection for which it was destined. This is to take place within the Christian church, where one can once again become fully human through the reception of the Holy Spirit, whose work it is to complete the process of perfection in the image and likeness of God.[39] An objection may of course be raised to the veracity of Irenaeus's claim that humanity was restored in the recapitulation of Christ by pointing out the mere fact that there remain countless individuals who are not members of Christ's church and thus do not have the Spirit dwelling within them, thereby making continual growth in the image and likeness of God impossible. To this, Denis Minns details Irenaeus's likely response:

> Irenaeus was not blind to the physical and moral imperfection of the human beings he saw about him, but he was able to attribute this imperfection to the fact that the purposes of God for humankind had not yet been fully realized. His optimism was tempered by realism; he did not believe that the will of all human beings would have to be turned back to God before God's purposes could be achieved, but he believed it was in the power of all human beings to be incorporated in the divine plan for the perfection of the earth creature in the image and likeness of God. Those who chose not to be part of this plan would simply cease to be part of any plan at all.[40]

Minns's point above is echoed by Gustaf Wingren, who writes that "even though the members of the Christian Church are relatively few in number compared with the unbaptised, this does not affect faith in Christ's absolute power, for it is not the sum total which counts but the function,

---

38. Wingren, *Man and the Incarnation*, 112.
39. Bounds, "Irenaeus and the Doctrine of Perfection," 170.
40. Minns, *Irenaeus*, 86.

the continuing expansion through preaching to new multitudes. This function is directly connected with the future—the cosmic perspective. Christ's dominion is irresistible and progressive."[41] Through Christ's recapitulation, therefore, God's plan of salvation is made available for all of humanity, but it is up to the human person to accept or reject this plan. While Christ renewed humanity and offered it once again the ability to continue to grow in the perfection of the image and likeness of God, each person can decide themselves whether or not to participate. But even in acknowledging such a reality, Irenaeus nevertheless continued optimistically to maintain a dynamic understanding of the work of Christ and his church, believing that it would eventually extend to all humanity, to the end of time, and even beyond.[42] Indeed, he understood that for an individual Christian in possession of Christ and the Spirit, progression in the image and likeness of God would itself be an eternal proposition. For no matter how much humanity grows in perfection, it will, in Minns's words, "never cease to be the creature of God, never cease to exist in the mode proper to creatures, in the mode of Becoming."[43]

Being created with an infinite capacity for growth is the ultimate promise of humanity; and eternal participation in an infinite God is the ultimate destiny for humanity. These are the fundamental insights offered by Saint Irenaeus of Lyons into how the human person can be theologically understood. Moreover, these are the insights that have stimulated John Hick's soul-making understanding of why evil and suffering exist in creation, and how they can possibly relate to the human person. As Marilyn McCord Adams writes in her analysis of Hick, "Drawing his inspiration from Irenaeus (as against Augustine), Hick assigns God, not a retrospective reason in terms of a past fall from perfection, but a prospective or teleological explanation in terms of God's developmental goal for created persons."[44]

In the statement above, Adams raises an important point, which must be revisited: namely, in establishing within the Christian tradition a theological foundation that can support the development of a soul-making theodicy capable of shedding new light onto how purgatory might be approached and understood, is it only appropriate to appeal—as Hick, among others, does—to this new "Irenaean" tradition, at the expense of all others? It will be argued that Augustine's understanding does not in fact mark a radical departure from the conclusions reached by Irenaeus, especially with regard

---

41. Wingren, *Man and the Incarnation*, 135.
42. Wingren, *Man and the Incarnation*, 141–42.
43. Minns, *Irenaeus*, 89.
44. Adams, *Horrendous Evils*, 50.

to the question of theodicy. Rather, the perceived discrepancies between the two can most often be traced back to a question of historical interpretation, often over basically (and perhaps surprisingly) non-essential points, rather than that of actual substantial differences between the authors themselves.

AUGUSTINE OF HIPPO

Augustine of Hippo wrote extensively on the question of human origins, and its connection to the problem of evil and suffering. The most comprehensive answer Augustine offers on this issue can be found in his later works, in which his understanding of original sin is key to his understanding of theodicy. Broadly speaking, the doctrine of original sin states that because of the sin of Adam and Eve, both them and their offspring (which is to say, all of humanity) have been personally affected by that action's consequences, which in turn can only be washed away by God's grace in the sacrament of baptism.

According to Gerald Bonner, there have traditionally been two theological points of view on the doctrine of original sin and the consequences it is understood to carry: the first is a medical perspective, which understands original sin as something like a hereditary disease, that is, something that blights the individual with the ill-effects of the original illness, without imparting personal guilt or culpability, leaving the person in need of healing through the aid of merciful and compassionate doctor; the second is a juridical perspective, which understands original sin as something like a heinous crime committed by an ancestor, the guilt of which is inherited by his descendants.[45] Notably, Augustine's understanding maintained both aspects.[46] He believed original sin to be both a crime and a disease, from which no person—other than Christ—was, or would be, immune.

Prelapsarian Humanity

It is necessary to situate Augustine's concept of original sin within his overall vision of human origins, the Fall, and eventual redemption. As such, Augustine's understanding of the Fall and its consequences was predicated principally upon his understanding of the prelapsarian human condition, which he understood to be pristine. "Man's nature," writes Augustine, ". . .

---

45. Bonner, *St. Augustine*, 370. Bonner later states that the former understanding would go on to broadly inform the understanding of human origins within the Eastern Christian theological tradition, while the latter would go on to dominate the Western Christian tradition.

46. Bonner, *St. Augustine*, 370.

was created at first faultless and without any sin."[47] In the beginning, humanity was created perfectly "good"—in the image of God (*imago Dei*), and in possession of a rational soul that was in total harmony with itself and God.[48] Yet unlike Irenaeus, who, as we have seen, ascribed a certain immaturity to this state, Augustine understood prelapsarian humanity to have its full intellectual faculties about it, and described this state of being as one characterized by an "undisturbed" love for God, "since the beloved object [God] was always at hand for their enjoyment."[49] With all of their natural desires satisfied by such a close proximity to the divine, Augustine would go on to declare that Adam and Eve were not bothered by any pressures or temptations that might serve as a cause to turn away from this relationship and fall into sin. As such, their existence was lived out in a state of total spiritual and intellectual tranquility, which afforded them the clarity of mind to freely enjoy an existence of perfect harmony with God and God's created world: "We conclude then that man lived in paradise as long as his wish was at one with God's command. He lived in enjoyment of God, and derived his own goodness from God's goodness. He lived without any want, and had it in his power to live like this for ever."[50]

Augustine held to a hierarchical understanding of the human person, at the summit of which exists the person's rational, intellectual soul, within which he believed the *imago Dei* to dwell. For him, it was the *imago Dei* that corresponded to humanity's goodness, as that is where the soul's basic activity of recognizing God as the source and summit of its being took place, which in turn formed and conditioned all other activities (including bodily and affective activity) according to this end.[51] Augustine understood that, as unencumbered intellectual creatures, prelapsarian humans were capable of carrying out their creaturely purpose of recognizing and living obediently to God, without any strain or exertion, for all of time. Yet this harmonious state of initial wholeness was not self-sustaining; indeed, it required a total dependence upon that same Creator. As Augustine writes:

> The Supreme Good beyond all others is God. It is thereby unchangeable good, truly eternal, truly immortal. All other good things derive their origin from [*ab*] him but are not part of [*de*] him. That which is part of [*de*] him is as he is, but the things he has created are not as he is. Hence if he alone is unchangeable, all

---

47. Augustine, "On Nature and Grace," ch. 3.
48. Augustine, "On Nature and Grace," ch. 3.
49. Augustine, *City of God*, 14, 10.
50. Augustine, *City of God*, 14, 26.
51. Drever, "Redeeming Creation," 148–149.

things that he created are changeable because he made them of nothing [*ex nihilo*]. Being omnipotent he is able to make out of nothing [*de nihilo*], i.e., out of [*ex*] what has no existence at all.[52]

Unlike God, creation did not by its own power possess the supreme, unchangeable Good. Since humanity was indeed created out of nothing, there therefore existed—in spite of its supposed "faultlessness" and perfection—an innate mutability within creation. Augustine understood creation's mutability as evidence of its incomplete (*informis*) nature, which was neither sinful nor immoral (and as such did not undermine creation's initial perfection) to the extent that it participated in the supreme, unchangeable Good (indeed, this *informis* served to delineate the fundamental ontological difference between the immutable Goodness of God and the mutable goodness of creation). Moreover, the nature of this relationship implies that if it were ever to be severed, the essential sustenance provided by God would too be cut off, resulting in a fracture of, among other things, human stability and identity as it descended into a state of being that could be described as considerably less than "good."

With such an understanding of creation in mind, it could therefore be said that Augustine considered the earliest, prelapsarian humans to have existed in a state of an active, if delicate, integrated wholeness—with regard to how they related to both themselves, creation, and their Creator. From the point of creation, Adam and Eve wholly possessed in their nature the divine image and likeness, which wholeheartedly desired—and serenely recognized—God as the source and summit of their existence. Moreover, by virtue of their mutable origins, the possibility existed for them to not just dwell, but to also grow in their natural human vocation: to remain in God's sustaining embrace and continue to be formed in communion with God's goodness. Yet at the same time, Adam and Eve's creaturely mutability also carried with it a more destructive potential that continually threatened their state of integrated wholeness, for they always carried with them the possibility to act out in ways contrary to this natural desire and reject their divine communion.

The Fall and Original Sin

In order to protect the inalienable goodness of God, Augustine maintained that God, as the supreme Good, consequently made all things

---

52. Augustine, "De Natura Boni," 25.885, 1. Quoted in Drever, "Redeeming Creation," 142.

"SOUL-MAKING" AND THE WESTERN THEOLOGICAL TRADITION

good, including human nature. However, there inexplicably arose within this good nature an evil will, a will that desired something other than the supreme Good; and it is from this will that sinful action followed.[53] Nico Vorster describes such evil willing as a self-originating act that cannot be explained in terms of causes.[54] Accordingly, Augustine's explanation as to how an uncaused evil will initially arose in a supposedly pristine and mature humanity remains somewhat mysterious. On the one hand, he understood humanity to exist in a state of serene rationality, immune from pressures, unnatural passions and temptations, as already discussed; but on the other, he is clear that in spite of its supposed perfection, due to the fact that human nature was created by God out of nothing, and depended upon God for its sustenance (without which it would descend into chaos), it is therefore subject to the possibility of change, within which a space is created for evil to emerge and corrupt human nature.[55] With such an understanding in mind, Augustine describes an evil will, in the form of pride, arising secretly in Adam, but fails to explain how an untroubled rational nature would allow such a will to arise in the first place, let alone succumb to it.[56]

Evil, then, arose not as an external, independent force but rather as an uncaused, self-originating defect of the will that had arisen in a good that was already created by God (Augustine used the term *privatio boni*, which translates into "privation of the good").[57] As Vorster points out, it has no substantial being in and of itself, but rather exists parasitically, as a fault created by a substance, that continues to dwell within the nature of that substance.[58] By eating fruit from the tree of the knowledge of good and evil, Adam voluntarily acted upon the evil desire of his will, thus instigating humanity's fall from grace. Augustine understood that this sinful action—along with every other sinful action—carried with it two principal consequences: firstly, there is the guilt of mortal condemnation, a personal culpability of severing humanity's intimate relationship with God, resulting in damnation—the "second death." Secondly, in addition to the direct penalty of gravely effecting their relationship with God, there also followed the penalty of the various secondary effects related to the sinful action that are temporally experienced by the sinner as a disordering of their entire personhood.

53. Augustine, *City of God*, 14, 11.
54. Vorster, "Augustinian Type of Theodicy," 30.
55. Augustine, *City of God*, 14, 11.
56. Augustine, *City of God*, 14, 13.
57. See Augustine, *City of God*, 14, 11.
58. See Vorster, "Augustinian Type of Theodicy," 29.

Adam had abandoned his primary activity of obedient recognition of God, choosing instead more unnatural preoccupations. And by choosing to indulge in those preoccupations, he in effect chose to sever himself from intimate relationship with God, and, as a result, also separated himself from the divine sustaining grace he needed in order to adequately maintain the integrity of that created perfection endowed to him by God. Without it, Adam no longer existed as he ought, that is, he no longer existed in the mode natural to his existence; consequently, a crisis of ontological identity ensued as the *imago Dei* imprinted upon his soul became severely distorted.[59] Its entire hierarchic structure became disordered: the will was weakened and its body—caught up by unnatural desires—turned against it; the natural world suddenly became a hostile place in which to live—danger existed all around, as was the specter of disease and the threat of bodily death.

Overcoming Concupiscence through Grace

In the unique case of Adam and Eve as the parents of humanity, it was not just they who reaped the consequences of this event, for Augustine was adamant that the calamitous ill-effects of that original sin would indeed be passed on to all of their offspring. How this "reign of death" was passed on seminally is a question of what Augustine would call "concupiscence," i.e., desire. For Augustine, desire is good in principle (*concupiscentia boni*); it informs the will's natural yearning for God by inclining it toward a number of natural goods proper for a life in obedience to God; in short, it is a desire "bound up with the very purpose of human existence; a life lived *propter Deum*."[60] So long as Adam lived obedient to God, he was able, by virtue of possessing a rational soul that was able to maintain command of his will and desires, to live in harmony, with both himself and his Creator.

For Augustine, this harmony would extend to all matters relating to sexuality. Before the Fall, Augustine would argue that any desire related to sexuality would have existed in conformity with Adam's rational will; as such, the sexual act itself indeed remained a free and natural act, as it would have been performed under total self-control, in a matter fully commensurate to its created purpose.[61] But that harmony was of course shattered with

---

59. Drever indicates that Augustine initially believed that the Fall in fact destroyed the *imago Dei* found within Adam, but would later go on to modify his claim to state that the *imago Dei* was only distorted (Drever, "Redeeming Creation," 149).

60. See Lamberigts, "Critical Evaluation," 178.

61. Augustine, "On Marriage and Concupiscence," 2, 26. Elsewhere, Augustine would vividly describe his understanding of prelapsarian sexuality (within the context

his fall from grace; nature, as already discussed, became corrupted through a disordering of the will, and weakened by pride, envy, and fear, the will would turn against that which was initially natural to it as it easily adhered to destructive earthly desires. Thus, the aforementioned disobedience of the flesh, and the corresponding shame and confusion over humanity's newfound lack of internal control would remain the two enduring effects—the enduring secondary consequence—of original sin: "When the first man transgressed the law of God," Augustine writes, "he began to have another law in his members which was repugnant to the law of his mind, and he felt the evil of his own disobedience when he experienced in the disobedience of his flesh a most righteous retribution recoiling on himself."[62] Augustine referred to this newfound unnatural bodily disobedience and attendant disordered desires as *concupiscentia carnis*, that is, fleshly desire. And while *concupiscentia carnis* (now commonly referred to as simply "concupiscence" or "lust") was not in itself sinful when ordered according to the greater desires proper to the rational soul, Augustine thought that these desires, now disfigured into lust by the Fall, could indeed occasion sin if indulged and acted upon by the individual. For Augustine understood that disordered concupiscence (that is, lust) as the context by which disordered and wounded human nature was transmitted. And since Augustine believed that disordered concupiscence would necessarily be present in the postlapsarian act of procreation, it could therefore be considered as "the means whereby Original Sin is transmitted."[63]

Augustine would maintain that every person conceived and born since the Fall of Adam was done so not according to the direction of a good will, but rather in a moment of lustful passion, brought about by a disordered concupiscence.[64] Any newborn child, therefore, is born not according to lawful nature, but rather according to a nature that has been both ontologically and relationally distorted by sin, a "reign of death" ruled over by Satan, from whom, Augustine declares, "no one—no, no one—has been delivered, or is being delivered, or ever will be delivered, except by the grace

---

of marriage) as existing entirely under "the command of the will for producing offspring—as the foot is for walking, the hand for labour, and the mouth for speech" (Augustine, "On the Grace of Christ," 1, 40).

62. Augustine, "On Marriage and Concupiscence," 1, 7. Later, Augustine would write that when "Adam sinned by not obeying God, then his body—although it was a natural and mortal body—lost the grace whereby it used in every part of it to be obedient to the soul" (Augustine, "On Marriage and Concupiscence," 1, 7).

63. Bonner, *St. Augustine*, 378.

64. Augustine, "On the Grace of Christ," ch. 42; see also, Augustine, "On Marriage and Concupiscence," 1, 7, and 2, 53.

of the Redeemer."⁶⁵ For Augustine, the only way an individual can escape the "reign of death" caused by original sin is through the grace of God, beginning in the sacrament of baptism. Baptism abolishes the mortal guilt of original sin and mitigates the accompanying woundedness and ill-effects experienced by the person.[66] However, it would seem that even with the grace of baptism, these ill-effects are not in themselves totally wiped away; rather, they would remain in the person for the rest of their life, thus resulting in a lifelong contest to gain mastery over the passions of concupiscence, the goal of which being the eventual rehabilitation of the person's interior hierarchy thereby restoring for themselves the *imago Dei*:

> The concupiscence of the flesh, however, is such that it remains in man warring against it through continence, even though its guilt, which was contracted by generation, has already been completely ended by regeneration. It remains in its action, not by drawing away and enticing the mind and with the mind's consent conceiving and bringing forth sins, but by arousing evil desires the mind must resist. For this excitement of desires is itself the action of concupiscence, even when, in the absence of the mind's consent, the effect does not follow.[67]

It must be emphasized that in spite of his attitudes regarding fallen human nature, Augustine believed that it was indeed possible for humanity—with the aid of God's grace—to not only successfully struggle against the unnatural passions with which *concupiscentia* regaled the will, but also to transcend the more base instincts of its fallen nature, for each successful act of resistance effectively diminished the power of concupiscence over the individual, thereby allowing the wound caused by original sin on the *imago Dei* to not only heal, but to grow once again in sanctity.[68] This, for Augustine, was a lifetime's work; but it was also the path of progress toward perfection, that is, toward an ever deeper, more intimate state of communion with the divine: "For we do not deny that human nature can be without sin," Augustine writes, "nor ought we by any means to refuse to it the ability to become perfect, since we admit its capacity for progress—by God's grace, however, though our Lord Jesus Christ. By His assistance we aver that it becomes holy and happy, by whom it was created in order to be so."[69]

---

65. Augustine, "On the Grace of Christ," ch. 34.
66. Augustine, "On Marriage and Concupiscence," 1, 28.
67. Augustine, "Against Julian," bk. 6, ch. 19.
68. Lamberigts, "Critical Evaluation," 186.
69. Augustine, "On Nature and Grace," ch. 68.

CONCLUSION AND IMPLICATIONS

With the basic outline of Irenaeus and Augustine's respective anthropologies established, we can now return to the question of whether both of these positions can allow for an interpretation capable of supporting a soul-making understanding of theodicy. Hick, for his part, believed that Augustine held no place in his particular understanding of theodicy, relying instead upon the insights of Irenaeus for inspiration. In addition to the practical considerations already detailed, this rejection also carries with it a certain symbolic significance. For Hick understood Augustine's ideas on anthropology and theodicy to have influenced the entire western theological tradition,[70] and by rejecting Augustine, Hick was also making a very clear statement regarding his opinion of the tradition that has followed. As such, Hick's choice of the relatively obscure Irenaeus as the so-called "patron saint" of his project provides the first indication that his soul-making vision of theodicy may have intended to have been more of a revolutionary departure from the field's established tradition than a mere evolution from within.

Such an approach has certainly borne fruit for Hick, whose vision has gone on to gain considerable influence. However, in an unpublished essay, Paul W. Gooch persuasively argues that the distinction between Augustine and Irenaeus's account of prelapsarian humanity and the Fall, although present, need not undermine the overall coherency of a basic shared understanding of the human person and the Fall present in both of their writings, as it is not strong enough to render their overall theological projects totally inconsistent. According to Gooch, it would seem that as far as theological anthropology is concerned, one can find within the work of both individuals the essential soul-making elements necessary for constructing an anthropological framework based on the premise of God's divine will desiring for us, over the course of time, to come to moral maturity and a spiritual perfection, with an ultimate eschatological realization.

With Hick's distinction in mind, Gooch responds to the seemingly irreconcilable question of primordial perfection by simply maintaining that in addition to the basic framework offered above, Augustine is adding his own belief that "ideal human nature was realized primordially as a graphic way of setting out God's original intentions for the human race."[71] Yet Gooch insists that this belief amounts to only "an addition to, not a contradiction of" a basic anthropological understanding that can allow for the belief in

---

70. See Hick, "Irenaean Theodicy," 42. This opinion is shared by Swinburne, *Providence and the Problem of Evil*, 38; Drever, "Redeeming Creation," 135; Minns, *Irenaeus*, 83; and Barrett, "Love Almighty," 107, to name a few.

71. Gooch, "Augustinian and Irenaean Theodicies," 6.

a theodicy in which the existence of evil can be justified by its place in the divine plan of soul-making.[72] For while holding to some form of primordial perfection would certainly have an effect on the overall question of tone, it would not in any way compromise any of the basic premises essential to soul-making, as laid out above, therefore leaving Gooch to conclude that "the two approaches [Augustinian and Irenaean] are not fundamentally incompatible on this particular question."[73]

Gooch goes on to challenge the very notion that Augustine held to such a seemingly strict understanding of primordial perfection. For if Augustine understood "perfection" to convey a sense of total indefinite completion, then the point of distinction between his and Irenaeus's respective understandings of human origins would indeed remain quite stark, regardless as to whether or not it exists as a mere addition; but, as already explained, Augustine believed that even in its perfection, humanity, due to its natural mutability, continued to remain open to change. It would seem that in using the word perfection in his description of humanity, Augustine understood the word in its "less robust sense," wherein "things may be exemplary and without fault or blemish without having to have an ontologically permanent perfection."[74] Returning to the actual event of the Fall itself, Gooch offers his own explanation that helps to clarify Augustine's own somewhat less than clear position:

> A more satisfactory route would be to consider the possibility that perfection in a creature must necessarily come within certain limitations, limitations which provide opportunity for (but do not compel) choices some of which can be wrong. For instance, a rational creature might, in appreciating its own kind of perfection, come to value a higher perfection more greatly. Suppose, as a reasonable result, it wished to embody that higher perfection, but that this is contrary to its own best interests. Its striving to become like God would therefore have some understandable motive; and the possibility that it make this choice a consequence of its freedom. In going wrong it would lose its perfection, but the process would not be incoherent and incomprehensible.[75]

Gooch's analysis of what is meant by prelapsarian perfection in the thought of Augustine manages to successfully challenge the notion that he believed it to merely indicate a sense of static, ontological completion, and

---

72. Gooch, "Augustinian and Irenaean Theodicies," 6.
73. Gooch, "Augustinian and Irenaean Theodicies," 6.
74. See Gooch, "Augustinian and Irenaean Theodicies," 7.
75. Gooch, "Augustinian and Irenaean Theodicies," 7.

in turn reveals a basic understanding similar to that of Irenaeus: that the earliest humans possessed a primary integral harmony, and due to their dynamic capacity as mutable creatures, were capable to further grow and flourish in that harmony; yet that mutability was abused, resulting in the Fall event. This, in effect, reinforces Denis Minns's conclusion that Irenaeus basically agrees with Augustine on a startling number of key anthropological premises: "He agrees that God alone is Being and that creation will always be in a state of Becoming; he agrees that free will is the pivot on which the creation can incline towards reality and be strengthened in its on existence, or incline towards non-being and begin to tumble into nothingness. He agrees that, because the creation is only Becoming and not Being, it is almost inevitable that the balance will tip towards nothingness."[76] This serves as an important qualification to Hick's supposed distinction between Irenaeus's and Augustine's respective understandings of prelapsarian humanity. For it is true that while Irenaeus was much more explicit regarding its spiritual innocence and childlike level of maturity, it would seem that Augustine, too, implicitly acknowledges some form of human primordial immaturity in admitting its possibility for growth and change.

However, in spite of this emerging sense of a fundamental similarity between the two theologians, Minns raises the point that Irenaeus and Augustine will ultimately go on to develop opposing general outlooks, namely, that while Augustine incessantly dwells upon and laments over "the instability inherent in the condition of Becomingness, Irenaeus emphasizes the possibility of growth and development inherent in it."[77] While their respective conclusions have indeed led to noticeable discrepancies with regard to overall tone, if we were to return to Gooch's main point, this distinction remains ultimately inessential to the basic soul-making understanding of anthropology present in both individuals. Take, for example, Augustine's conception of disordered concupiscence, one of the principal enduring secondary effects of the Fall in his *Privatio boni* understanding of evil in the world. While this has traditionally been interpreted theologically as evidence of our now-inherent sinfulness and broken relationship with God and the rest of creation, there also exists a very significant opportunity for these lingering and all-pervasive disharmonies to be understood as a source of soul-making.

Acknowledging that the consequences of the first sin remain present in every aspect of a human person's interaction with the world, an Augustinian model of soul-making appears able to interpret the trials that emerge from

---

76. Minns, *Irenaeus*, 84.
77. Minns, *Irenaeus*, 84.

concupiscence, along with resistance to them, integration of them, and transcendence over them, as opportunities that can also lead to moral and spiritual growth. According to Augustine, disordered concupiscence is "remitted, indeed, in baptism; not so that it is put out of existence, but so that it is not to be imputed for sin. Although its guilt is now taken away, it still remains until our entire infirmity be healed by the advancing renewal of our inner man, day by day, when at last our outward man shall be clothed with incorruption."[78]

Soul-making for Augustine, then, centers upon the concept of healing and transcending our fallen natures by withstanding and overcoming the trials of disordered concupiscence, the lingering effect of humanity's first sin. Admittedly, as Minns has pointed out, Augustine does seemingly refer back to an idealized prelapsarian state as the model upon which to return. However, and in contrast to Minns's point raised above, the path back to this state does not seem to be characterized strictly by lament over humanity's fallen nature in this condition of Becomingness; rather, it seems to be characterized by a deep insight into the actual and ongoing woundedness of postlapsarian humanity, and possessed of a real hope that these wounds can indeed be healed. This is important in that it can perhaps temper an expectation that soul-making is somehow a totally linear process, on an ever-upward, ever-pleasant, trajectory; instead, Augustine's concept of disordered concupiscence emphasizes the frailty and capriciousness of fallen human nature, underlines the immense difficulties of the soul-making journey, and, indeed, casts necessary attention upon the messiness inherent in the very idea of soul-making itself.

Augustine, therefore, injects a certain realistic empathy into his understanding of the human person—that is to say, a particular appreciation regarding the ongoing struggles and temptations that are carried by human nature in its ongoing journey of soul-making. Indeed, Augustine will go on to actually acknowledge the importance of encountering adversity in one's personal development: "If there is no war there will be no victory. And if we do not obtain victory over the faults that strip against us there will not be any cleansing from faults, for, if we conquer temptation in these snares of our body, we are purged of the strife of passions that war against us."[79] This is an important insight that ought to be considered in the future construction of any soul-making anthropology, theodicy, or conception of the afterlife. Moreover, in reviewing these later writings of Augustine, what also emerges is a growing realization that in spite of the clear emphasis placed

---

78. Augustine, "On Marriage and Concupiscence," 1, 28. This insight will be explored in the following chapters as we begin to develop Hick's soul-making concepts into a Catholic, sanctification-based, understanding of purgatory.

79. Augustine, "Against Julian," bk. 2, ch. 6.

upon human woundedness and the difficulties of the soul-making journey, Augustine nevertheless managed to maintain a certain sense of forward-looking hopefulness for humanity's ability to grow in spiritual maturity through the grace of God: "For we do not deny that human nature can be without sin; nor ought we by any means to refuse to it the ability to become perfect, since we admit its capacity for progress—by God's grace, however, though our Lord Jesus Christ. By His assistance we aver that it becomes holy and happy, by whom it was created in order to be so."[80]

It would appear then that the basic teleological structure of Augustine's anthropological understanding coheres with that of Irenaeus, yet also remains in possession of its own unique perspective. For while Irenaeus's understanding is much more explicit and sympathetic to the various immaturities present within prelapsarian humanity, Augustine's is characterized by a particular sensitivity to the trials and challenges to be faced by postlapsarian humanity. Thus, in spite of the particular emphasis each has placed upon their own understanding of humanity, this does not appear to be in itself strong enough to seriously compromise a shared set of overarching foundational principles. Regardless of the questions of primordial perfection and assignation of responsibility for the Fall, both authors nevertheless propose the essential elements of a soul-making vision of the human person within their overall theological projects: humanity is dynamic and evolving; our previous or present state of being is not the ultimate condition that God desires for us; and that rather it is God's will, over the course of time, to bring us to moral maturity and spiritual perfection, which will ultimately be realized eschatologically.[81] To qualify the analysis of Hick and Minns—both Augustine and Irenaeus offer surprisingly not incompatible theological visions, at least as far as a soul-making understanding of humanity is concerned. Both present a basically teleological account with an eschatological resolution. And with this basic compatibility now established, we can once again return to the central question of how a broader, more theologically inclusive understanding of soul-making can relate to contemporary reflection on theodicy and the doctrine of purgatory.

REASSESSMENT OF IRENAEUS AND AUGUSTINE'S CONTRIBUTIONS TO THE CONCEPT OF SOUL-MAKING

In light of the similarities now identified between these two theologians, it may be helpful to return to Irenaeus, and consider the theological emphases

---

80. Augustine, "On Nature and Grace," ch. 68.
81. Gooch, "Augustinian and Irenaean Theodicies," 6.

present in his anthropology, as well as the language he used to express these emphases. Indeed, more so than for his early oblique references affirming the existence of an intermediate state, Irenaeus's true significance in our present exploration rests in the sense of compassionate understanding and optimism that his ideas have injected into the question of theological anthropology (compassionate understanding regarding the immaturity of primordial humanity, and optimism regarding its ability for growth and development), which can, in turn, directly influence new ways in which the doctrine of purgatory can be approached. Perhaps this can be most clearly seen in the terminology he chose to employ when describing the earliest humans. By simply using the metaphor of a child to describe humanity's prelapsarian state, and crucially in his description of humanity during the Fall event, Irenaeus was able to better humanize the concept.[82] The effect is one of a more compassionate understanding of the human condition and perhaps a more accurate grasp of the human evolutionary process, which has no doubt contributed to the appeal of a sanctification-based understanding of theological anthropology—and for that, Irenaeus certainly deserves some credit.

Also of importance are some of the details that Irenaeus chose to provide in his explanation of how the process of sanctification can take place:

> Since God, therefore gave [to man] such mental power (*magnanimitatem*) man knew both the good of obedience and the evil of disobedience, that the eye of the mind, receiving experience of both, may with judgment make choice of the better things; and that he may never become indolent or neglectful of God's command; and learning by experience that it is an evil thing which deprives him of life, that is, disobedience to God, may never attempt it at all, but that, knowing that what preserves his life, namely, obedience to God, is good, he may diligently keep it with all earnestness. Wherefore he has also had a twofold experience, possessing knowledge of both kinds, that with discipline he may make choice of the better things.[83]

Irenaeus places a clear emphasis on the importance of experience—for better or for worse—in one's journey of sanctification. By clearly mentioning how a concrete experience of evil or suffering can lead an individual to greater spiritual growth, Irenaeus makes explicit a nuance that should be considered in any conversation regarding a sanctification-based understanding of

---

82. Irenaeus, *Against Heresies*, 2.28.1, 4.38.1; see also Irenaeus, *On the Apostolic Preaching*, 12, 14, 47.

83. Irenaeus, *Against Heresies*, 4.39.1.

the human person. Augustine, on the other hand, is perhaps less explicit in articulating the constructive potential of personal struggle, or experiences of suffering. It must be pointed out, however, that this concept is not totally absent in the thought of Augustine. Indeed, one can find in his writings an insistence that personal progress is in fact possible through God's grace, even during times of great personal struggle: "because in the very offering up of such a prayer [of help and deliverance] there is a struggle against the tempter, who fights against us concerning this very necessity; and thus, by the assistance of grace through our Lord Jesus Christ, both the evil necessity will be removed and full liberty be bestowed."[84] Elsewhere, he is perhaps even more explicit: "If there is no war there will be no victory. And if we do not obtain victory over the faults that strip against us there will not be any cleansing from faults, for, if we conquer temptation in these snares of our body, we are purged of the strife of passions that war against us."[85] The distinction that one can perhaps draw is that while Irenaeus understands experiences of evil and temptation—whether succumbed to or triumphed over—to both provide opportunities for learning and growth, Augustine tends to only emphasize the utility of those against which the individual resisted and overcame.

Perhaps unsurprisingly, it is generally the points raised and emphasized by Irenaeus that would go on to be incorporated by Hick as defining characteristics of a soul-making post-mortem intermediate state within his broader vision of a soul-making theodicy, in which the intermediate state becomes the place in which the person and their experiences become transformed by God's love to a point of total maturity and perfection. By clearly holding to certain key Irenaean concepts, as well as by employing a terminology that would so easily resonate with contemporary values and sensibilities, one can perhaps understand why John Hick would name Irenaeus as the patron saint of his soul-making vision of anthropology, theodicy, and the afterlife. Irenaeus's undeniably attractive tone has raised renewed interest in his work among contemporary theologians, which in turn has injected some much-needed energy into the present debate surrounding the topics of anthropology and theodicy. For those reasons, it seems only fitting that Irenaeus remains the patron saint of this current project, as well.

However, a word of caution appears in order, for along with Irenaeus's clear optimism regarding the human condition and the soul-making process also lurks the potential of over-simplification when interpreted for the purpose of constructing a contemporary soul-making theodicy. Such

---

84. Augustine, "On Nature and Grace," 79.
85. Augustine, "Against Julian," bk. 2, ch. 6.

a generalization may perhaps be inclined to see Irenaeus's optimistic belief in the *possibility* for the moral and spiritual development of the human person from childhood to full adulthood to become an *inevitability*, in which the journey of soul-making resembles something akin to an irresistible force, with its success guaranteed at the expense of the person's freedom of agency.[86] For as mentioned earlier, Augustine's perspective carries with it a certain emphasis on the lingering frailty of postlapsarian humanity—an important insight that can perhaps serve as a reminder to those tempted to ascribe an overly optimistic interpretation to Irenaeus and his understanding of the human condition. In insisting upon the presence of disordered concupiscence within each person, Augustine is in turn insisting that even though soul-making is teleologically oriented toward an eventual state of wholeness and maturity, its journey is fraught with setbacks, temptations, and pitfalls—including the very real possibility of failure. As a result, Augustine can help to clarify the possible misconception of a universalized, linear trajectory of soul-making, that perhaps can be envisioned in an overly simplistic reading of Irenaeus.

Augustine's potential for positively contributing to our project reaches beyond the possibility of complimenting the theodical interpretation of Irenaeus; for in addition to the question of theodicy, Augustine provided greater detail regarding the role and function of the purgatorial state within his writings,[87] which carries important implications in the development of an expanded sanctification-based understanding of purgatory within the Western Christian—specifically Catholic—theological tradition. For while Augustine's role in purgatory's development has commonly been considered according to the concepts of suffering, satisfaction, and punishment for the lingering impure effects of a person's sin-history, our investigation into the soul-making possibilities of his anthropology can allow for a reevaluation of his understanding of the intermediate state and its implications for our project. And although much focus has been placed upon Augustine's use of the word "punishment" when describing purgatory, it would also seem that Augustine's position of the post-mortem purifications encountered in the afterlife, while on the one hand reflecting the clear societal and legal values of his time,[88] may, on the other, also contain room for greater nuance than has been traditionally understood.

---

86. Gooch warns against such an understanding, pointing out that the main purpose of soul-making is "growth into responsible freedom" (Gooch, "Augustinian and Irenaean Theodicies," 10).

87. See, for example, Augustine, *Enchiridion*, 109; *City of God*, bk. 21.

88. See Moreira, *Heaven's Purge*, 39–41.

Augustine understood the word "punishment" to mean the corresponding spiritual consequence that an individual will experience in proportion to the lingering effects of their sins. Crucially, however, he also notes that the experiences of these consequences range from excruciating to perhaps even pleasant. In the *Enchidirion*, for example Augustine writes: "During the time, moreover, which intervenes between a man's death and the final resurrection, the soul dwells in a hidden retreat, where it enjoys rest or suffers affliction just in proportion to the merit it has earned by the life which it led on earth."[89] While it therefore seems clear that some sort of post-mortem suffering is the expected lot for most individuals in the intermediate state, the fact that Augustine mentions a range of possible experiences calls into question the notion that these same experiences exist *solely* to punish the individual, and *nothing else*. Moreover, Augustine also indicates in his writings the belief that the intercessory prayers of the faithful on earth can have an efficacious effect on the souls in the intermediate state:

> Nor can it be denied that the souls of the dead are benefited by the piety of their living friends, who offer the sacrifice of the Mediator, or give alms in the church on their behalf. But these services are of advantage only to those who during their lives have earned such merit, that services of this kind can help them. For there is a manner of life which is neither so good as not to require these services after death, nor so bad that such services are of no avail after death; there is, on the other hand, a kind of life so good as not to require them; and again, one so bad that when life is over they render no help. Therefore, it is in this life that all the merit or demerit is acquired, which can either relieve or aggravate a man's sufferings after this life.[90]

Accordingly, it becomes difficult to conclude that the post-mortem experience of purification is to be experienced exclusively as punishments *solely for their own sake* if the prayers and intercessions of the living are in some way able to alleviate the suffering involved. Again, such a passage seemingly indicates that these post-mortem "punishments" are not something wholly objective and externally imposed, but rather are personally tailored to the person, and take into consideration the various circumstances of their life. Thus, while Augustine certainly did not explicitly endorse that which has come to be described as a principally sanctification-based understanding of

---

89. Augustine, *Enchiridion*, 109. This opinion is corroborated in the *City of God*, in which Augustine writes that "death came into being through the perpetration of the first sin; and it may be that the period which follows death brings to each one an experience suited to the 'building' he has erected" (Augustine, *City of God*, bk. 21, ch. 26).

90. Augustine, *Enchiridion*, 110.

purgatory, it seems difficult to claim that he was, on the other hand, a proponent of a strictly satisfaction-based understanding. At the very least, it can be argued that he understood what would come to be known as purgatory as something more than merely a venue to be punished for the sake of being punished, and that beyond the need to satisfy any remaining injustice done toward God through personal sin, there also existed in these punishments a glimmer of an opportunity for continued improvement, correction, and discipline. As such, we are able to find in Augustine, not only an articulation of a soul-making based understanding of the human person, but also a window of opportunity to further interpret and develop the relationship between a soul-making understanding of the human person and the afterlife. Although many additional steps needed to take place in order for this to happen, it appears that we are able to observe at this point that, just as Gooch was able to show how the respective theological anthropologies of Augustine and Irenaeus remained basically not-incompatible, so too the relationship between Augustine's belief in the post-mortem intermediate state and the notion that salvation can be achieved *through* punishment (and not simply *because* of—or *after*—punishment) is likewise not-incompatible.

Thus, Hick and Gooch present two key points for our consideration: that Irenaeus is the principal expositor of what can be interpreted as a soul-making theodicy, and that, whether or not one views Irenaeus to be more explicit in his formulation, there nevertheless remains no basic competition between Irenaeus and Augustine for the purpose of interpreting their respective ideas into a soul-making theodicy. In addition, we can now add a third point: that although Augustine may have been less explicit than Irenaeus with regard to soul-making, Augustine more clearly presents in his writings an opportunity to form a connection between his own soul-making understanding of anthropology and theodicy, and a belief in a post-mortem intermediate state (which, again, appears to be an object of belief shared by both Irenaeus and Augustine). And within the context described above, it is possible to interpret this Augustinian notion of punishments as the means by which, one way or another, the person can, through God's grace, find final victory in their battle with disordered concupiscence within the broader process of post-mortem purification. This development will have positive implications upon an expanded sanctification-based understanding of the doctrine of purgatory within the Catholic tradition, as it allows for any future interpretation to draw from the insights of both Irenaeus and Augustine.

By departing from Hick in drawing Augustine into our reflections on an expanded sanctification-based (soul-making) understanding of purgatory, we are in effect situating these reflections more firmly upon a foundation that can be found within the Christian church's theological tradition—something that remains important for this project. And now that this tradition has been more clearly identified—and indeed strengthened—through the mutual inclusion of both Augustine and Irenaeus, it now becomes possible to properly examine how their initial soul-making contributions have later informed contemporary theologians and explore in what ways these contributions can inform a more robust understanding of the doctrine of purgatory. Although we will return to those initial insights when articulating a new vision of a soul-making understanding of purgatory within the Catholic tradition, we will first return to John Hick and observe how and in what ways he and his contemporaries have been able to build upon this foundation (even if only partially recognized) in their development of a sanctification-based, soul-making understanding of the post-mortem intermediate state. By exploring the details of Hick's soul-making theodicy in greater depth, we will be able to gain a deeper understanding of how his own valuable insights into an expanded role and function of the intermediate state can—and in what way—be brought into conversation with the doctrine of purgatory.

4

Soul-Making Influences within a Catholic Context

As WE HAVE NOW seen, John Hick principally locates the foundation for later soul-making interpretations of anthropology and theodicy within the writings of Irenaeus of Lyons. Yet, it has also been demonstrated that those foundations were not restricted to just one segment of the Christian tradition but could indeed be discerned across a broader theological landscape. While perhaps not entirely cognizant of that point, Hick would nevertheless go on to build upon those foundations in the development of his Irenaean-inspired, soul-making theodicy.

THE ROLE OF PURGATORY IN CONTEMPORARY SOUL-MAKING THEODICY

First published in 1966, Hick's *Evil and the God of Love* would prove highly influential. In it, Hick takes inspiration from Irenaeus's writings to develop a basic theodical theme, namely, that God fashioned a world in which both good and evil were allowed to commingle, thereby creating an environment within which humanity could gradually develop, in freedom and grace—and not without effort—toward an intended perfection.[1] While by no means seeking to minimize the terrifying, destructive force that is evil, or the horrific injustice that can accompany suffering, Hick would maintain that God ultimately possesses the final redemptive word over evil and

---

1. Hick, *Evil and the God of Love*, 215.

suffering: "That God mysteriously overrules the malicious deeds of the wicked . . . and eventually brings good out of evil, and indeed brings an eternal and therefore infinite good out of a temporal and therefore finite evil, is a thought of great promise for Christian theodicy."[2]

Hick argues that a world in which evil exists but is finally defeated is better than a world in which there exists no evil at all—that, in other words, the world we inhabit is somehow better for the possibility of suffering than it is without: "It would be an intolerable thought that God had permitted the fearful evil of sin without having already intended to bring out of it an even greater good than would have been possible if evil had never existed," Hick writes. "It must, then, be the case that sin plus redemption is of more value in the sight of God than an innocence that permits neither sin nor redemption."[3] With that in mind, Hick's particular theodicy rests upon the notion of humanity being created through an evolutionary process, wherein it would grow in maturity by purposefully engaging a challenging, character-developing (soul-making) world, made possible through the existence of evil and the freedom of personal choice. As such, each human person has to "grow into" its personhood (in a moral, intellectual, and spiritual sense), as that is not something that is fully present or developed at the very beginning of an individual's life. For Hick, this journey of engagement and growth culminates ultimately in the communal eschaton, in which God finally brings creation to perfection.

Hick's inclusion of an eschatological dimension in his theodicy is of great importance, as he believes it is what guarantees the ultimate success of any Irenaean type of theodicy.[4] For while he maintains that instances of suffering within a soul-making understanding of the world can serve as opportunities for constructive personal meaning-making and moral/spiritual growth, there also exist instances in which it is very difficult to sift any constructive benefits out of an experience of suffering, and others in which it would appear to be simply impossible, leaving Hick to admit that, ultimately, "so far as we can see, the soul-making process does in fact fail in our own world at least as often as it succeeds."[5] Therefore, in order for God to have the final word over evil and the greater good to be successfully extracted from the realities of lived suffering, the process of soul-making must continue in the afterlife, where it will find its eventual resolution.[6]

2. Hick, *Evil and the God of Love*, 89.
3. Hick, *Evil and the God of Love*, 176.
4. Hick, *Evil and the God of Love*, 237.
5. Hick, *Evil and the God of Love*, 336.
6. Hick, *Evil and the God of Love*, 339.

Although it appears that Hick does not in fact ascribe a name to this post-mortem soul-making process, it is clear that he understands it to take place in between the points of bodily death and final blessedness. Based on Hick's description, one could perhaps return to the term "post-mortem intermediate state" to refer to his understanding of the venue for these afterlife-based opportunities, in which a person continues the soul-making process until they are spiritually capable of fully experiencing the joys of heaven. By positing an intermediate state between bodily death and final beatitude where a person, by God's grace, continues—and ultimately resolves—the process of moral and spiritual growth that had begun on earth, it would seem that Hick is indeed proposing something strikingly similar to the contemporary Catholic understanding of a sanctification-based model of purgatory, as examined in the second chapter of this book. Yet it would also seem that Hick's particular understanding of the intermediate state marks something of a development upon the sanctification-based understanding of purgatory. Although already proposed by certain Catholic theologians in an attempt to examine how eschatology can be reapproached and understood from within the Catholic tradition, their respective emphases upon the purifications of purgatory as a means of sanctification was perhaps most significant for the mere fact that it marked a departure from the satisfaction-based model of purgatory long-held within the Catholic tradition. As we have observed, the legacy of a general understanding of an eschatology grounded in the categories and concepts of satisfaction still lingers. However, by operating outside of this tradition (and by instead operating within a Protestant tradition that has been historically very skeptical of anything resembling a post-mortem intermediary state), Hick has been able to bypass much of the residual historical issues that have accompanied purgatory's place in eschatological reflection, leaving him free to develop his own positive understanding of an intermediate state by grounding it as an essential component in his broader anthropological, theodical, and eschatological vision.

One aspect of Augustine's thought (and the tradition of theodicy that has drawn upon him for inspiration) of which Hick has been highly critical is his supposed reliance upon what Hick characterizes as overly philosophical and abstract concepts in his explanations of human nature, rendering it an abstract study of metaphysical essences and substances that tends to generalize and objectify any understanding of the human person and their relationship with the world.[7] In response to this, Hick maintains that any constructive Christian theodicy must be "centred upon moral personality

---

7. Hick, *Evil and the God of Love*, 53.

rather than on nature as a whole, and its governing principle must be ethical rather than aesthetic."[8] As an extension of his theodicy, Hick's understanding of the post-mortem intermediate state is also conceived through this ethical, person-centered perspective. As such, by constructing an ethical understanding of eschatology as an essential component of his ethical theodicy, Hick is in fact answering one of the demands earlier posed by Dermot A. Lane (one of the aforementioned Catholic proponents of a sanctification-based model of purgatory), which is that any credible attempt at answering the eschatological question must now also account for the various social pressures existing in the present word that remain in need of resolution, including global poverty, the threat of nuclear weapons, and the ongoing ecological crisis.[9] Although it cannot be said that Hick directly addresses each of the points enumerated by Lane, the overall point remains clear: that with regard to both theodicy and eschatology, ethical, subject-oriented questions concerning the individual person, the ongoing state of their moral personality, and the ongoing state of their relationship to their interpersonal surroundings, their moral, spiritual history, and their environment must all be considered.

It would appear, at first glance, that by positing within his own eschatological system a post-mortem intermediate state that recognizes and addresses the various external environmental pressures encountered by a person within a world of soul-making, Hick offers a cohesive ethical approach in understanding the human person's relationship to both theodicy and eschatology that might be able to shed new insights into how a sanctification-based model of purgatory might be understood. However, it has already been pointed out—and will be further explored in this chapter—that Hick is operating decidedly outside of the mainstream Christian tradition. Thus, it will be important to ascertain exactly what aspects of Hick's understanding of the post-mortem intermediate state cohere with, and indeed compliment, an understanding of death and the afterlife as has been received and passed down within the Christian tradition. It is the purpose of this chapter to examine both Hick's concept of "soul-making" and its relationship to the intermediate state in greater depth, and then analyze in what ways it is able to be brought into conversation with the contemporary understanding of the Catholic doctrine of purgatory.

---

8. Hick, *Evil and the God of Love*, 198.
9. Lane, *Keeping Hope Alive*, 7.

THE ROLE OF THE INTERMEDIATE STATE IN HICK'S THEODICY

In developing his understanding of theodicy, Hick argues that in order for any theodicy to be deemed "successful" it must first be considered both possible and plausible. Possibility, for Hick, means that the proposed theodicy must be internally coherent, while plausibility indicates a consistence between both the data of the religious tradition upon which the theodicy is based, and the data of the natural world, as revealed by the facts of scientific inquiry and the sociological facts of contemporary humanity's ethical, psychological and religious sensibilities—particularly those regarding the question of the existence of evil.[10] Accordingly, Hick believes that the so-called Augustinian approach to theodicy, characterized by an apparent insistence upon humanity's primordial perfection and a decisive fall event, to be theoretically possible, but decidedly implausible. On the other hand, he sees both possibility and plausibility in the Irenaean approach, which according to Hick, successfully operates out of "a framework of thought within which a theodicy became possible which does not depend upon the idea of the fall, and which is consonant with modern knowledge concerning the origins of the human race."[11] Based upon Irenaeus's insistence that God created an immature humanity capable of freely growing in relationship with its Creator through moral and spiritual progress, Hick allows Irenaeus's insights to form the foundation of his own evolutionary understanding of humanity "as an immature creature living in a challenging and therefore person-making world."[12]

The basic value undergirding Hick's insistence upon the necessity of a soul-making conception of the world is that the attainment of goodness and perfect relationship with the Creator by encountering and eventually transcending temptations, setbacks, and hardships through responsible, compassionate, decisions in concrete situations, is more rich and valuable (in a moral and spiritual sense) than would be the case if one was created to exist in a perpetual state of serene, if ignorant, virtue.[13] In elaborating upon this point, Hick writes that if God wanted to create finite persons embodying the *greatest* kind of moral and spiritual goodness, God could not have created them as already perfect, but rather was obligated to create them with both some degree of imperfection, *along with* the capability of achieving a greater

---

10. Hick, "Irenaean Theodicy," 39.
11. Hick, "Irenaean Theodicy," 41.
12. Hick, "Irenaean Theodicy," 40.
13. Hick, *Evil and the God of Love*, 255.

goodness according to the developmental contributions of freely chosen, hard-won insights and virtues: "a moral goodness which exists as the agent's initial given nature, without ever having been chosen by him in the face of temptation to the contrary, is intrinsically less valuable than a moral goodness which has been built up through the agent's own responsible choices through time in the face of alternative possibilities."[14]

Hick maintains that humanity was not created with the intention of living out a static, finitely perfect existence, but rather, by the will of God and through the forces of nature, it was created with a certain immaturity, in which not only its knowledge of self and its relationship with the Creator was imperfect, its very awareness of God himself was not entirely evident. Hick terms this lack of awareness as existing within an "epistemic distance" from its Creator, according to which the presence of God in the world remains obscure, thereby allowing for the movements and powers of the natural world to remain ambiguous as to their origins and purpose.[15] Yet Hick goes on to insist that in spite of this distance, humanity, from its very origins, nevertheless possessed a certain preternatural inclination toward the divine, no matter how obscured by the Fall and its consequences, which might be termed—although Hick does not do so himself—as a certain operative grace from God, permanently present in the person and continually working to incline them toward God. And in so doing, it therefore allows for the possibility for the specifically *soul-making* quality of various experiences or actions encountered or performed by the person by allowing for those experiences or actions to potentially bring about further moral and/or spiritual growth, and ultimately growth in relationship with God. It would seem that this is then achieved through particular instances of what could generally be termed as cooperative grace, whereby the person freely chooses to respond positively to these various experiences in such a way so as to uncover God's divine presence embedded within them and is able to integrate them into their own personal identity. In so doing, that is, by choosing to recognize the divine presence in these life experiences, along with the spiritually-constructive potential that they may offer, a person engaged in the journey of soul-making is therefore continuously striving—with God's help—to bring their own will closer to God's, gradually developing the ability to see God's presence (and God's desire for each person) in each experience, as well as the desire to come closer to God through each of these experiences.

---

14. Hick, "Irenaean Theodicy," 44.
15. Hick, "Irenaean Theodicy," 43.

However, while this preternatural inclination toward God indeed remains obscured by our human limitations, Hick argues that this, too, is for an intended purpose, as ambiguity necessarily guarantees that humanity operates with some degree of genuine freedom and authenticity as it journeys, however tentatively, to fulfill its innate desire for intimacy with God. The world, Hick writes, as the environment of a person's life, will be by design religiously ambivalent, "both veiling God and revealing Him—veiling Him to ensure man's freedom and revealing Him to men as they rightly exercise that freedom."[16] As such, within Hick's understanding of primordial humanity, the first humans were not acting according to some sense of perfect knowledge and awareness, nor were they acting out of a sense of fear of obligation toward God; instead they came into consciousness as primitive, self-referential creatures, yet creatures capable of—and invited to—move beyond instinct and enter into relationship with the divine by making decisions, performing actions and integrating experiences to the end of transcending their basic orientation of self-regard into a self-giving orientation of love for the other (both divine and creaturely).

To this end, one can find in all of creation the qualities necessary for abetting humanity's inherent dynamism. In other words, the world into which humanity was created—and presently finds itself—was itself created for the purpose of stimulating humanity's progress. It was created as the arena within which human persons could make the hard-won decisions and receive the hard-won experiences that are conducive to both moral and spiritual growth. To use Hick's terminology, it was created for the purpose of soul-making. As such, the principal criteria by which the goodness of the world (and by extension, God) ought to be judged is not the mere "quantity of pleasure and pain occurring in it at any particular moment, but by its fitness for its primary purpose, the purpose of soul-making."[17]

It is with this criterion of soul-making in mind that Hick approaches the reality of evil, and the relationship between its existence and that of a loving, good Creator God. Briefly put, Hick believes that a world of soul-making is impossible without the existence—and perceived problem—of evil:

> Thus the hypothesis of a divine purpose in which finite persons are created at an epistemic distance from God, in order that they may gradually become children of God through their own moral and spiritual choices, requires that their environment, instead of being a pain-free and stress-free paradise, be broadly the kind of

---

16. Hick, *Evil and the God of Love*, 282.
17. Hick, *Evil and the God of Love*, 259.

world of which we find ourselves to be a part. It requires that it be such as to provoke the theological problem of evil.[18]

Thus, while Hick freely admits that God, as the author of creation, remains ultimately responsible for the existence of the evils of pain and suffering, these are permitted as necessary evils for the even greater goods of achievement, success, and triumph to exist with any sense of value or moral worth. In other words, God only permits the existence of evil in order to make possible the existence of even greater good, achieved through the soul-making endeavors of God's creation.[19] This is the good that humanity has freely chosen to search out and strive toward, even in the face of challenge, exertion, and adversity.

Such an acknowledgment should in no way mitigate evil's chaotic, savage character; Hick insists it remains a positively destructive force that does not possess any value intrinsic to itself in God's divine plan.[20] Rather, its value in that plan is to be found in the soul-making activities whereby it is overcome, namely in and through the work of humanity's redemption from sin and mutual self-service amid instances of adversity and suffering. Nevertheless, Hick acknowledges that the question may be posed of whether God could have simply created a better world and do away with the existence of pain and suffering altogether, even if they serve a supposedly constructive purpose. Hick responds with his own question and reiterates his main point: "Better for what? We have to specify the general aim or purpose which has motivated the act of creation, and then ask whether the world could have been better in relation to that purpose."[21] If the world was indeed devoid of pain and suffering, then human existence, according to Hick, "would involve no need for exertion, no kind of challenge, no problems to be solved or difficulties to be overcome, no demand of the environment for human skill or inventiveness. There would be nothing to avoid and nothing to seek."[22] Indeed, Hick sees such an ideally perfect world, in spite of its supposed tidiness, as vastly inferior to our own messy world of soul-making, as it leaves no opportunities for any sort of the aforementioned greater goods to emerge, leaving him to conclude that while human life in a world devoid of evil may appear idyllic, "the race would consist of feckless

---

18. Hick, "Irenaean Theodicy," 48.
19. Hick, "Irenaean Theodicy," 50.
20. Hick, *Evil and the God of Love*, 323.
21. Hick, *Evil and the God of Love*, 308.
22. Hick, *Evil and the God of Love*, 306–7.

Adams and Eves, harmless and innocent, but devoid of positive character and without the dignity of real responsibilities, tasks, and achievements."[23]

If then, one is able to accept Hick's premise that a soul-making world is morally better than a non-soul-making world, then it follows that one must accept along with that premise the necessary ingredient allowing for the very concept of authentic soul-making to have any purchase, namely, the existence of evil. It is the existence of evil, with its attending potential for risk, for woundedness, and for failure, that guarantees the freedom and authenticity of the individual's journey toward sanctification.

Of course, in light of the above explanation, Hick anticipates the following question: While one may accept the need for some degree of pain and suffering to exist in a world of soul-making, must the degrees of pain and suffering that one can potentially experience be as intense as they are? While one may accept the calamities brought about by moral evil as the consequence of a humanity endowed with a genuine freedom of choice, in what ways do the calamities of natural evil, that is, the destructive powers found in the innate forces of our environment (such as natural disasters and crippling disease) contribute to soul-making? In response, Hick has already pointed out that the world formed by these natural forces also includes a humanity formed by these same forces; that these destructive natural forces helped to bring about our natural evolution as well as our "epistemic distance" from God is a point that Hick sees as crucial to guaranteeing our independence of action and authenticity of growth. But with regard to the problem of the intensity of these natural evils, Hick proposes the following: "Concerning the intensity of natural evil, the truth is probably that our judgments of intensity are relative. We might identify some form of natural evil as the worst that there is . . . and claim that a loving God would not have allowed this to exist. But in a world in which there was no cancer, something else would then rank as the worst form of natural evil."[24]

Hick admits that this might sound like cold comfort to someone who has experienced instances of extreme suffering; however, he maintains that he is unaware of any other alternative theory that could provide a better explanation as to why certain individuals or groups suffer as they do—as such, the only remaining appeal to this question within his Irenaean framework is to that of mystery.[25] Perhaps, in order for humanity's epistemic distance from God to be authentically maintained, there must always remain in the soul-making process some degree of uncertainty, unpredictability, and

23. Hick, *Evil and the God of Love*, 307.
24. Hick, "Irenaean Theodicy," 49.
25. Hick, *Evil and the God of Love*, 333.

unknowability, so as to render virtuous human actions good in themselves, and guarantee that they were not attained through the forces of coercion, fear or obligation. Additionally, Hick points out that the undirected and haphazard way in which certain instances of natural evil are encountered is itself sometimes necessary so as to allow for a world in which greater good can be found in spontaneous acts of mutual caring, aid, and love.[26] As such, to live with this mystery is to live according to a certain, ongoing challenge, to see to what extent the person chooses to persist in their self-centeredness, or whether they have adequately advanced in the path of soul-making to a basic disposition of love and regard for the other.

That is conceivably the function that pain and suffering—including the pain and suffering that stems from instances of natural evil—can play in a world of soul-making: that even when it is as randomly distributed as it is, and in such varying intensity, it can still, in some way, serve a constructive role in a person's moral, spiritual, and intellectual development. But, on the other hand, it is also very easy to recount specific instances of encountered pain and suffering that have served absolutely no conceivable constructive purpose, occurring instead as an entirely destructive force. This is something that Hick candidly acknowledges when he writes that "so far as we can see, the soul-making process does in fact fail in our own world at least as often as it succeeds."[27] Such an admission underlines one of Hick's principal points: that reflection on theodicy cannot remain an entirely abstract endeavor, in which such instances of destructive suffering find a cool and detached explanation for their existence within a larger theodical system. Rather, its ethical dimension must be honestly maintained, and ethically speaking, such instances of destructive suffering ultimately remain inscrutable to logical attempts at explanation, and their resolution demands more than a sound intellectual argument. It is for that reason that Hick turns to the eschaton to find some sort of resolution for all instances of encountered evil, of both the constructive and destructive variety:

> We have to say simply that the incomprehensible mingling in human experience of good and evil, virtue and vice, pain and pleasure, grief and laughter, continues in all its characteristic and baffling ambiguity throughout life and ends only with death. . . . If there is any eventual resolution of the interplay between good and evil, any decisive bringing of good out of evil, it must lie between this world and beyond the enigma of death.[28]

26. Hick, "Irenaean Theodicy," 49.
27. Hick, *Evil and the God of Love*, 336
28. Hick, *Evil and the God of Love*, 339.

Hick believes that the validity of his soul-making theodicy rests on the premise that the existence of evil can only tolerated for the sake of the ultimate greater good that will necessarily emerge from it; thus, when considered at an individual level, a person's journey of soul-making must likewise render the pain and suffering personally encountered throughout one's life somehow worthwhile, even experiences of a destructive nature. Yet, as we have seen, he also realizes that for the vast majority of persons, it is almost impossible to successfully complete the soul-making process during one's earthly life. Therefore, by sheer necessity, he posits a certain post-mortem intermediary state of existence between earthly life and final beatitude in which each person's soul-making journey finds resolution: "In short," Hick writes, "the fulfillment of the divine purpose, as it is postulated in the Irenaean type of theodicy, presupposes each person's survival, in some form of bodily death, and further living and growing towards that end-state. Without such an eschatological fulfillment, this theodicy would collapse."[29] Yet it is not simply resolution that the person seems to receive in this state, but rather a sense of triumph over—and a deeper appreciation of—the sometimes-difficult events of one's life, made possible through the attainment of an ever-growing maturity of perspective. According to Hick: "We must affirm in faith that there will in the final accounting be no personal life that is unperfected and no suffering that has not eventually become a phase in the fulfillment of God's good purpose. . . . For if there are finally wasted lives and finally unredeemed sufferings, either God is not perfect in love or He is not sovereign in rule over His creation."[30]

In light of such an understanding, Hick maintains that the extent to which the presence of evil in God's soul-making plan of salvation is justified depends wholly upon the degree of completeness achieved by that same plan of salvation. This, for Hick, is an all-or-nothing proposition: either the existence of evil is justifiable, or it is not; either God's plan of salvation is successful, or it is not. An infinitely loving and powerful God, who made humanity for fellowship with himself, must not, ethically speaking, let some parts of that humanity fall by the wayside due to the existence of evil and suffering as some sort of by-product of God's soul-making world. As such, Hick is particularly insistent that all instances of unjustified pain, inexplicable suffering—in other words, all seemingly destructive frustrations to God's divine plan—must somehow be redeemed and therefore proposes that the continued soul-making processes of the post-mortem intermediary state be made available to every person, throughout all of history, no matter

---

29. Hick, "Irenaean Theodicy," 51.
30. Hick, *Evil and the God of Love*, 340.

what happened to transpire during their earthly life: "All experience of evil, in the forms both of wickedness and suffering, will have been turned by its end into a history that has led to the Kingdom of God. But if that eschaton is to be unqualifiedly good, no preceding sin or pain must be left outside the scope of its retrospective justification."[31]

Hick thus repudiates the possibility of an eternal hell for the reason that its very existence as a place of eternal torment implies that either God does not will to save all of God's creation (in which case God is not fully good), or that certain individuals managed to elude God's plan of salvation (in which case God is not all-powerful).[32] Nevertheless, it seems undeniable that certain persons do indeed die in a state of profound woundedness or alienation from God—therefore, from God's perfect power and goodness, Hick deduces that in the end those persons "will somehow be drawn freely to open [themselves] to [their] Maker."[33] In the place of hell, Hick proposes that the role and function of the post-mortem intermediate state be expanded, seeing in it an opportunity for all of God's human creation to continue—and complete—the soul-making process (whether as victims of destructive suffering, or as perpetrators, or both), throughout which "God will never cease to desire and to actively work for the salvation of each created person." God, Hick continues, "will never abandon any as irredeemably evil. However long an individual may reject his Maker, salvation will remain an open possibility to which God is ever trying to draw him."[34]

In elaborating upon his understanding of the post-mortem intermediate state as another venue in which God can work to draw a person closer to himself, Hick writes that "it seems morally (although still not logically impossible that the infinite resourcefulness of infinite love working in unlimited time should be terminally frustrated, and the creature reject its own good, presented to it in an endless range of ways, . . . but despite the logical possibility of failure the probability of His success amounts, as it seems to me, to a practical certainty."[35] In effect, Hick is proposing an understanding of a post-mortem intermediate state in which—and through which—every person is guaranteed salvation. For although Hick might acknowledge that it *does seem logically possible* that a person will ultimately "perish" if they choose to remain closed off to God's sustaining presence, the notion that there are elements of God's creation that can potentially exist in an eternal

---

31. Hick, "Problem of Evil," 598.
32. Hick, *Evil and the God of Love*, 342.
33. Hick, "Problem of Evil," 600.
34. Hick, *Evil and the God of Love*, 343.
35. Hick, *Evil and the God of Love*, 344.

state of suffering and torment, and that these sufferings can never lead to "any constructive end beyond themselves," amounts, in Hick's eyes, to nothing more than pointless, interminable torture, something antithetical to his entire concept of soul-making and of the loving, creative God behind it.[36] Thus, in accordance with his twin beliefs in a humanity oriented toward God via a process of soul-making and a loving, creative God who is both the author, sustainer, and consummator of this process, Hick proposes a temporally bound post-mortem existence where every person might receive the graces necessary to complete their own soul-making journey. For some individuals, this might simply involve some extra time to grow in the good already present in their lives and tie up the so-called "loose-ends," for others, this might apparently necessitate an extended period of appropriating, and indeed reclamation of, certain setbacks—and even outright failures—that might have occurred, so that they may be transformed into constructive elements of God's divine plan. For others still, who lived a life of seeming detachment from God, it might involve a longer process of moral and spiritual purgation that may take on a possibly painful, self-reformative character, through which the individual will eventually grow in an awareness to see God's divine presence in their own history, and eventually come to identify with that presence. Therefore, in every instance, no matter what the circumstances, the intermediate state can serve as an opportunity in which everyone will receive the transformative graces required to freely choose to enter into an eternal relationship with the Creator.

Such an understanding bears a striking similarity to that of Origen, almost eighteen hundred years earlier.[37] Returning once again to this early "father" of purgatory,[38] it can once again be pointed out that like Hick, Origen, too, was notable for his unique and controversial opinions on the afterlife—most famously, the belief in universal salvation and the temporary nature of hell.[39] As we have seen, Origen's understanding of hell took on certain purgatorial characteristics, in which all of the evil present in creation would eventually be expunged, until there is only the purified good that remained.[40] Again, Origen conceived of this process as something akin to a period of healing from spiritual illness, as well as personal correction, allowing the person to grow in the virtues necessary to freely enter into full

---

36. Hick, *Evil and the God of Love*, 341.
37. See chapter 1 of this book.
38. Le Goff, *Birth of Purgatory*, 52.
39. Le Goff, *Birth of Purgatory*, 55.
40. Origen, *On First Principles*, 3.5.3–7. For an explanation of Origen's understanding of hell, see chapter 1 of this book.

communion with God. The similarities between Origen and Hick's respective understandings of hell are obvious. However, the similarities between Origen and Hick are not limited to issues involving the afterlife. Indeed, with Origen, one can almost see in Origen the beginnings of an almost proto-soul-making understanding of the human person, in which they are understood to navigate a world full of challenge in an attempt to become more and more like God. Origen believed that while the world undoubtedly contains struggle and difficulty, its purpose remains "fundamentally beneficent" in that it was created by God with the intention for "rational spirits to become like God voluntarily and through their own efforts."[41] Origen would also maintain that in spite of its fallen nature, the human spirit nevertheless possesses a natural longing for God, which God would not have allowed to exist unless he intended for it to be ultimately satisfied.[42] Thus, for Origen—like Hick—the purpose of human life is to respond to this desire so as to grow in intimacy and become more like God, with the goal of ultimate union in the afterlife.

Yet in spite of these numerous similarities, Hick curiously refrains from naming Origen as the major inspiration behind his soul-making theological project. This point was raised by Mark S. M. Scott who, after noting their presence, asked Hick why it was the case that Origen received from him so little attention. Hick wrote in response that while it is indeed the case that Origen's thought, for the reasons outlined above, is much nearer than Irenaeus to his own contemporary soul-making understanding of theodicy and the afterlife, he would nevertheless keep Irenaeus as his "patron saint." One reason for this was what Hick would characterize as Origen's "eccentric" understanding of the preexistence of souls; another was that Irenaeus was active before Origen, who he believed ended up taking some of Irenaeus's more implicit themes and developing them more explicitly. Finally, Hick would also mention, rather pragmatically, that Irenaeus is already a saint and Origen is not, which makes Irenaeus a more attractive candidate from a "PR point of view." Thus, due to reasons that Scott would describe as "practical and political," Hick would continue to maintain Irenaeus as the patron saint of his soul-making theodicy, even though it may align closer to Origen theologically.[43]

Yet just as Origen's understanding of the afterlife was not without its critics, neither has been Hick's (despite his deliberate PR concerns). In response to the concerns that the intermediate state exists as a tool of

---

41. Trigg, *Origen*, 28.
42. Trigg, *Origen*, 29.
43. Scott, "Suffering and Soul-Making," 333.

coercion, in which everyone will choose to embrace God, no matter what, Hick maintains a relative understanding of what is meant by "coercion," in that, practically speaking, no act of human will has ever been carried out in a vacuum of perfect freedom, but rather has always occurred in interaction with various forces, circumstances, and situations beyond itself and its choosing.[44] Therefore, although an individual may have, within their own context, freely chosen to develop an orientation fundamentally turned against God, the intermediate state effectively provides a new context in which it becomes far more likely—indeed, inevitable—that within this new set of circumstances, the individual will experience a desired reorientation their life toward the divine through a continuous exposure to God's divine grace.[45]

The post-mortem intermediate state therefore serves an essential role in Hick's soul-making understanding of anthropology, theodicy, and the afterlife: it provides the context within which every individual can continue, with the aid of divine grace, their own journey of soul-making to the point of a blessed conclusion. Hick's understanding of the intermediate state ensures that no instance of pain or suffering ultimately goes unanswered by guaranteeing further soul-making opportunities for individuals who might have experienced instances of pain and suffering and were unable to constructively resolve the spiritual and psychological effects of those actions while on earth. Moreover, it offers an expanded understanding of how these post-mortem opportunities might operate by mentioning possible instances of self-awareness and reformation, continued growth and even healing. Finally, in stressing the ultimately communal awareness that is derived from soul-making and how a soul-making afterlife will be a collective experience in the broadest sense, in which everyone will participate, Hick's understanding of the post-mortem intermediate state decisively expands the eschatological horizons in which it is situated and orients it toward a hopeful future conclusion. For these reasons, Hick's soul-making model of the intermediate state offers possible new insights into how a contemporary, sanctification-based understandings of purgatory might be conceived; but on the other hand, there remain certain elements within his thought—especially elements that have emerged over the course of his later academic career—that raise definite issues for their reception within a Christian, specifically Catholic, context. Therefore, it would seem that further investigation of his soul-making post-mortem intermediate state is required.

---

44. Hick, "Problem of Evil," 600.
45. Hick, "Problem of Evil," 600.

ANALYSIS

Before any attempt can be made to determine exactly how John Hick's soul-making post-mortem intermediary state can inform how purgatory may be thought to operate within its present doctrinal understanding, an important point must first be addressed: namely, the progression of Hick's own theological and philosophical perspectives over the course of his life. As David Cheetham states on the first page of his introductory work on the thought of John Hick, "Hick's work could be described as a journey. Readers of his books will not find a static thinker, rather his work might be characterized as an ever-expanding exercise"[46] This is especially true with regard to his understanding of death and the afterlife, including the role and function of the intermediary state.

In the time between the publishing of *Evil and the God of Love* (1966 CE)—Hick's first major work on the subject of creation, theodicy, and the afterlife—and *Death and Eternal Life* (1976 CE), in which those themes are revisited, Hick seemingly immersed himself in the teachings of other world religions and became increasingly comfortable in expressing a religiously pluralistic worldview.[47] Accordingly, his thoughts on the subject of death and the afterlife evolved from the position of a Christian-informed universalism facilitated through a post-mortem intermediate state capable of providing every person further opportunities to continue and conclude the process of soul making, to a universalism understood to occur by means of a series of reembodied conscious personalities, in which the period between the reembodiments becomes a recurring space wherein each person can process and integrate each of their experiences between each reembodiment.

Although Hick continues to maintain the basic argument found in *Evil and the God of Love* regarding the need for a universalist understanding of soul-making,[48] it would appear that since the writing of *Death and Eternal Life*, he would become dissatisfied over certain points within his previous understanding—specifically over the notion of just how effective

---

46. Cheetham, *John Hick*, 1.

47. A very basic biographical outline of Hick's personal religious journey might shed some light upon his own intellectual movement. Born in 1922, he had a conversion experience in college (whereupon he developed what he considered to be certain "fundamentalist beliefs," from which he only gradually drifted away), and was ordained in the Presbyterian Church of England (now United Reformed Church) in 1953. It was during this time that he came to develop strong views on religious pluralism as well as the historical reality of certain aspects of the Christian faith. Toward the end of his life he identified as an "irregular attender" of URC services and Quaker meetings (Hick, *Autobiography*, 323).

48. See Hick, *Death and Eternal Life*, 200–201.

and authentic the process of soul-making could be in a post-mortem, disembodied, intermediate state. According to Hick, in order for a person to authentically choose God through the process of soul-making, it must be done "freely," that is, emanating from a person's innate creaturely freedom, even though it may be circumscribed by circumstances, or the person's own immaturity: "creaturely freedom always occurs within the limits of a basic nature that we did not ourselves choose; for this is entitled by the fact of having been created."[49] Thus, he would ultimately conclude that moral and spiritual growth could only occur within the context of finite embodied life, "bounded by birth and death, because it is the pressure of these boundaries that makes time precious and development possible."[50]

This increasing insistence that soul-making can only authentically occur within the created temporal confines of an embodied life would lead Hick to question his previous position of looking toward the post-mortem intermediate state—in which the disembodied soul becomes an essentially receptive agent of God's grace—as a means for concluding the soul-making process. Instead, finding inspiration in the approaches to the afterlife found in the world's eastern religions, Hick would eventually go on to conclude that a person's soul-making journey will thus take place over the course of multiple lives, each, according to Hick, "bounded by something analogous to birth and death, lived in other worlds and spaces other than that in which we now are."[51]

For Hick, the opportunities of multiple physical lives would solve his earlier concern over the seemingly fleeting opportunities for a person to freely and progressively engage the soul-making process during their time on earth. And in response he would go on to postulate a process of retrieval and preservation of the "dispositional continuant" (which is not to say the individual consciousness) of each person, which can be carried over from one life to the next.[52] For Hick, a person's dispositional continuant existed beyond each person's conscious self, and was something akin to their unconscious collection of memories, conditioned by any accumulated moral/

---

49. Hick, "Irenaean Theodicy," 52.

50. Hick, *New Frontier of Religion and Science*, 198.

51. Hick, *Death and Eternal Life*, 456.

52. See Hick, *New Frontier of Religion and Science*, 199. This was one of the last major works before Hick's death, in which he would further refine his position to offer the following explanation: "What we should take from Hinduism and Buddhism, I suggest, is the thought that in the unconscious depth of the present personality there is a deeper moral/spiritual essence which can survive bodily death and be re-embodied in a new conscious personality—or indeed in a series of new conscious personalities" (Hick, *New Frontier of Religion and Science*, 196).

spiritual growth or deterioration stemming from previous actions and responses of previous lives. The reembodied person, then, is not simply a reincarnation of the present conscious self, but, according to Hick, "a new personality formed by all the genetic and environmental circumstances which makes each of us the unique individual that we are, but embodying the dispositional continuant at the basis of this new individual."[53]

Within this reformulated understanding, the role and function of the intermediate state is accordingly modified. Whereas Hick previously understood it to serve as a post-mortem opportunity for an individual to continue their soul-making journey, leading to eventual resolution, the intermediate state now becomes a sort of post-mortem opportunity to appropriate and integrate any lived experiences before the person becomes reembodied into a new bodily life, within a new soul-making environment so as to continue the process.[54] Hick specifically indicates his appreciation of the Tibetan Buddhist concept of *bardo* (literally "between two") in helping to understand how an individual dispositional continuant can be objectively evaluated after death and continuously transferred over the course of multiple lives. For Hick, *bardo* is the belief that the post-mortem world is created by the mind in accordance with its own respective beliefs, and that after death, "released from the pressures and threats which sustain our self-image in this life, the mind realistically appraises itself in a kind of psychoanalytic experience and the outcome reaches consciousness in the imagery provided by one's religious faith."[55] Accordingly, Hick would go on to adapt this insight to his own evolving understanding of the afterlife, specifically the role and function of the post-mortem intermediate state:

> I am assuming, then, that when the physical organism dies the conscious personality continues to exist. And I speculate that in the first phase of its post-mortem existence it is not embodied, and accordingly receives no new sensory input, but experiences a kind of dream environment built out of the materials of memory by the molding power of conscious and repressed desires developed in the course of its earthly life. This will be a period of self-revelation and self-judgment, a kind of psychoanalytic experience in which we become aware of our own character, so largely hidden from us in this life, and perhaps as a result form new and different hopes and aspirations.[56]

53. Hick, *New Frontier of Religion and Science*, 199.
54. Hick, "Present and Future Life," 13. A more detailed explanation of this process can be found in Hick, *Death and Eternal Life*, 403–21.
55. Hick, *Death and Eternal Life*, 403.
56. Hick, "Present and Future Life," 12.

However, unlike certain understandings of reincarnation found in various eastern schools of thought, Hick would maintain the strong divinely oriented teleological component of soul-making found in *Evil and the God of Love* and accordingly adopted this new understanding of reembodiment to his previous position that even though a person may experience numerous spiritual achievements and setbacks throughout their series of reembodiments, the person's aforementioned preternatural inclination toward the divine fundamentally orients their journey in a direction that ultimately gravitates toward God.[57] The soul-making cycle that Hick would therefore come to envision is one of life, death and appropriation within an intermediate state, followed by another—possibly otherworldly—life,[58] death, further appropriation, and so on as the person progressively transcends their initial spiritual and moral immaturity, culminating in an ultimately selfless, corporate existence in which the person will become "so transparent to the divine life that [they will] no longer live as separate self-enclosed individuals."[59]

The description offered above is a very basic outline of Hick's much more complex understanding of the afterlife that developed during the middle to latter part of his career. It has been kept intentionally brief, for the simple reason that while undoubtedly thought-provoking, its content simply falls too far outside the imposed parameters of this project to warrant further consideration. Our purpose is to investigate and identify in what ways Hick's initial soul-making understanding of the intermediate state can inform our revisiting of the present doctrine of purgatory. Although not without its own set of problems that will need to be addressed, it will ultimately be argued that Hick does indeed provide certain key insights into how the present doctrine could be approached and understood. However, it would seem that these insights are to be largely found within Hick's earlier work on the subject, where a constructive conversation with what he is proposing appears at least possible. This does not appear to be the case with Hick's latter conclusions; for while these conclusions could undoubtedly yield some unique insights into how this doctrine might be considered, they also pose extreme—almost certainly insurmountable—challenges in

---

57. See Hick, "Present and Future Life," 14.

58. Hick interprets the overall lack of collective moral progress in the history of humanity as evidence that a soul-making process of continuous reembodiments is indeed not occurring on this world; thus, he postulates that "movement towards human perfection should occur in the personal histories and interactions of individuals through the successive par-eschatological worlds" (Hick, "Irenaean Theodicy," 66. See also Hick, "Present and Future Life," 13, and *Death and Eternal Life*, 284–88, for further statements indicating support of an understanding that reembodiment is to occur over a plane of multiple worlds).

59. Hick, *Death and Eternal Life*, 446.

any attempt to harmonize them with Catholicism's, or indeed, mainline Christianity's present attitude toward the idea of reincarnation, or any variation thereof.

The updated 1994 edition of the *Catechism of the Catholic Church* unequivocally offers the following statement on the subject: "Death is the end of man's earthly pilgrimage, of the time of grace and mercy which God offers him so as to work out his earthly life in keeping with the divine plan, and to decide his ultimate destiny. When 'the single course of our earthly life' is completed (*Lumen gentium* 48:3), we shall not return to other earthly lives: 'It is appointed for men to die once (Hebrews 9:27).' There is no 'reincarnation' after death."[60] More recently, Bradley Malkovsky points out that for all of its clarity, there is not much by way of explanation behind this pronouncement other than its direct reference to Scripture.[61] He goes on to suggest that the reason for the Catholic Church's hostility toward the doctrine may lie in its traditional affirmation of the resurrection of the whole person, iterating that Christianity has traditionally considered reincarnation to be unnecessary in light of God's merciful preservation and transformation of the human person in its entirety after death: "The Christian position, and not just the specifically Catholic position, is that God's love for each human being is so great that every person is called into permanent union with God *as this particular human* individual."[62]

The fundamental problem with reincarnation (at least from the perspective of the Catholic theological tradition), then, is that by suggesting there will exist multiple bodies for each individual soul, what is effectively being affirmed is that a person is simply either a soul or an unchanging consciousness alone, thereby contradicting Christianity's basic affirmation that the human person exists as a unique and particular composite of both body and soul. Accordingly, while reincarnation or reembodiment indicates the resuscitation and transference of "a person" (which may be conceived of as "a soul," or as a pure changeless consciousness, or as a "dispositional continuant" [to borrow Hick's terminology], depending on how one understands the process) from one body to the next in approximately the same manner of existence as before, resurrection indicates a total transformation and integration of the "entire" human person, both body and soul. In the words of Malkovsky, it "entails the completion of the human person in a new liberated mode of existence and awareness, a total integration and full participation of the human person in the life of the divine, whereby each

60. Catholic Church, *Catechism of the Catholic Church*, 1013.
61. Malkovsky, "Belief in Reincarnation," 6.
62. Malkovsky, "Belief in Reincarnation," 2.

person perfectly reveals the glory and beauty of the creator in a unique and singular way."[63] It is as a unique human being—a unique creature composed of a particular body and a particular soul—that we are called into relationship with God. By postulating multiple bodies for every individual, the uniqueness of each person becomes fundamentally diluted and the resurrection event itself becomes an absurdity—hence the unambiguous declaration found in the *Catechism*.

In his evaluative introduction to the thought of John Hick, David Cheetham mentions that Hick himself has been critical of individuals who have challenged one aspect of his thinking by regarding it in isolation from the rest of his thought, or have neglected to consider the revisions and qualifications that have been added at a later date.[64] Nevertheless, in taking a closer look at Hick's views on death and the afterlife, it would seem that a certain degree of isolation nevertheless remains necessary, as there are certain elements within his earlier thought that can indeed inform and constructively challenge the contemporary theological understanding of purgatory. However, there are also elements, largely emerging from the latter part of Hick's academic career that, for the time being, remain basically incompatible; his advocating for the belief in reembodiment would fit into that latter category.

Undoubtedly, these speculations authentically stem from Hick's personal convictions; however, for our purposes, they run the risk of terminally effecting any attempt of introducing his fundamental Irenaean soul-making insights into any Christian, particularly Catholic, discussion of the afterlife. Therefore, it would seem that Hick's earlier spirit of optimistic restraint must instead be channeled in the discussion to come, mindful that it will include Hick's already-mentioned insights into soul-making, as well as the lessons learned from our earlier exploration of purgatory's doctrinal history. Thus, our ongoing exploration of Hick's thought will instead focus on the core issues raised by Hick in the earlier stages of his academic career; for while certain issues will unquestionably arise regarding the compatibility of even some of these earlier positions and how death and the afterlife are understood in the greater Christian theological tradition, there nevertheless remain certain insights unique to Hick that can undoubtedly inform the present understanding of the role and function of purgatory within a broader, contemporary eschatological system.

---

63. Malkovsky, "Belief in Reincarnation," 4.
64. Cheetham, *John Hick*, 1.

CONTRIBUTIONS

Perhaps Hick's most significant contribution to this discussion is in proposing an understanding of the intermediate state in which its role and function most directly responds to John E. Thiel's earlier point that, in order to maintain its relevancy within a Catholic context, any further speculation on purgatory must somehow harmonize itself with an eschatological understanding present in a "Pauline" spiritual culture. Returning once again to this crucial point raised in chapter 2, it can be recalled that as opposed to what he broadly characterized as the competitive "Matthean" spiritual culture previously dominant in Tridentine and pre-Tridentine Catholicism, the culture out of which the formal doctrine of purgatory emerged, Thiel describes the Pauline spiritual culture as one which emphasizes the presence of sin as an equalizing, shared reality within the human condition, thereby necessitating a universal need for divine grace. This grace bypasses any hierarchical understanding of grace and salvation that had privileged the merit of individual action and personal placement at the time of judgment, thereby rendering such distinctions irrelevant. The soteriological focus within this context is removed from the individual situation of rewarded personal merit and is instead placed upon authentic responses arising from a universal condition toward a universal call, tending toward a more universally minded resolution in the eschaton. As such, the eschatological dynamics of fear and self-obsession associated with a competitive, merit-based understanding are effectively replaced by a dynamic of solidarity and hope, in which not only one's own destiny, but the destiny of all creation is finally transformed and consummated by God's divine grace.

Thiel points out that this general theological culture—and specific eschatological outlook—has been closely associated with classical Protestantism, which, in keeping with its obvious emphasis on unmediated grace and suspicion toward notions of works-righteousness, has historically rejected the salvific value of purgatory as a place where an individual can eventually gain perfection through intense punishments that have been judged appropriate according to the detailed accounting of personal value and sin as found within a Tridentine eschatological system of merit. Moreover, as already mentioned, Thiel goes on to convincingly identify this same Pauline sense of spirituality as the predominant spiritual culture that has emerged within the Catholic Church since the time of the Second Vatican Council, thereby leading to his theory that popular belief and theological relevancy of how and why the doctrine of purgatory diminished as it struggled to transition from an earlier, Matthean understanding to a post-conciliar, Pauline understanding.[65]

While theologians within the Catholic tradition have so far been working to adapt a Matthean understanding of purgatory to an emerging Pauline spiritual culture, Hick, on the other hand, has instead been able to directly adopt key elements of this Pauline spirituality as a hermeneutic in postulating and developing a particular understanding of a post-mortem intermediate state within his larger anthropological, theodical, and eschatological system. He has been able to explore the possibility of a post-mortem intermediate state according to an understanding that maintains the premises that (a) humanity was created in a state of moral and spiritual immaturity, always existing in a state of epistemic distance from God (although, as we have seen, Hick would not maintain the existence of a "fallen" humanity as such, he would identify a universal human "immaturity" and need to engage in a personal soul-making journey toward God), and (b) at the end of a person's earthly life of soul-making, God will meet that person and provide them with the grace needed (in the form of further moral and/or spiritual development, healing, etc.) in order to enter into perfect union with God. In other words, Hick has based his soul-making system upon the twin premises that the human race is engaged in a process of becoming, and with God's grace, which God always imparts, each person experiences a continuation of that process, finding eventual completion in the eschaton. In so doing, Hick closely adheres to the Pauline spiritual tenets outlined earlier: he acknowledges the reality of a spiritually and morally incomplete person existing in an epistemic distance from God, as well as the ultimate saving power of God's unmediated grace in helping that person through the soul-making process, up to the point of final eschatological consummation.

Therefore, in postulating an understanding of the intermediate state that has been guided by these so-called Pauline spiritual principles of direct relationship between a humanity in the process of becoming and a loving, ever-graceful God, Hick has been able to effectively develop an essentially Pauline understanding of the intermediate state "from the ground up," that is, without any reference to—or impositions from—a traditional hierarchical authority. He has not been required to acknowledge and account for centuries of historical and theological points of consideration that must be necessarily acknowledged and accounted for whenever the doctrine of purgatory is considered within a Catholic context. Instead, Hick is able to bypass the need to address and accept certain received doctrinal points

---

65. See Thiel, *Icons of Hope*, 99–101, which was discussed at greater length in chapter 2 of this book.

present in the Catholic understanding of purgatory and can engage it from a perspective entirely unencumbered by the complexities of working within a received history and tradition. This has arguably allowed him to approach the intermediate state with an entirely fresh perspective, and in so doing, has been able to freely develop a clear and consistent understanding of the intermediate state within a Pauline spiritual context. Accordingly, Hick's understanding offers a number of concrete insights into how a sanctification-based understanding of purgatory can continue to be developed within a contemporary Catholic context.

The principal reason why Hick remains able to inform the Catholic understanding of purgatory is because both he and the post-conciliar church share a basically hopeful eschatological outlook. Even though Hick expresses his hope within a universalist context, both nevertheless look toward the eschaton with hopeful trust in the renewing and consummating power of a loving and merciful God.[66] Yet within these respective eschatologies of hope, Hick has had more success in integrating his understanding of the intermediate state for the following reasons: he has (a) articulated an understanding that minimizes the sense of eschatological anxiety that individuals may feel when considering the afterlife, he has (b) sought to foster a deeper understanding of the communal dynamics present when considering the eschaton, and he has (c) continued to develop the way in which the mechanics of its purifications may be more broadly considered as multifaceted expressions of divine grace.

Firstly, by identifying the post-mortem intermediate state as the next positive stage in a person's soul-making journey, Hick has been able to successfully articulate its basic function in a context in which it is *not* intended to alleviate the eschatological anxiety of the faithful (for in Hick's universalist context, there is ultimately no reason for any person, "faithful" or not, to feel any real eschatological anxiety). To that end, Hick postulates an understanding of the intermediate state that reflects the belief that the opportunity of growing in relationship with God throughout one's life remains basically available to every person and in turn recognizes the unique importance of that person's own journey of relationship, within their own set of circumstances. Yet, it is important to point out that this foundational belief can also be found in the Second Vatican Council's universal call to holiness as found in *Lumen gentium*:

> Therefore, all in the Church, whether they belong to the hierarchy or are cared for by it, are called to holiness, according to the

---

66. Hick, *Evil and the God of Love*, 339–40; see also, Second Vatican Council, *Lumen gentium*, #48.

apostle's saying: "For this is the will of God, your sanctification" [1 Thess 4:3; cf. Eph 1:4]. This holiness of the Church is shown constantly in the fruits of grace which the Spirit produces in the faithful and so it must be; it is expressed in many ways by the individuals who, each in their own state of life, tend to the perfection of charity, and are thus a source of edification for others...[67]

Although some discrepancies might exist between Hick and the Council members regarding their respective understandings of the human person, the basic point upon which both can seemingly agree is the belief that whatever their condition, all persons are called to greater intimacy with God. However, when a person's earthly attempt at answering that call is over, Hick clearly does not anticipate any imposed set criteria by which a person may be judged, or against which a person may be compared, when assessing that attempt; instead, it would seem that the main lens through which he believes this journey will be assessed is that of personal authenticity—that is, in what way was the person able to grow and mature in the particular environment and circumstances in which that person found themselves. This rule of authenticity is crucial, in that it frames for Hick the key soul-making function of the intermediate state: it becomes the place where the person is able to receive the grace necessary for continued growth, maturity, and ultimately a transcending of their particular environment or circumstances, thereby bringing them ever closer in relationship with God. It is clear to Hick that at no point ought the intermediate state be considered a means for alleviating existential fears over the afterlife, for he would consider those fears to be unfounded in the first place. Accordingly, Hick's conception of the intermediate state does not even consider the principal reasons that justified much of its historical existence—the person's life will not be judged according to an objective standard, over and against everyone else; the need for jockeying as persons vie with one another to meet the standard set by Christ and the saints is therefore negated. Rather, the implied rule against which every person will be measured is their own, that is, to what extent has this person become who they were called by God to be.

But as has already been mentioned, it is possible to interpret the decrees of *Lumen gentium* as part of the Second Vatican Council's attempt at dispelling those same eschatological fears—and its attending competitive spirituality—as well. Indeed, in the 1994 edition of the *Catechism of the Catholic Church*, it is stated that regarding the final judgment of an individual, "the truth of each man's relationship with God will be laid bare. The

---

67. Second Vatican Council, *Lumen gentium*, #39.

Last Judgment will reveal even to its furthest consequences the good each person has done or failed to do during his earthly life."[68] The use of the word "relationship" is important in describing the nature of the judgment. Relationship implies deep intimacy between two persons (in this case the individual person and Christ), and it is within the context of this relationship that an outcome will be found. Although it must be noted that Hick would not necessarily adhere to a belief in a final judgment as such in his own understanding, what is significant is that in both articulations, afterlife considerations are not being made according to an imposed set of objective criteria against which believers must compete for a favorable judgment, but rather to the degree of personal authenticity according to which one lived one's own life and grew in relationship with God.

It would therefore seem that in light of the developments of the Second Vatican Council, the area where Hick's own soul-making understanding can serve to further inform the Catholic understanding of purgatory is by helping it to more explicitly frame purgatory's role and function within the context of growth in authenticity and relationship. In so doing, Hick presents a possible understanding of purgatory that essentially *works* for the person, enabling them to become a more authentic version of themselves, thereby allowing them to enter more fully into relationship with the divine that to some extent has already begun. It is an understanding that does not necessarily seek to scrutinize in what way every individual action in every set of circumstances may or may not have been an offence against God, but rather seeks to integrate those actions and circumstances into the greater narrative of the person's own relationship with God. And in pointing to the intermediate state as the venue where the individual's growth in these graces continues, Hick effectively demonstrates exactly how purgatory might be conceptually considered within a non-competitive, non-Matthean spirituality of the afterlife in which eschatological anxiety is no longer a major concern. In other words, Hick is able to articulate an understanding of the intermediate state that is able to contribute toward a constructive eschatological response to a person's experiential and historical concerns within a Pauline spirituality of the afterlife. It successfully accounts for the question of whether or to what extent a person has been able to live a life of authentic right-relationship within their own environment and offers them as guiding principles for an understanding of purgatory within a correspondingly optimistic eschatology of hope.

Secondly, in addition to postulating an understanding of the intermediate state that more effectively responds to the personal eschatological

---

68. Catholic Church, *Catechism of the Catholic Church*, 1039.

concerns presented within a Pauline spiritual culture, it also seems more able to respond to increased concerns regarding the communal dynamics present in the eschaton. As observed earlier, the Second Vatican Council invited its participants to reflect more deeply on the eschatological significance of the scope of Christ's grace in his desire to transform the world:

> The promised and hoped for restoration, therefore, has already begun in Christ. It is carried forward in the sending of the holy Spirit and through him continues in the church in which, through faith, we learn the meaning of our earthly life while, as we hope for the benefits which are to come, we bring to its conclusion the task allotted to us in the world by the Father, and so work out our salvation. Already the final age of the world is with us and the renewal of the world is irrevocably under way.... [69]

The above passage not only appears to confirm the importance of the already touched-upon themes of authenticity and relationship in the person's faith journey and afterlife experience, it also raises a new eschatological theme as attention is shifted away from an almost-singular concern for individual salvation. As observed earlier by Henry Novello, while the Second Vatican Council did not abandon Catholicism's traditional eschatological teachings, it did nevertheless signal a move away from a near-exclusive preoccupation with individual destiny "when it sought to acknowledge the universal dimensions of the Christ event and the meaning and value of this earthly life, so that individual destiny and hope is portrayed as bound up with the destiny and hope for the whole of humanity and the entire universe."[70] Thus, as the Council members began to articulate a stronger sense of both the universality of Christ's grace and God's desire to bring all of creation back to God, they simultaneously began to focus less exclusively on the importance of personal destiny in their eschatological considerations. In other words, as an eschatological posture of future-oriented and other-oriented hope was emphasized, a culture of self-regarding eschatological anxiety became increasingly marginalized.

The main concrete effect this shift had on the way in which the doctrine of purgatory was considered can be found in the Council's brief declaration on its place within the already-existing eschatological doctrine of the Mystical Body of Christ—specifically, as the place where, through prayer, the deceased person is able to remain connected to the living and continues to participate in the "acquisition of sanctity" through the grace of God as they wait for both the completion of their personal sanctification and the

---

69. Second Vatican Council, *Lumen gentium*, #48.
70. Novello, "Eschatology Since Vatican II," 415.

final sanctification of all things in the eschaton.[71] The Council's raising of the communion of saints is significant, for it is precisely this communion-centered aspect of purgatory that is strengthened by Hick's reflections on the communal dynamics of the post-mortem intermediate state.

Without any concern of eschatological anxiety to address, the overall posture offered by Hick is not one in which persons on the soul-making journey behave as spiritual competitors, but rather as spiritual companions: fellow-travelers journeying from a shared point of immature, volatile self-regard to a destination of final integration and unity with God and creation. Although each person is perhaps on their own path, the growth and awareness engendered by this journey only leads to the realization that the paths continuously intersect, and ultimately converge, on the way to that final destination. Hick's insights therefore seem to offer a basis upon which the doctrine of purgatory could come to be understood primarily as a post-mortem context within which a person's own respective call to holiness—within a larger community of traveling companions—will ultimately be brought to fulfillment: "This end-state is conceived of as one in which individual egoity has been transcended in communal unity before God. And in the present phase of that creative process the naturally self-centered human animal has the opportunity freely to respond to God's non-coercive self-disclosures, through the work of prophets and saints, through the resulting religious traditions, and through the individual's religious experience."[72]

Although worked out at the subjective level, the result of soul-making is a greater communal awareness as the fearful, wounded, and self-referential "I" is gradually transformed by God's loving grace into a condition totally free from the trapping, self-enclosing effects of sin (be it sin perpetrated, sin experienced, or structural sin in which one lived) and totally open toward the other. Hick thus proposes the post-mortem intermediate state as an opportunity for that process of transcendence to reach completion, that is, it becomes the locality where, after a lifetime's journey, a person's base egoism is finally transformed into an authentic relationality that is open to all of creation. In effect, Hick is postulating an understanding of the intermediate state in which it serves as an instrument of communion, wherein God's grace has the time to complete its work of bringing about a new creation. It is the place where a collection of more or less self-enclosed individuals gradually become a living community of interconnected beings resting in God.

---

71. Second Vatican Council, *Lumen gentium*, #50–51.
72. Hick, "Irenaean Theodicy," 51.

This above understanding relies upon a very strong belief in the power of God's grace, which serves as the guiding force behind Hick's understanding of the intermediate state. Whether or not this reliance might be too strong will be discussed shortly; however, in the meantime it is important to note that in emphasizing the point that growth in authenticity and orientation for right-relationship developed within the soul-making journey will ultimately find completion in the afterlife, resulting in an increasingly transparent selflessness as the person is moved to adhere ever more closely to God, Hick is able to cultivate an understanding of the intermediate state that effectively captures the emphasis placed on eschatology's communal dynamics by the Second Vatican Council. As such, he is able to offer insight into how a Pauline conception of purgatory can be considered as not just a locality for growth in authenticity and right-relationship through God's grace, but as a locality where growth in authenticity and right-relationship necessarily begets an openness to the "other" in the most radical sense—that is, an openness to all of creation, and ultimately, an openness to God himself.

Moreover, in demonstrating how a sanctification-based understanding of purgatory may be situated within a Pauline eschatological context, Hick might also be able to further illuminate how the mechanics of such an understanding—that is, how the purifications of purgatory may be thought to operate in cleansing a person from the residual effects of sin—are able to successfully bring about a person's full transformation into a spiritually mature and aware being, totally oriented toward authentic right-relationship. For as noted earlier, the word "purification" has gradually come to replace "punishment" in contemporary discourse on how the effects of sin are purified from a person.[73] Indeed, this shift marked a crucial point in the doctrine's history, in which it has now come to be understood primarily as a post-mortem opportunity for the deceased to receive whatever sanctifying graces that they may need in order to "mature the soul for communion with God."[74] Such an understanding is in itself basically complementary to that of Hick's; however, within the Catholic context, we have also seen that "purification" still tends to be interpreted to imply primarily (if not exclusively) an experience of personal reformation—that is, a purification of the soul from the accumulated layers of a person's so-called "compromises with evil" so that their true, perfect self can emerge.[75] To a certain extent, this focus on purification through reformation continues to engender a

---

73. See chapter 2 of this book.
74. Benedict XVI, *Spe Salvi*, #45.
75. Benedict XVI, *Spe Salvi*, #46. See also chapter 2 of this book.

certain past-oriented understanding of purgatory's role and function: the emphasis basically remains on the individual gaining awareness of—and being cleansed from—their past wrongs, in their full implications, before they are able to enter into heaven. Thus, while the language of purification marks a definite evolution in thought, some residuals remain from the previous, satisfaction-based understanding of the doctrine, that is, a lingering preoccupation with the past and strong emphasis on purification *from* its enduring negative consequences.

On the other hand, the "purifications" within Hick's soul-making understanding of the intermediate state are able to be considered within a broader context. For while they can still of course refer to growth in a spiritually mature authenticity and desire for right-relationship by purifying of the soul from past sins through increased self-awareness and reformation, Hick's sensitivity to the human condition and his emphasis on the importance of this often-messy, sometimes hazardous journey implies an understanding more inclined to regard an individual's past in light of the world's deliberately challenging, soul-making reality. As such, while purification from the lingering consequences of past, un-constructive actions is still considered, the ultimate focus remains on the value and eventual promise of soul-making itself. Thus, while the Catholic understanding of purgatory may at times struggle to decide its eschatological orientation, Hick's view firmly faces toward the future, in which any notion of post-mortem purification is regarded unequivocally through the lens of a graced continuation of moral and spiritual growth toward God. It is grace that meets a person at their death, providing exactly what that particular person might need in order to complete their own soul-making journey. And while the purificatory qualities of this grace can take the form of already-mentioned self-awareness and reform, they can also include the ability to continue progressing in already-developed moral and spiritual graces, and perhaps, if need be, even healing from instances that have severely distorted a person's ability to be in authentic right-relationship with either themselves, others, or God.

Within Hick's understanding, the intermediate state therefore serves as not just an opportunity for purification from previous wrongs, but also as an opportunity to grow in the good that has yet to be fully developed. In other words, the purifications of the intermediate state can be equally understood to further develop and magnify what is essential, and not just remove what is inessential. Thus, within Hick's eschatological system, the meaning of the word "purification" carries with it a clear meaning: for in addition to being considered as a synonym for self-reformation, it can also refer to personal development, a growth in maturity developed on the path of becoming a being entirely oriented in authentic right-relationship toward both God and creation.

Finally, in establishing such a framework wherein the full implications of the notion of purgatorial purifications may be explored, Hick also provides a speculative context within which we can conceive of the intermediate state as involving a form of healing for past wrongs that might have been done to a person. This may be a situation where the person has done nothing wrong, and yet has been seemingly failed by the soul-making process. In such a case, God's grace may descend upon that person in the form of compassion and healing, so that in time, that person may have the capacity to both authentically recognize God's love for them and choose to enter into relationship with God. This particular insight is an expansion of Hick's understanding of sanctification which underlines the main point that post-mortem purifications can occur in ways other than that of purification from sin, but it also maintains the fundamental belief that God remains a God of love and is actively seeking to perfect all of creation and bring it back to God. This crucial point will be explored further in the following chapter.

Thus, in developing a soul-making understanding of the post-mortem intermediate state that does not seek to merely find relevancy within a Pauline eschatological system, but in itself exists as an essential, fully integrated component, Hick is able to further illuminate the nature of the possible role and function of a Catholic understanding of purgatory as a realm of love and compassion within a broader eschatological system guided by the principles of a Pauline spiritual culture. Hick effectively touches upon the same broad eschatological themes that have emerged as guiding principles since the Second Vatican Council (a deeper communal consideration, and a more robust optimism regarding its processes and mechanics),[76] and has applied them to the development of his own understanding of the intermediate state; however, by explicitly incorporating them from the onset into his own understanding, Hick has been able to offer concrete suggestions regarding how these same themes may be more explicitly expressed within a Catholic theological context. Therefore, if Hick's relatively modest insights into these issues were to be further considered or adapted to such a context, they could possibly go a great way in allowing the doctrine of purgatory to likewise become comfortably situated within a broader Catholic eschatology of hope.

---

76. See chapter 2 of this book.

CONCLUSIONS

In postulating an understanding of the post-mortem intermediate state within a basic Pauline eschatological framework of hope, Hick effectively manages to go a considerable length in bringing the doctrine back to its theological origins. His approach in attempting to understand the intermediate state somewhat mirrors the attitudes and aspirations of the early Christians, from whom belief in the post-mortem intermediate state began to take hold: both developed their respective understandings (a) as a natural response to the lived reality of loss and suffering, (b) with a strong awareness that the communal dimensions governing earthly life will continue into the afterlife, and, perhaps most importantly, (c) from a basic spiritual posture of hope, that is, out of a simple, genuine faith in a merciful, loving God who through grace is actively seeking to comfort those who are suffering or have suffered, and to find new avenues to bring to salvation those who may have strayed.[77]

In strongly emphasizing these above eschatological themes, Hick manages to recapture much of the intentionality of the early Christians and largely succeeds in returning the intermediate state to its theological and spiritual roots. In turn, Hick has been able to inject into subsequent reflection on the intermediate state a certain energy and enthusiasm present in its nascent formation—an energy and enthusiasm which may sometimes seem lacking in contemporary Catholic reflection on the doctrine of purgatory. For while its present emphasis on sanctification ought not to be discounted, it would still appear possible for the current Catholic understanding of purgatory to be further informed and enriched by Hick's soul-making understanding of the intermediate state. Specifically, Hick is able to offer a vision of how purgatory might operate in a Catholic Pauline spiritual culture that tends to privilege a stronger, more universal understanding of divine grace and its availability by choosing to emphasize and further develop what ended up being the key eschatological themes that emerged from the Second Vatican Council: namely that ongoing eschatological reflection ought to take into account decidedly more communal considerations, realizing that its consideration is not an essentially self-referential affair, and secondly, a more robust optimism and insistent understanding that hope becomes the chief theme and operational principle that would guide all further eschatological thought.[78]

---

77. For a more detailed explanation of early Christianity's relationship with the post-mortem intermediate state, see chapter 1 of this book.

78. For more on the conciliar and post-conciliar developments in eschatological thought, see chapter 2 of this book.

By more radically exploring these key concepts, Hick is able to provide some answers to the questions that have long bedeviled those who sought to develop an understanding of purgatory consistent with contemporary Catholic eschatological thought. In developing an understanding of an intermediate state "from the ground up" within a Pauline spiritual system, Hick has been able to identify some important characteristics that could possibly, in turn, be adopted into a contemporary Catholic understanding of purgatory without any risk of compromising its doctrinal integrity. Therefore, one can conclude that Hick's soul-making understanding of the post-mortem intermediate state indeed offers clear insights into how a contemporary Catholic sanctification-based understanding of purgatory could be further developed and consistently integrated into contemporary eschatological discourse—thereby increasing its theological relevancy, and hopefully, its pastoral relevancy as well. However, there remain some impediments to full adoption of Hick's ideas, even from within his earlier work. This remains true not just within a Catholic context, but even within the Protestant tradition, where a number of theologians have been inspired by Hick's postulation of a more theologically sensitive and ecumenically acceptable post-mortem intermediate state, but still find some of his theological positions problematic. Thus, after identifying the potentially controversial issues with Hick's soul-making thesis, the work of these later theologians will be explored in order to better understand exactly how—and to what degree—Hick's soul-making insights can be further developed within a more contemporary setting, in order to gage to what extent they may ultimately be incorporated into the present Catholic theological context.

5

Challenges with Hick's Understanding of Soul-Making and Further Developments within a Protestant Context

IN THE PREVIOUS CHAPTER we were able to demonstrate the feasibility of applying soul-making's key principles within a particularly Catholic context. Moreover, we were also able to offer concrete examples of how John Hick's soul-making understanding of the human person, theodicy, and the afterlife can indeed stand to inform contemporary reflection on the Catholic doctrine of purgatory by uniquely strengthening various aspects of its established sanctification-based approach. However, we were also able to identify certain features within Hick's understanding, even within its earlier articulations, whose implications remain problematic from a Catholic—and indeed, broader Christian—perspective. These effectively amount to two principal points: his insistence on a strict, original-sin-denying "Irenaean" interpretation of theological anthropology (over and against a so-called "Augustinian" model),[1] and an insistence that an all-powerful, all-loving God is obligated to meet all instances of suffering and evil with an ultimately greater good—a position that would lead to Hick's eschatological belief in universal salvation.[2] Thus, before we articulate our own conclusions regarding how Hick's key soul-making insights can contribute to a more clear and robust understanding of the doctrine of purgatory, we must first investigate these more controversial points and determine the effect that they might

1. See chapter 3 of this book.
2. See chapter 4 of this book.

have on our overall ability to adopt Hick's more constructive elements into a Catholic setting. And finally, to help further inform these conclusions, we will also investigate the various ways in which other contemporary Christian theologians have developed a sanctification-based understanding of an intermediate state—which may or may not include the soul-making themes elucidated by Hick. This analysis will assist us in perhaps uncovering any details that might have been overlooked in Hick's soul-making context, as well as offer some insight regarding potential ecumenical possibilities that a revisited sanctification-based understanding of purgatory may hold in ongoing Catholic-Protestant dialogue.

ANTHROPOLOGICAL AND ESCHATOLOGICAL CHALLENGES

Returning to the ongoing dialogue between Hick, soul-making, and the contemporary Catholic theological context, we are now able to return to the first point raised above. We argued in chapter 3 that it is indeed possible to challenge Hick's belief that soul-making's key insights could only be developed from within a very narrow element of the broader Christian tradition. This was essential in establishing first and foremost that soul-making, as a general concept, remained viable within a theological context less isolated and less revolutionary than what Hick was proposing. Drawing on the thought of Paul W. Gooch, we were able to demonstrate that soul-making's key anthropological and theodical concepts could indeed be authentically developed within the breadth of a tradition that includes a so-called "Augustinian" perspective, and that an uncompromising adversarial posture toward that tradition that Hick includes in his own understanding of soul-making is not in fact necessary for its consideration within a Catholic setting.[3]

This point, ostensibly anthropological, in fact concerns a far bigger question: the role and function of the broader Christian tradition in its relationship with the idea of soul-making. Likewise, as we now turn our attention to the second point, we shall see that while it too ostensibly concerns a soteriological and eschatological point of contention that carries with it certain doctrinal challenges from a Catholic point of view, behind it lies a more fundamental question regarding our understanding of God, divine goodness, and the overall objective of God's divine plan for creation. And it is precisely this question which must be addressed in Hick's work in order to determine the further suitability of his soul-making insights within a Catholic theological context.

3. This was explored in greater detail in chapter 3 of this book.

As already stated, Hick believes that in order for the concept of soul-making to have credibility, every instance of evil and suffering must eventually be understood to somehow contribute toward the ultimate end of perfect goodness and perfect union with God, which itself will justify every one of those instances of evil that have occurred along the way of history. Again, a failure to do so would indicate either an unwillingness or inability on God's part to bring about their transformation, which for Hick would call into question not only God's perfect love and omnipotence, but the legitimacy of God's entire plan for creation as well. And it is fundamentally for that reason that Hick proposes an eventual eschatological resolution in the form of a universal reconciliation of humanity with God as the means by which any lingering instances of evil and suffering will be transformed.[4]

However, in response to Hick's basic claim that God chose to create significantly free human beings who, through God's divine plan of soul-making, *will eventually choose to grow in the goodness found in union with himself,* David Cheetham offers a provocative possible counter-proposal: "what if God created significantly free human beings not because he wanted them to develop into good persons, but because he wanted them to develop into *full* persons?"[5] Cheetham, in his work on John Hick's life and thought, clearly expresses his sympathy with Hick's soul-making hypothesis, and offers the following assessment as to why Hick's hypothesis might be considered so attractive:

> What appeals to Hick's theodicy is the fact that it seems to steer away from tyrannical and juridical pictures of an omni-perfect God who exacts punishments for evil. Instead, it portrays God as very much a personal (even "parental") Being who wishes to authentically interact with human beings. The effect of this is that it seems to bring God more *into* the world of the sufferer; that is, God accepts ultimate responsibility for evil and is perceived to work *within* the process to bring all people into a limitlessly good outcome for their lives.[6]

However, while Cheetham concludes that Hick's understanding of soul-making remains "an insightful attempt to understand the human condition and its purpose," which "seeks to consider human life as it is actually

---

4. This is detailed in greater length in chapter 4 of this book.

5. Cheetham, *John Hick*, 53. Although Cheetham does not offer a precise definition of what he means by "full," he seems to indicate that it would refer to individuals who have been able to come freely to express and live their innermost desires and values in the gradual construction of their personal identity.

6. Cheetham, *John Hick*, 63.

experienced and felt,"[7] he nevertheless goes on to pay particular attention to the arguments criticizing Hick's belief in universalism, and raises the general point that while he offers a strong case for emphasizing the power of divine love within his soul-making hypothesis, it consequently becomes very difficult to "do justice" to any espousal of authentic human freedom within such an articulation.[8] Cheetham further develops the question posed above upon an argument initially proposed by Linda Zagzebski, who has attempted to demonstrate that the effectiveness of a soul-making understanding of the world is indeed found *not* in the ends it is designed to achieve, but rather in the motivations that created it in the first place.

Zagzebski, too, is sympathetic to the concept of soul-making, and seems to agree with its basic premise: that human persons are created with the capacity to develop—in and through their environments—into full moral agents with the ability to enter into and maintain full and loving relationships with both others and with God. Moreover, in her response to a number of philosophical arguments made against the problem of excessive or destructive evil within a soul-making conception of the world, Zagzebski defends Hick's point that it is logical to maintain the validity of soul-making while simultaneously acknowledging that more evil exists in the world than is necessary for the purposes of soul-making itself. Like Hick, Zagzebski also reasons that if there was no such thing as an excess of evil, there would be nothing for a person to strive against and overcome—that is, if evil was simply mild and predictable, it would effectively become domesticated and more easily accommodated for within a person's moral/spiritual life, thereby providing no motivation for them to exert themselves in trying to transcend the adverse circumstances of their life. Zagzebski concludes that it is impossible to establish a threshold to determine when evil is *excessively* excessive, but that a soul-making world contains whatever evil is necessary in order for persons to rationally believe that there indeed exists an excess of evil in the world, thereby creating a morally ambiguous environment out of which they are able to perform good and virtuous actions.[9]

However, unlike Hick, she does not ground this understanding upon a belief that this evil is ultimately permitted for the sake of a certain good, namely the validity and eventual success of soul making, upon which the goodness of God consequently depends. Instead, she understands that the presence of evil—even excessive evil—is permitted because the very

---

7. Cheetham, *John Hick*, 64.

8. Cheetham, *John Hick*, 58. For further details on Cheetham's criticisms, see Cheetham, *John Hick*, 51–58.

9. Zagzebski, "Critical Response," 126.

capacity for evil is a constituent component of the free will that guarantees the "personhood" of every human person as they embark on a journey of soul-making, and it is exactly such a person who God, out of God's love, desired to create. As such, Zagzebski understands soul-making's validity to not rest in an inherent "good" it is destined to achieve, but rather that it is quite simply the appropriate means by which a loving being would act in creating human persons and an environment capable of respecting and developing human personhood:

> To love a person logically requires permitting that person to be a person. To allow a person to be a person requires that he be allowed to contribute to his own soul-making through his free will. This is justified not because the existence of free persons is good, nor because love is good, nor for the sake of good in any other way, but simply because loving persons is something good persons do and loving persons in such a radical way that any evil is permitted for the sake of their personhood is something a perfectly good person would do.[10]

Cheetham would later present Zagzebski's basic points in the form of the following argument: (a) Within a soul-making understanding of humanity, evil exists so that there can be persons; (b) creating significantly free persons is more valuable than eliminating evil if eliminating evil entails the elimination of significant personhood; and (c) maintaining personhood is therefore more valuable than the elimination of evil.[11] To help further illustrate this essential point, Zagzebski presents an analogy of a relationship between a loving parent and their child, in which God resembles the parent and the human person resembles a child: a good parent loves their child and because of that love, wants the child to develop into a "full" person; thus, to that end, the gradual granting of autonomy by that parent to the child becomes imperative. Yet that autonomy is not granted simply because doing so would somehow make the child morally better, or that it would contribute to the overall good in the world: "If any of these reasons were [the parent's] motivation," Zagzebski writes, "she would be treating her child as a means to an end—the end of producing good."[12] Thus, for Zagzebski, the hallmark of a truly loving parent is quite simply respect—respect to allow the child to make their own basic decisions in life so as to truly become what they want to be (for better or for worse), and not to become whoever the parent has decided that that child ought to be:

10. Zagzebski, "Critical Response," 128.
11. Cheetham, *John Hick*, 53.
12. Zagzebski, "Critical Response," 127.

> It seems to me . . . that the parent would want this [basic autonomy] for her child even if the child did not use his autonomy to do good and even if much less good is produced in the world overall. She acts this way because she loves her child. It is also true that her love is good. But she does not act this way *because* her love is good. . . . Goodness does not figure in her motivation at all. Instead, she loves her child as an end in himself and would continue to do whatever contributes to the development of his personhood whether or not it leads to good. What parent would ever agree to turn her child into a non-person or even less of a person because her child is bad.[13]

Although it is without question that Zagzebski would prefer for her child to be a *good person*, her point in the above passage is that before they have any hope of developing an authentic moral sense of personhood, that child must first necessarily be regarded as a *person*. And for Zagzebski, love for the child as a *person* necessarily includes respect for that child's personhood, and respect for personhood, in turn, necessarily includes respect for that child to express their own desires and then use their innate—if perhaps imperfect or uninformed—freedom to ultimately choose to become the kind of person they would like to be. It does not, on the other hand, include coercive or manipulative activity so as to guarantee that the child will become whatever the parent wants them to be, regardless of the child's own deeply held and expressed desires or any actions that child has taken to actualize those desires.

According to Zagzebski, if one is to believe that a human person, at her or his most basic level, is actually in possession of free will, the consequences effected by that free will—as well as the personal desires that underpin it—must also be acknowledged and not deliberately manipulated or ignored out of existence: "It seems to me that we cannot evaluate the soul-making hypothesis unless we are clear on what a soul actually is. If the existence of souls is impossible without the degree of free will which actually exists, it would also be impossible without whatever amount of evil such free will produces."[14] As such, *the parent's goodness* does not therefore rest on the degree to which the parent is able to successfully increase the extent to which the child is adhering to its parent's own desires and participating in the parent's sense of goodness, but rather rests on the unconditional love and respect that that parent shows toward the child by allowing them to embark upon their own process of personhood, which necessarily entails respect

---

13. Zagzebski, "Critical Response," 127.
14. Zagzebski, "Critical Response," 129.

for the decisions that they make along the way, whether that parent agrees with those choices or not. Out of love, a parent does what the parent can to help their child to mature and develop, but they do so knowing that that love may not be reciprocated. This therefore becomes the risk of a parent's love: although the parent can join love with force in order to try to secure its success, the parent instead refrains from doing so and chooses to let their love stand freely. The parent, in this case, offers their love wholly over to the child with the knowledge that that child can respond with indifference or even rejection—and if that is the case, there is nothing that a parent can do to make it otherwise. It becomes, therefore, a love joined with vulnerability. As such, a genuinely loving parent might be disappointed with the child's choices, and may express that disappointment; the parent, however, is not entitled to use their love as a pretext for translating that disappointment into actions that are somehow intended to coerce or manipulate that child to act according to the parent's desires.

Thus, a parent's love can of course be manifested in their earnest contribution toward the child's developing sense of personhood, but however that may be expressed, it must necessarily include that true sense of risk present in any authentic act of love, which is grounded in the child's fundamental freedom to accept or reject that love as that child continues to construct their own basic identity, with all of its constituent desires, values, and relationships. As Zagzebski writes: "To love a person logically requires permitting that person *to be* a person. To allow a person to be a person requires that he be allowed to contribute to his own soul-making through his free will. This is justified . . . simply because loving persons is something good persons do and loving persons in such a radical way that any evil is permitted for the sake of their personhood is something a perfectly good person would do."[15]

To help further illustrate her point, Zagzebski offers herself as a hypothetical example. While considering the possibility of one of her own children remaining perpetually estranged from her, Zagzebski offers the following response: "If one of my children did not know that I loved him I would be deeply grieved and would do everything I could to reconcile him to me, but I would stop short of interfering with his personhood, even if I had the power to do so."[16] While Zagzebski does not further elaborate on her example to illustrate exactly how a parent might interfere with the child's personhood, one can imagine it taking the form of a parent, under the veneer of parental love and affection, employing certain psychological tools,

15. Zagzebski, "Critical Response," 128.
16. Zagzebski, "Critical Response," 129.

such as guilt, fear, or obligation in order to ensure some form of continuing relationship with the child. It could also include a parent working incessantly behind the child's back to engineer certain employment, residential, and relational opportunities that the parent thinks are in the child's best interest, or perhaps sabotaging other opportunities that the parent thinks are not in the child's best interest. This could even take the extreme form of a parent—again, under the auspices of parental love—physically restraining their child so as to "protect" them from certain perceived dangers or risks in the world. In all of these instances, the parent may be working under the genuine but misguided belief that these are acceptable actions that a concerned, loving parent may perform under certain extreme circumstances; of course, the reality is that they ultimately degrade the child by both undermining the child's ability to freely form authentic, lasting relationships, and to freely construct their own personal identity.

Such an understanding of course contrasts with Hick's implied understanding of human freedom, and how he understands its operations within God's plan of divine union with all of humanity. Hick would of course maintain that a person can indeed continue to possess authentic liberty of thought and action and yet remain virtually guaranteed to freely choose to grow in that goodness that God offers them—if not in this earthly life, then, crucially, in the afterlife.[17] For Hick this is somehow possible because he understands that the human will is never exercised in pure isolation; rather, it always takes place in interaction with "circumstances and powers" beyond itself.[18] In the afterlife, those circumstances and powers include a post-mortem landscape of unremitting divine love that will bear down on the person until they are finally able to fully recognize that love and choose to adhere to it: "This process," Hick writes, "in which the infinite resourcefulness of infinite love will sooner or later find a way to us, depends upon the fact that it is God who has created us and that he has created us for himself."[19]

Yet even if we consider Hick's point as valid that no human desire is ever exercised in isolation, but rather within a certain set of circumstances external to the individual, it would seem that the set of circumstances that he understands to be present in the afterlife (the active and infinite resourcefulness of God's infinite and omnipresent love) are so extreme that it becomes unreasonable to suggest that even a relative degree of freedom is present in the formation of the individual's desires. Their extremity lies

17. Hick, "Problem of Evil," 600.
18. Hick, "Problem of Evil," 600.
19. Hick, "Problem of Evil," 600.

in the fact that they are designed to guarantee only one result: effectively captive in the face of unremitting divine love, there is ultimately no room for an individual to choose what kind of person they would like to be. Instead, the only option for even the most wayward of souls is acquiescence, and an inevitable—if contrived—form of reciprocation. It is by such means that the evil carried by such a soul will eventually be eliminated; God will ultimately succeed in God's soul-making plan for creation by *making* that particular soul inevitably choose to love God. Thus, while Hick and Zagzebski both understand freedom of choice to be an intrinsic component of the human person, Zagzebski considers respect for a person's sovereignty to be the ultimate expression of love and guarantor of divine goodness, whereas Hick's understanding implies that, ultimately, personal freedom can only be thought of as something relative, and subordinate to the greater good of God's divine plan for humanity's salvation.

It is in response to this uncompromising care for the individual's ultimate welfare that Cheetham offers yet another provocative question: "Is the universalist's love self-interested? Perhaps the universalist's love is a love which is too jealous to lose, too sentimental to allow free persons to make serious choices. Perversely, perhaps, we might charge the universalist's God as one who cannot tolerate final refusal from any creature. If such action is love then surely it is possessive love which in seeking to protect the beloved, protects only itself."[20] It would seem that Cheetham's description of a "jealous lover" can appropriately be applied to Hick's understanding of God, who appears governed by an obligatory impulse to transform every existent evil into something good. While God ostensibly does so for the sake of the victims of suffering, God's extension of this saving, redeeming "love" to persons who have basically decided over the course of their lives to maintain a broken relationship with either themselves, others, or the divine, ultimately results in them becoming a mere means to a predetermined end so as to satisfy God's seemingly selfish love (and ultimately, Hick's predetermined understanding of divine goodness, which remains the root cause for such an understanding).

By suggesting instead that divine goodness may be measured by God's ability to respect God's own fundamental desire that all of humanity develop into unique, free and "full" persons, Zagzebski—with help from Cheetham—manages to reassert the importance of human freedom in any consideration of soul-making, thereby providing a constructive alternative lens through which one can continue to regard and hold the essential elements of a soul-making understanding of the human person, theodicy, and

20. Cheetham, *John Hick*, 54.

the afterlife that still maintains both God's divine goodness and sovereignty, yet without needing to subscribe to the more coercive elements of Hick's understanding of soul-making that inescapably lead toward universalism. It thus remains possible to consider a soul-making understanding of purgatory that continues to maintain its essential coherency without the need to adopt the same role and function for it as envisioned by Hick within his universalist understanding. Such an alternative maintains the basic soul-making principles of theodicy already identified, and are more readily able to be applied within the framework of a Catholic eschatological context.

CHALLENGE OF DESTRUCTIVE SUFFERING

As alluded to earlier, Hick demands that all instances of suffering and evil that have occurred within creation must somehow ultimately contribute to the fulfillment of the greater, all-justifying good that God has planned for creation. But this principle is not limited strictly to individuals in the afterlife who, for one reason or another, have insisted on persisting in their rejection of relationship with God; it extends as well to those who encountered some form of destructive suffering during their earthly lives and have died without finding an opportunity to integrate those experiences, into either their understanding of themselves or into their understanding of—and relationship with—God. For Hick, as we have observed, God's goodness demands too that their experience of the seemingly unredeemable evil present in those instances must still be transformed into a constructive, spiritually positive experience that not only helps to facilitate their gradual openness to God, but will also positively contribute to the greater good of God's realized plan for creation, writing that within his so-called Irenaean theodicy, "God's purpose of good must be universally fulfilled; or else, to the extent to which it has been thwarted the divine sovereignty is shown to be limited. An eternally persisting evil would represent a definitive failure on the creator's part . . . If the universe contains these permanently unredeemed evils, it follows that God is limited either in goodness or in power."[21] To that end, if such a reclamation remains impossible for those individuals during their earthly life, the post-mortem intermediary state will become for them a venue in which that process could occur.

Once more, such an insistence appears problematic to our present project, and again for the same reasons touched upon above: the coercive impact that Hick's insistence on the necessity for the reclamation and redirection of every instance of evil has on the basic integrity of the human

---

21. Hick, "Problem of Evil," 598–99.

person. However, in *Reclaiming Theodicy: Reflections on Suffering, Compassion and Spiritual Transformation*, Michael Stoeber presents an argument against the theodical necessity of divine reclamation of destructive suffering in a manner that effectively runs parallel to Cheetham and Zagzebski's earlier point: in order for God to respect human beings precisely as human beings within his divine plan of soul-making, God must respect humanity's intrinsic freedom of thought and action (including the consequences of humanity's intrinsic freedom—both for good and for utterly destructive evil). Thus, with regard to the question of God's respect for human freedom when it is being misused by an individual to inflict suffering upon others, Stoeber maintains that while it may be fairly easy to understand how and why this respect be maintained when such misuses of freedom are somehow able to contribute toward a constructive end, that same respect must necessarily be extended to those extreme, incomprehensible instances when humanity abuses its freedom in such a way that it becomes impossible for any constructive end to ever result.[22]

In order for the true significance of destructive suffering to hold in any soul-making understanding of the world, it must be considered in light of the same radical freedom in which those acts were perpetrated and/or received; to do otherwise would be committing an injustice against the terrible respect that they deserve—both as singular events in and of themselves and within the larger soul-making context. For that reason, if a person, in their freedom, chooses to commit an act that results in destructive suffering—or if a person were to experience an act that resulted in destructive suffering for themselves—God's love for humanity is such that God will respect these actions by acknowledging them for what they truly are: destructive, in the sense that they remain "without transformative impetus for the victims of it . . . it remains a great evil."[23] For Stoeber, the possibility of destructive suffering is the ultimate risk in the creation of a humanity capable of authentic soul-making—that the radical freedom which God imbued humanity in order to make authentic love possible could be so radically abused as to make hate, and a lived, enduring experience of hate, possible as well. As Stoeber observes, the great tragedy of our world is that "destructive suffering is a condition of the fundamental freedom that is essential to our spiritual transformation and redemption, yet its personal experience does not contribute towards this religious ideal and can even radically inhibit it."[24]

22. Stoeber, *Reclaiming Theodicy*, 70–71.
23. Stoeber, *Reclaiming Theodicy*, 72.
24. Stoeber, *Reclaiming Theodicy*, 72.

By advocating for the exact opposite of what Stoeber is suggesting, that is, by insisting that in order to preserve divine goodness and sovereignty within the context of soul-making, every instance of so-called destructive suffering must carry with it some sort of transformative impetus for its victims, Hick's proposal manages inadvertently to trivialize their true horrific nature by undermining the basic freedom in which these acts were committed, thereby effectively undermining the human dignity of the person (or persons) involved in those actions and, by extension, the dignity of humanity in general. In his seeming need to find resolution for every possible "loose end" within his understanding of theodicy, it would appear that Hick attempts to eliminate evil at the expense of human personhood, whose identity is inextricably linked to its sense of authentic personal freedom and, crucially, the effects that it creates—including instances of utterly destructive suffering. By undermining or rearranging the effects that that freedom is able to achieve, Hick calls into question the legitimacy and value of that freedom itself, which in turn calls into question the legitimacy and value of human personhood itself.

Hick's desire to regard the intermediate state as a further opportunity to wrap any lingering instances of suffering and evil up into God's divine plan for his creation is born out of a basic impulse: to help render intelligible a soul-making theodicy predicated on the belief that every instance of suffering and evil will eventually become subsumed into a greater, all-justifying good. If we return to Hick's criteria for assessing what he terms to be the success of a given theodicy, it should be noted that while his own response does indeed appear to possess the coherence necessary for a *possible* response (in that it manages to maintain an internal logical coherence), it manages to fall short within his own criteria of *plausibility*, which he roughly defines as a consistence between both the data of the religious tradition upon which the theodicy is based, and the data of the natural world, as revealed by the facts of scientific inquiry and the sociological facts of contemporary humanity's ethical, psychological, and religious sensibilities, particularly those regarding the question of the existence of evil.[25] For in his attempt to effectively respond to these profound questions of human suffering and God's goodness with a coherent message of hope, Hick's impulse is certainly commendable; however, we have seen that in pursuit of that goal, he has tied his various problematic "loose ends" into a theodical understanding in which spiritual truths about human freedom and suffering are sacrificed for the sake of developing an intellectual coherence around a highly disputable point. In so doing, Hick's failure to fully grasp both the necessarily

---

25. Hick, "Irenaean Theodicy," 39. See also chapter 4 of this book.

horrifying nature of destructive suffering as well as the necessary importance of authentic freedom ultimately undermines the effectiveness, or "success," of the theodicy that he is proposing.

With the particular question of success in mind, Stoeber provides a helpful way forward by reassessing the role and function of the intermediate state in articulating an intelligible response to the particular issue of destructive suffering that manages to honor both its terrifying reality as well as the Christian belief in a loving, all-powerful God. In describing the need for an effective theoretical theodicy, Stoeber writes: "The hope in theoretical theodicy is that the love, wisdom, and justice of God can be reconciled with the evils of destructive suffering. Perhaps the most significant aspect of such reconciliation is the healing and redemptive overcoming for the victims of destructive suffering, through the power of God. A Christian theist hopes for this healing and redemptive overcoming for the victims, and effective themes of theodicy will give intelligible voice to it."[26]

Rather than maintaining that human suffering is necessarily *transformed* by God into a greater good that can somehow make the experience of suffering ultimately worthwhile, Stoeber holds that through a process of healing and reconciliation, a sense of personal *recovery* of an experience is indeed possible. This process can occur through many different mediums, perhaps especially through encountering the compassionate love of God that has its source in the passion of Jesus Christ. According to Stoeber: "Jesus experiences a brutal, alienating rejection and pain, not simply in acknowledgement of suffering, but the actual heartaching experience of the reality. Suffering in this view, even for the God-man, is the basic stuff of life, painful experiences that are only redeemed in the power of divine love."[27] This intensely personal experience of suffering allows God to be fully present when members of God's own creation are suffering; it allows for a bond of compassion to be struck between God and the person in their suffering, who may come to know that their suffering is not—and has not been—experienced alone. Yet, conceding that, for a variety of reasons, this reality might not have been immediately (or even remotely) evident for many victims of destructive suffering, Stoeber crucially suggests that for those unfortunate enough to experience instances of destructive suffering, this divine compassion may also be experienced as a form of psychological and spiritual healing. This can occur both in this life and, if necessary, in

---

26. Stoeber, *Reclaiming Theodicy*, 68. For further discussion regarding Stoeber's own belief in the possibility of achieving a "successful" or "effective" theodicy, as well as opinions on gauging the effectiveness of a given theodicy, see Stoeber, *Reclaiming Theodicy*, 64–68.

27. Stoeber, *Reclaiming Theodicy*, 46.

the post-mortem intermediate state, to support a person's necessary moral and spiritual development: "If the victims of destructive suffering are not to be unfairly removed from this possibility [of redemption through spiritual growth and transformation], there must be contexts of healing which give them further opportunities for transforming purification. What is required is a life-condition suitable to healing and continued spiritual development, so the destructive horror does not unjustly remove the victim finally or permanently from the redemptive dynamic."[28]

This is not to say that such destructive suffering is transformed into a good but rather that God's grace has the power to effect human healing and recovery from such horrors. Stoeber believes that an ongoing experience of this divine compassion will not somehow "compensate" the person for their suffering; it will not, in other words, somehow transform it into something that they might eventually look back upon it with a peculiar sense of gratitude. It will, however, help the person overcome the painful effects of that experience by guiding them through a process of healing from that suffering, which can in turn lead to that person's eventual recovery through a gradual reorientation away from an insular, wounded self-regard, and toward a restored understanding of their own unique worth and dignity as a beloved child of God. As Stoeber writes, a person's "own suffering is never forgotten or transcended in this process of spiritual transformation." Instead, it is "transmuted into an ongoing active concern for others. Through one's own suffering 'in Christ' one is spiritually moved, and able, to help and heal others in the way that it is modeled by and experienced spiritually in the compassionate Christ."[29]

Stoeber's insight that the post-mortem intermediate state can serve as a venue for further healing and personal transformation from destructive suffering is of great importance. It compliments Cheetham and Zagzebski's alternative soul-making model of the afterlife, one that values above all the opportunity for the human person to freely grow to become their true self by offering a glimpse into how an all-loving, all-powerful God can still care for God's creation even though its members experience instances of destructive suffering, while at the same time respecting humanity's inalienable dignity as human beings to choose their spiritual path. Through the contributions of Cheetham, Zagzebski, and Stoeber, this alternative soul-making model stands as an effective counter-point to Hick's own understanding: not only does it overcome, from the Roman Catholic perspective, some of the more doctrinally problematic elements of soul-making, it is also able to

---

28. Stoeber, *Reclaiming Theodicy*, 74.
29. Stoeber, *Reclaiming Theodicy*, 53.

both identify and provide alternatives for an implausible assumption central to Hick's theodicy—namely, his belief that God created significantly free human persons to operate within a plan for creation that above all else, has been designed to bring it to an all-justifying greater good—that would eventually lead to the aforementioned doctrinal discrepancies.

With aid from the thought of Cheetham, Zagzebski, and Stoeber, it indeed becomes possible to adapt Hick's basic soul-making understanding of theodicy and the afterlife to a Roman Catholic context, so that his key insights (as identified earlier) may be allowed to engage and inform the doctrine of purgatory. This will be fully articulated in the following chapter; however, before we do so, it is important to briefly review recent developments within the Protestant tradition that have followed upon Hick's initial work on the concept of purgatory/intermediate state. This will serve to offer further refinements to our reflections and also shed some light on the ecumenical possibilities that a revisited Catholic doctrine of purgatory may have in dialogue with the broader Protestant tradition.

STATUS OF THE POST-MORTEM INTERMEDIATE STATE WITHIN PROTESTANT THOUGHT

The doctrinal status and perceived role of a post-mortem intermediate state within the Protestant tradition might be described as tenuous, at best. As Jerry L. Walls points out, Protestant belief in purgatory was largely rejected by the early Reformers for two basic reasons: it was not clearly taught in Scripture, and it seemingly suggested a soteriological model of works-righteousness according to a process of sanctification and not that of justification by faith.[30]

Martin Luther (1483–1546 CE), who initially professed a strong—if critical—belief in the doctrine, would gradually over the course of his life ultimately come to reject it as a humanly constructed idea that is unfaithful to the gospel and what it teaches about the nature of grace and salvation. Initially, Luther would appear to have taken purgatory's existence for granted, restricting his criticism toward its abuses (such as the selling of indulgences, and the claims of the pope to have continuing jurisdiction over those who have died).[31] However, his dissatisfaction with purgatory continued to grow as the theological tension between the concepts of sanctification and justification increased within him. As he found psychological solace and spiritual liberty in the notion that simply by his faith (understood by Luther

30. Walls, *Purgatory*, 53.
31. Luther, "95 Theses," 27, 13, 22, respectively.

as a totally free gift of God's grace) he could be assured of salvation, his understanding of purgatory as a liminal place where a person's salvation was worked out in degrees eventually led him to view it as a source of unnecessary uncertainty and anxiety over the sense of assurance one had of one's own salvation—a feeling that was exacerbated by certain unsavory elements within the pre-Reformation Catholic Church, which were keen to inflame fearful attitudes toward the afterlife for the purpose of financial gain.[32] Thus, by 1521, even though Luther continued to maintain a personal belief in purgatory, he began to hold that it was a matter of personal opinion; moreover, he found it very difficult to find any scriptural evidence for its existence, and would eventually come to develop the notion that the purgatorial pains of salvation were primarily experienced here on earth and not in the afterlife.[33]

Shortly thereafter, Luther began to express more grave doubts, resulting in more direct attacks against purgatory's scriptural veracity and its abuses by the Catholic hierarchy. And finally, by 1535, with his theological outlook now fully matured, Luther wrote his *Lectures on Genesis*, wherein the doctrine was finally denounced as "the greatest falsehood" and characterized it as an invented instrument of oppression by the papacy that sought to undermine the reality of humanity's total dependency of God's grace by denying the salvific value of faith and suggesting, as he saw it, a limited efficacy of Christ's death on the cross for the salvation of all sins.[34]

John Calvin (1509–1564 CE), on the other hand, forcefully opposed the doctrine of purgatory from the very beginning of his public life. Like Luther, Calvin was concerned about its non-scriptural foundations; however, it would seem that his primary concern was over how its demands for further post-mortem "satisfactions" for sins would threaten the efficacy of Christ's death on the cross to provide complete satisfaction for all sins. As Calvin writes, if one believes that "the blood of Christ is the sole satisfaction for the sins of believers, the sole expiation, the sole purgation, what remains but to say that purgatory is simply a dreadful blasphemy against Christ?"[35] However, unlike Luther, Calvin rejected the concept of "soul sleep," a term referring to a period of dormancy experienced by the disembodied soul in an undefined location between bodily death and the general resurrection, thereby leaving him to develop a position that maintained that after death, the souls of the righteous would ascend immediately into heaven and experience its peace in the divine, yet nevertheless remained incomplete as they

---

32. Walls, *Purgatory*, 38–39.
33. See Luther, "In Defence and Explanation," 95–98.
34. Luther, *Luther's Works*, 315.
35. Calvin, *Institutes*, 3.5.6. Quoted in Walls, *Purgatory*, 41.

progressed through a period of spiritual growth that began on earth and would be perfected in time for the general resurrection.[36] This leaves Calvin with a position that acknowledges that the spiritual condition of the righteous is gradually perfected through a drawn-out post-mortem process, but that this process is situated in the eternal realm of heaven in the presence of God (where temporality does not exist), and not in any distinct place specifically intended for this task.

It must also be stated that the doctrine of purgatory would go on to be rejected in principle within Anglicanism as well, with any reference to praying for the dead being eliminated through Thomas Cranmer's reforms of the liturgy in *The Book of Common Prayer*, followed by the doctrine's forceful rejection in Article XXII of the Anglican Church's foundational *39 Articles of Religion* in 1571, which states that "the Romish Doctrine concerning purgatory . . . is a fond thing, vainly invented, and grounded upon no warranty of Scripture, but rather repugnant to the Word of God."[37] Thus, from the initial hostility of the early Reformers toward the doctrine emerged a general theological and popular religious culture that too was hostile, and for the most part remained so well into the twentieth century. With a few notable exceptions, such as the relatively sympathetic attitude expressed toward the doctrine by the Anglo-Catholics of the Oxford Movement during the nineteenth century, it was not until the mid-twentieth century that certain groups and individuals within the Protestant traditions appeared willing to revisit the doctrine and positively consider its possible role and function within their own respective understandings of the afterlife.

There are a number of factors that have contributed to this development. Firstly, one might point to the spirit of ecumenism that emerged within both Protestantism and Catholicism during the twentieth century, which, after centuries of mutual hostility and suspicion, began to allow for a free and open exchange of beliefs over any number of theological issues with the intention of finding common understanding, if not convergence, on these issues. Thus, for the first time in centuries, Protestant theologians were invited to consider how the doctrine of purgatory might be understood within their own respective traditions, and not be regarded as a concept totally alien and antithetical to their beliefs. Secondly, it would seem that while certain Catholic theological positions were either routinely affirmed or criticized within the various Protestant traditions by its early leaders, those same positions were rarely formally codified as an essential element of their faith. For example, while the doctrine of purgatory was condemned

---

36. See Calvin, *Soul Sleep*, 64–69.
37. Anglican Church of Canada, "39 Articles of Religion," article 22.

within Anglicanism's *Thirty-Nine Articles*, the Anglican Church of Canada acknowledges, in a preamble to the articles, that they "have never been officially adopted as a formal confession of faith in any province of the Anglican Communion, but they serve as a window onto the theological concerns of the reformed English church."[38]

Thus, at least with regard to purgatory, while its legitimacy has often been attacked throughout the history of Protestantism, there would often remain an opening through which it could be reapproached and reexamined. This appears to have been the case especially within the Anglican tradition, where a relatively significant number of individuals, such as C. S. Lewis and John Macquarrie, have openly expressed their belief in a postmortem process of growth and development within an intermediate state. Lewis, for example, while acknowledging the definite limitations of the classical Catholic satisfaction-based model of purgatory of which he would have been most familiar, nevertheless expresses concerns for the well-being of his deceased loved ones, a desire for spiritual cleansing, and a recognition that this would take place in the form of a process; it is for this reason that he explicitly expresses his belief in purgatory, albeit more akin to the later sanctification-based understandings.[39] Lewis's treatment of the subject is notable in that he approaches it as a lay theologian. He is not, so to speak, engaged in any formal theological dialogue, and his proposal is not taking place in the relative isolation of academic debate. Rather, Lewis is writing in his capacity as a well-informed and dedicated member of the laity and is likely writing to and for other members of the broader Christian church. In such a setting, Lewis is, to a certain extent, representing a popular opinion on the spiritual role that purgatory might play within the lives of the lay faithful. As such, he is not debating its finer doctrinal points or its place within the Church of England's formal teaching on the afterlife, but rather is expressing, from the perspective of a dedicated layperson, the same basic hopes and desires that had undergirded belief in the doctrine as it emerged within the early church. Whether he is aware of it or not, Lewis is demonstrating that the same beliefs that precipitated purgatory's initial adoption and development within Christianity have remained just as strong and just as relevant many centuries later.

Like Lewis, John Macquarrie also maintained a strong belief in purgatory, writing that it seems difficult "to understand why Protestant theologians have such a violent prejudice against this conception, for it seems to me to be indispensable to any reasonable understanding of Christian

---

38. Anglican Church of Canada, "39 Articles of Religion."
39. See Lewis, *Letters to Malcolm*, 107–11.

eschatology."⁴⁰ Yet while Lewis envisioned an understanding of purgatory as a component in a more conventional framework that included a distinct and eternal heaven and hell, Macquarrie understood the afterlife to exist as a sort of singular continuum containing hell, purgatory, and heaven, through which one may move from near-annihilation due to sin toward total union with God.⁴¹ Macquarrie's understanding of the afterlife thus tends towards a strong—if not dogmatic—universalist outlook,⁴² in which all of creation is thought to move through this continuum toward ultimate reconciliation with God. Purgatory, in this understanding, provides "the dynamic, moving element into the traditional [eschatological] scheme, where heaven and hell could easily be mistaken for fixed immutable states."⁴³ Published at roughly the same time as Hick's *Evil and the God of Love*, Macquarrie's *Principles of Christian Theology* thus provides a surprising compliment to Hick's early eschatological beliefs, in that it too envisions an understanding of the intermediate state that facilitates an individual's transformation through divine grace within an overtly universalist context.

Strikingly similar to Macquarrie's understanding of purgatory is the Committee on Christian Faith of the United Church of Canada's articulation of the afterlife as proposed within *Life and Death: A Study of the Christian Hope*. A document that outlines the eschatological beliefs of the United Church (and predates Macquarrie and Hick by about five years), *Life and Death* discusses the intermediate state at length. Describing the Catholic understanding of purgatory at that time as "not Biblical" and "unacceptable" due to its supposed belief that the sufferings of purgatory were considered penal as well as cleansing, the Committee proposes another view "which sets forth the possibility of a place or condition of remedial discipline and growth in grace rather than of penal suffering."⁴⁴

The Committee's approach to this question is fascinating, in that it rejects the notion that post-mortem cleansing and growth takes place in some sort of intermediate state after a person's ultimate destiny has been determined at the particular judgment, and maintains instead that the particular judgment merely reveals and confirms the state of a person's soul as it continues the life that it lived on earth until the end of time. As such, it does not render as definitive the question of that person's salvation, nor does it precipitate an instantaneous and total sanctification of the person; rather,

---

40. Macquarrie, *Principles of Christian Theology*, 367.
41. Macquarrie, *Principles of Christian Theology*, 367.
42. Macquarrie, *Principles of Christian Theology*, 366–67.
43. Macquarrie, *Principles of Christian Theology*, 367.
44. Committee on Christian Faith, *Life and Death*, 37–38.

it reveals to that person the full reality of who they really are as spiritual beings at that particular moment, so as to provide further opportunities for repentance, personal reformation, and spiritual growth before the end of time.[45] The Committee thus proposes that heaven and hell are not two distinct realities entered into immediately after the personal judgment, but rather a reflection of a person's personal disposition within the same postmortem reality, which can change as they inevitably grows in God's grace. Clearly foreshadowing Macquarrie's own considerations of the role and function of the intermediate state within a context sympathetic toward universalism, the Committee's understanding is notable for ultimately denying the existence of any sort of "intermediate state" as such, yet nevertheless proposes an understanding of a person's post-mortem life as a direct continuation of their earthly life, in the form of a process of growing in divine grace and integrating that life in communion with God. Thus, it too serves as a unique—although very likely unrelated—precursor to Hick's own universalist soul-making conception of the afterlife that he will propose in less than a decade later.

Whether Hick was aware of these particular developments or not, a broader theological context was nevertheless being established in which he and other contemporary Protestant theologians became able to explore the possibilities of a post-mortem intermediate state—a context that, admittedly, continues to remain relatively marginal within Protestantism yet nevertheless is producing an increasing number of individuals keen to express belief in some form of an intermediate state within their own approaches to eschatology. Perhaps one of the most notable Protestant proponents of a post-mortem intermediary state is Marilyn McCord Adams, an Episcopal priest who, working within the Anglican tradition, would identify closely with Hick in her own extensive work on articulating a Christian response to the problem of evil and suffering (indeed, *Christ and Horrors: The Coherence of Christology*, one of her last books, is dedicated to Hick, whom she described as an "excellent mentor"). Adams demonstrates a clear sympathy to Hick's understanding of human origins, specifically its ability to highlight the developmental, evolutionary nature of humanity as well as the presence of—and ongoing vulnerability to—evil within the primordial human condition.[46] However, choosing to distance herself from possible theodical explanations as to why God would allow evil and suffering to exist in God's creation, Adams instead concentrates her attention on God's relationship

---

45. Committee on Christian Faith, *Life and Death*, 41–43.

46. Adams, *Horrendous Evils*, 32–43. See also Adams, *Horrendous Evils*, 50–52, where Adams favorably describes Hick's soul-making theodicy.

with the existence of horrendous evils within God's creation, which she defines as "evils the participation in which (that is, the doing or suffering of which) constitutes *prima facie* reason to doubt whether the participant's life could (given their inclusion in it) be a great good to him/her on the whole."[47]

Throughout her body of work, Adams will often refer to these horrendous evils as simply "horrors," and it would seem that her basic theological project is to explore in what way God compensates humanity for permitting the existence of these horrors. It is within this context, that of God's relationship to these horrors, that Adams dramatically builds upon a number of key points raised by Hick. Taking issue with his earlier attempt to find meaning in destructive suffering by proposing that, although mysterious, its existence is nevertheless necessary in an environment basically conducive to soul-making, Adams states that the mere notion that "God would permit some to participate in horrors in order that others might profit from a better soul-making environment seems a poor defence of Divine goodness to the participants. For horrors not only fail to advance the participants' progress, but also *prima facie* defeat the positive significance of their antemortem careers."[48] In response to this perceived omission in Hick's theodicy, Adams contends that any attempt to find an instrumental reason as to why God might permit destructive suffering/horrors is ultimately counterproductive, in that it attempts to find a reasonable answer to something that is—and always will be—inherently unreasonable to our minds: "Horrors," Adams writes, "resist domestication in terms of 'morally sufficient' reasons (reasons compatible with perfect goodness, knowledge, and power) of why God permits them . . . I want to insist that horrors are so bad that to treat any of the reasons why we can think of as reasons God found (or would have found) sufficient turns God into a monster, an evil genius of worse than Cartesian proportions."[49]

Instead, Adams wishes to establish that, in spite of the reality of horrors, and acknowledging their horrendous impact upon human existence, God nevertheless remains fundamentally *for* us, that is (as she describes it) God remains basically "good" toward us. For Adams, God can only be considered good if God is able to overcome and defeat these horrors by integrating them into the lives of the horror-participants in such a way that they become overwhelmingly good—not just within the context of the world as a whole, but also within the context of the participant's personal life

---

47. Adams, *Horrendous Evils*, 26.
48. Adams, *Horrendous Evils*, 52.
49. Adams, "Horrors in Theological Context," 470.

history.[50] Indeed, for Adams, every horror ever perpetrated or experienced by humanity must be caught up in this process if God's plan for creation is to be considered in any way successful. She elsewhere refers to the reasoning behind God's obligation to responding to horrors as the "logic of compensation."[51] This process of compensation, she maintains, is carried out in a three stage process: firstly, each person comes to be able to personally recognize God's intimate presence with them during periods of horror participation; secondly, the horror participant's positive meaning-making capabilities are restored through a further process of divine healing and development; and thirdly, transformed by this process, the horror participant is ready to reengage their own environment in such a way that they are no longer vulnerable to horrors.[52]

So convinced is Adams about the thoroughness of this transformation process, she writes that with the renewed perspective that it affords, the realization of divine solidarity with the person in horror participation is what allows those particular horrors to be gathered into that person's "on the whole and in the end beatific relationship with God, so that [they are] integrated into something immeasurably beneficial and meaningful."[53] "Once," she continues, "we recognize our own horror participation as an episode of intimate togetherness in our—on the whole and in the end—beatific life together with God, we would not retrospectively wish it away from our life histories."[54] Thus, like Hick, Adams envisions a world in which the victims of soul-making receive just compensation; however, it would seem that Adams exceeds Hick by even more strongly emphasizing the necessity of this compensation to reach back over the entirety of a victim's life and transform even their most horrific moments into something positive and actually welcomed.

To that end, Adams notes, like Hick, that this process of compensation is rarely—if ever—accomplished at the point of a person's death, thus proposing "new and nourishing environments where they can profit from Divine instruction on how to integrate their participation in horrors into wholes with positive meanings."[55] And also like Hick, Adams would add that in order for God to truly defeat horrors, this process of compensation will

50. Adams, *Christ and Horrors*, 45.

51. Adams, "Ignorance, Instrumentality, Compensation," 17.

52. Adams, *Christ and Horrors*, 47–48. See also Adams, "Horrors in Theological Context," 476.

53. Adams, "Ignorance, Instrumentality, Compensation," 20.

54. See Adams, "Ignorance, Instrumentality, Compensation," 20.

55. Adams, *Horrendous Evils*, 83–84. See also Adams, "Ignorance, Instrumentality, Compensation," 21.

necessarily occur for every horror-participant, both victim and perpetrator (who also clearly possess a compromised ability to form and derive positive meaning-making within their own lives), eventually resulting in an ultimate reconciliation between the entirety of creation and the Creator.

Adams, it would seem, is also operating under the same basic assumption that Cheetham has identified in Hick, namely that God created humanity with the basic intention that it will develop to become good persons, according to which God's goodness is to stand or fall. Thus, she writes: "My own estimate is that for an omnipotent, omniscient, and perfectly good God . . . universal salvation is required. To be true to Godself, God must accomplish God's purpose in creation for each and every created person God has made."[56] However, Adams draws a distinction in the process of restoring meaning-making for both victim (whose process will be characterized more by healing and integration) and perpetrator (whose process will be characterized more by painful, curative rehabilitation). In spite of the particularly painful form of compensation a perpetrator of horrors will have to endure in order for them to effectively integrate their experiences and fully participate in the divine life, Adams seems willing to offer such persons a considerable amount of sympathy, noting that God created humanity "as personal animals in a material environment of real and apparent scarcity"—conditions, she believes, that are not ideal for right-relationship with either creation or God.[57]

Adams concludes that these inherited primordial conditions effectively minimize the voluntary aspect of most human actions, in that humanity simply does not possess the basic competency to bear responsibility when it does ill. To help further illustrate her point, she also provides an example of a mother and child—similar to that of Zagzebski, but argued to a startlingly different conclusion: "My suggestion is that what the mother does by way of training and controlling the child in its earliest stages is agency-developing and enabling; it cannot count as manipulation until the child's agency is better formed."[58] Within this example, it would seem that the child's agency never becomes better formed; instead, Adams explains that since the "metaphysical gap" between God and humans is so unfathomably large, it means that no matter how developed human agency may seem in relation to other humans, it never moves beyond (or even perhaps reaches) the "infantile stage" of maturity in relation to God.[59] Unlike Zagzebski's

---

56. Adams, *Christ and Horrors*, 206.
57. Adams, *Christ and Horrors*, 226.
58. Adams, *Horrendous Evils*, 104.
59. See Adams, *Horrendous Evils*, 104.

metaphorical parent who eventually—if reluctantly—lets their child go in order to discover the world for themselves, Adams presents a parent who seems totally unwilling to take that same risk, who, behind a veneer of love, remains incapable of respecting their child's basic human dignity by refusing to believe that that child is ever capable of making a responsible decision for themselves.

Thus, even though Cheetham's question of whether a universalist's conception of God's love is too jealous and too sentimental to allow free persons to make responsible choices was intended primarily for Hick, it would seem that Adams's parental example depicts even more clearly just how jealous and how sentimental that love can be when it is allowed to be carried toward its logical conclusion. And accordingly, in spite of their philosophical differences over the question of the utility of theodicy construction, the basic similarities between Hick and Adams over the positive eschatological resolution of destructive suffering/horrors suggests that the general criticisms already raised against Hick can be equally applied to Adams—specifically Stoeber's, who, while sharing her belief that the experience of Christ on the cross allows God to compassionately enter into a person's own experience of destructive suffering/horrors, specifically insists that this divine solidarity leads to healing and an engendering of compassion on the part of the person, and that proposing some sort of transformative impetus for each instance of destructive suffering effectively trivializes its true horrific nature and attacks the basic dignity of the human person by undermining the freedom out of which these acts were committed and experienced.

This point is further developed by Andrew Gleeson, who takes particular issue with Adams's especially robust articulation of the positive transformative dynamics of the intermediate state. In response, Gleeson acknowledges that, as a premise of Christian hope, while it may be reasonable to argue that certain individuals who suffered tremendous evils may nevertheless regard the world as manifesting God's love and their lives as a meaningful positive good, and while he—with great humility—may accept that in some cases a victim may come to see their sufferings as a moment of intimacy with the divine love that suffered on cross and might no longer wish such events out of their own life, nevertheless rejects the impulse to universalize such a reaction, making it mandatory for every participant.[60]

As Gleeson suggests, Adams's attempts at establishing order and intelligibility by demonstrating that evil indeed has real—if latent—positive aspects, betrays the same theoretical tendencies that she warned against earlier: she recognizes that by simply allowing victims of horrors to accept their

---

60. See Gleeson, "On Letting Go of Theodicy," 10–11.

lives as great goods in spite of what has happened to them leaves a certain part of their life history as "absurd," and in response proposes an abstract, catch-all solution by which that absurdity is overcome. However, as Gleeson points out, what is abstractly possible may be morally or personally impossible for the victim: "The idea that the holocaust might take on a 'positive aspect', so much so that its victims no longer wished it out of their lives, is, they may well claim, at least for themselves, *unconscionable*; and the notion of their succumbing to such a view as a fruit of post-mortem divine largesse is ruled out as a diabolical vision of treason to evil's victims."[61]

Gleeson concludes that Adams has not let go of constructive theodicy's counter-productive tendency to "airbrush from the universe the *offensiveness*, the *incongruity* of evil. That impulse will not let her be content with simply observing the real possibility of believers accepting their lives and the world as great goods, despite (not because of) horrendous evils they have suffered, and *leaving it at that*."[62] Thus, in spite of Adams's repeated insistence otherwise, it would nevertheless seem that there is validity to Gleeson's observation that Adams's exploration of horrors does indeed verge on theodicy; and if that is the case, we may then return to Stoeber's earlier point about the dangers of denying experienced horrors through a well-intentioned felt need of transforming evil into good and conclude that it too lacks the overall effectiveness that we are ultimately seeking. Therefore, we are left able to judge that her conclusions on the role and function of the intermediate state as part of God's plan in responding to horrors will not be of direct benefit to our current project, as—distinctions aside—they generally tend to highlight and develop the most problematic elements of Hick's own response, and in so doing, further reveals just how incompatible these elements are with our attempt to articulate a soul-making understanding of purgatory within a Catholic context.

CONTEMPORARY PROTESTANT DEVELOPMENTS

While Marilyn McCord Adams has chosen to develop John Hick's understanding of the post-mortem intermediate state in such a way that it would end up highlighting some of its more problematic elements, there have also emerged a number of other contemporary Protestant theologians who remain intrigued by the notion of an intermediate state and believe that—under certain conditions—it might serve a constructive eschatological role. These individuals ought to be mentioned, if only very briefly, for they

61. Gleeson, "On Letting Go of Theodicy," 11.
62. Gleeson, "On Letting Go of Theodicy," 12.

provide further evidence for the ongoing viability and increasing popularity of the intermediate state's theological consideration within a broad range of contemporary Protestant thought. Moreover, by touching upon how they have come to understand the intermediate state within their own thought, we may uncover new insights into how a sanctification-based understanding of purgatory might be further developed within a Catholic context and may also shed new light on recurrent or convergent themes present in their approaches to the afterlife that could prove fruitful in ongoing ecumenical dialogue.

Among these individuals are noted theologians such as John Polkinghorne and Jürgen Moltmann. Although approaching the subject from the perspectives of different theological traditions, both affirm their belief in some form of a post-mortem intermediate state. And although neither focus extensively upon the subject, their respective reasons for postulating its existence are remarkably similar to those of Hick, Adams, and Stoeber. Offering a more cosmological perspective, Polkinghorne clearly indicates a belief in a "suitably de-mythologized concept of purgatory,"[63] pointing out that since the history of this universe has been unfolding in what could be understood as an ongoing process, we have every reason to believe that God, who Polkinghorne describes as a "patient and subtle Creator," intends for the afterlife to likewise take on the character of a similarly unfolding process.[64] This includes a dynamic quality to our eternal participation in God's divine being, as well as a proceeding process of purgation as the finite material of our present life is transformed into the eternal material of the afterlife.[65]

Moltmann, on the other hand, acknowledges that for most persons, the journey of our lives and our history with God remains "unfinished" at the point of death. This is especially true for those whose lives ended up being excessively burdensome or were cut tragically short, which in turn raises for Moltmann a particularly dire implication: "The idea that for these people their death is the finish would surely plunge the whole world into absolute absurdity; for if their lives had no meaning, have ours?"[66] Hence, Moltmann believes that God's history with the individual will continue after death and proposes "a kind of 'intermediate state'" as a "wide space for living, in which the life that was spoiled or cut short here can develop freely . . . as the time of a new life, in which God's history with a human being can

---

63. Polkinghorne, "Eschatology," 41.
64. Polkinghorne, "Eschatology," 40.
65. Polkinghorne, "Eschatology," 41.
66. Moltmann, "Is There Life after Death?," 252.

come to its flowering and consummation."[67] Moltmann clearly understands the intermediate state as something inextricably linked to the theological question of suffering, and as Miroslav Volf points out, it would seem that like Hick and Adams, Moltmann's understanding of the intermediate state would extend beyond further opportunities for personal meaning-making, and would indeed serve to facilitate his stated belief in the universal reconciliation of all creation with God.[68]

Although Volf does not engage such concepts as "purgatory" or "intermediate state" within his own eschatological reflections, he nevertheless clearly indicates belief in a period of post-mortem transition toward a final, joyful, eschatological fulfillment. In order for this fulfillment to be considered joyful, Volf believes that it must possess an "unperturbed peace between past and future in all presents," which is achieved by each individual through a period of transition into a state of "new innocence" in which the human will is liberated by the love of God to the extent that it becomes effectively "unaware" of anything else other than the good before it, thus removing from the consciousness an abstract, theoretical, knowledge of goodness *as* good and leaving the person aware only of the goodness in which they uniquely subsist.[69] It is perhaps Volf's position that contrasts most clearly with Adams's, for while they both maintain that every person will arrive at a blessed final joy in heaven,[70] Adams insists that the transformation of each person's memory of destructive suffering within their history will eventually come to contribute to that joy whereas Volf suggests that that joy will be attained through the non-remembrance of all such memory from each person's personal history.[71] Describing his proposal as a "thought experiment" that is merely exploring an idea that he believes to be possible within the Christian theology of redemption, Volf declares that "such memory of wrongs suffered—a particular example of the memory of sin—will not come to the minds of the citizens of the world to come because they will be fully immersed in the love that God is and that God will create among them. Non-remembrance of wrongs suffered is the gift God will give to those who have been wronged. It is also a gift they will gladly share with those who have wronged them."[72]

67. Moltmann, "Is There Life after Death?," 252.
68. Volf, "Enter into Joy!," 271. For Moltmann's statement on Universal Salvation, see Moltmann, *Coming of God*, 255.
69. Volf, "Enter into Joy!," 274.
70. See Volf, "Enter into Joy!," 275.
71. See Volf, *End of Memory*, 141–42.
72. Volf, *End of Memory*, 141–42.

Volf would come to see the receiving of this non-remembrance as post-mortem event, the culminating moment of a larger eschatological project of universal reconciliation, which will necessarily involve the redeeming of the histories of both perpetrator and victim:

> Reconciliation with one's estranged neighbors is integral to the reconciliation with God. The divine embrace of both the victim and the perpetrator has, in a sense, not come to completion without their own embrace. But how can people who have transgressed against each other embrace? How can their common past be redeemed so that they can have a new future? If one assumes personal continuity between a person as a sinner and as a recipient of grace and affirms the irreversibility of life, creation of a completely new past is out of the question. Rather, their past must be redeemed through reconciliation between them. Dealing adequately with sins suffered and committed is *a social process*, involving individual persons and their fellow human beings.[73]

Noting that human beings are, by nature, social creatures, whose identities are unavoidably shaped by how they relate to others and how others relate to them, Volf goes on to explain that while all sins are by definition against God, most sins are committed "in dealings with others," creating "a kind of perverse bond between persons."[74] For Volf, it is not enough for these bonds to simply be undone through a post-mortem seeking out and bequeathing of forgiveness between involved parties; rather, full participation in the divine life in heaven demands true reconciliation, which will not have taken place until "one has *moved toward one's former enemies and embraced them* as belonging to the same communion of love."[75] So all-pervading is this communion of love that persons bonded together within it will finally able to leave behind the last lingering effects of their experiences of sin and step into a world "in which each enjoys the other in the communion of the Triune God and therefore all take part in the dance of love freely given and freely received."[76] Citizens of this world, Volf maintains, will consequently be graced with a certain "not-coming-to-mind" of particular memories of wrongs suffered or perpetrated. These memories, he stresses, are not simply deleted, as though they never happened, but rather "simply fail to surface in one's consciousness" (Volf contrasts this with the term "forgetting,"

---

73. Volf, "Final Reconciliation," 101.
74. Volf, "Love Your Heavenly Enemy," 96.
75. Volf, "Final Reconciliation," 104.
76. Volf, "Final Reconciliation," 104.

which he rejects on the grounds that it connotes human activity over divine grace—activity, moreover, that could perhaps take the form of repression).[77]

Intriguingly, Volf situates these events not within the realm of a post-mortem intermediate state, claiming that the Catholic doctrine of purgatory remains unable to "compellingly [address] the social aspect of the transformation" that will need to happen in the afterlife.[78] Rather than attempt to nevertheless engage the doctrine and develop an understanding that is able to accommodate such a process, Volf instead decides that they will take place during the moment of the Last Judgment,[79] thereby rendering this "period" of post-mortem transition exceedingly brief. In a recent article, Jesuit theologian Nathan O'Halloran praises Volf for offering an eschatological vision that takes into account the demands raised by a serious consideration of its communal dynamics, yet would go on to take issue with Volf's specific decision to locate these aforementioned events in the moment of the Final Judgment, pointing out that the reordering of something as personal and complex as a person's identity would necessarily take some time, for if such an all-encompassing change were to happen suddenly, in the briefest of moments, it could only result in severe psychological damage for the person.[80] The need for a post-mortem reordering of a person's identity to be understood specifically as a *process*, as well as O'Halloran's particular insights into how purgatory might be understood in light of present eschatological developments, will be explored further in the following chapter. Important now is simply to point out Volf's contribution to our present exploration, namely, his clear articulation of how a person's death and post-mortem purification can be considered a communal, as well as a personal, event. Although Volf chooses not to situate this event within the realm of a post-mortem intermediate state, it would seem that his eschatological reflections nevertheless offer insight into how its communal dimension, so insisted upon by the Second Vatican Council and numerous other contemporary theologians, might be concretely considered within the purifying dynamics of purgatory. This, too, will be explored in the following chapter.

Finally, it is important to conclude this survey by spending some time to review the work of certain theologians who have sought to demonstrate how the existing Catholic doctrine of purgatory might be incorporated into their own respective Protestant traditions and reconciled with its existing

---

77. See Volf, *End of Memory*, 145–47.
78. Volf, "Love Your Heavenly Enemy," 95.
79. Volf, "Love Your Heavenly Enemy," 95. See also Volf, "Final Reconciliation," 102.
80. See O'Halloran, "Purgatory," 707.

theological tenets. David Brown, for example, presents a more developed argument for belief in an intermediate state within an Anglican context, in which he manages to persuasively respond to the early Reformers' concerns over purgatory's relationship to the supposed need to render further post-mortem satisfaction for a person's sins. Brown applies the medieval juridical distinction between the concepts of *culpa* (guilt/fault) and *poena* (reparation/penalty) in his understanding of how a sinful act is "satisfied" and eventually resolved in the afterlife. Demonstrating an understanding of sin very similar to that of Augustine's,[81] Brown points out that while the personal guilt created by sin remains as its primary effect and calls into question a person's justification before God, a "necessary consequence or penalty of wrong-doing" also exists as its secondary effect—which does not in itself effect the person's state of justification, but nevertheless has a very real effect on the person's spiritual and moral condition, and will consequently need to be purged before that person could be considered "good," or "perfect."[82] Brown recognizes that in order to guarantee any continuation of a sense of self for an individual between their sinful earthly life and life of presumed perfection in heaven, a sense of connectedness must be established between those two identities; however, an instantaneous transition would lead to a "profound identity crisis" as a lifetime's worth of accumulated memories, experiences, and attitudes, would undoubtedly become alien to the transformed body that carried them.[83] Thus, he proposes purgatory as a place where a person may cooperate with divine grace in a manner appropriate with their temporal condition, so as to develop—through an often painful process of self-awareness—the natural dispositions, habits, and virtues that constitute spiritual goodness.

More recently, Justin D. Barnard has advocated a sanctification-based model of the intermediate state as a possible solution to what he understands to be the philosophical inadequacy of the traditional Protestant belief that a justified believer is wholly and immediately sanctified by God at the point of death so that they may enter directly into heaven. Calling this belief "provisionism," Barnard contends that while he has no issue with the notion that saving faith is the necessary condition for entry into heaven, the conclusion must not be drawn that a person possessing saving faith is necessarily equivalent to a person possessing a full morally sanctified nature (Barnard defines "sanctification" as the "process by which one's moral condition is brought into conformity with one's legal status before God"),

---

81. See also chapter 3 of this book.
82. See Brown, "No Heaven without Purgatory," 455–56.
83. See Brown, "No Heaven without Purgatory," 451–53.

which life in heaven also demands, yet which most people do not possess at the point of death.[84] This leaves Barnard to conclude that death is something more like an interruption and not the conclusion of that process and the momentum it carries. Thus, while Barnard believes that it is indeed possible that God could immediately make the provision for those who have died to become immediately sanctified, he follows Brown in concluding that such a sudden intervention would arbitrarily cut short that process, and the drastic ontological change that would have to occur as a result of that intervention would often be so violent to the continuity of an individual's sense of personal identity from this life to the next that it would seem impossible to realistically consider them to be the same person.[85]

In response, Barnard proposes an understanding of purgatory by which the person is able to continue their process of sanctification until it reaches a natural conclusion. According to Barnard, purgatory "makes it possible for the Lapsable to become persons who possess the settled virtuous disposition characteristic of the Sanctified before enjoying union and fellowship with God in heaven. Thus, heaven preserves its essential moral perfection, while the possession of saving faith is maintained as a sufficient condition for eventual eternal union and fellowship with God in heaven."[86] Barnard explicitly distinguishes a sanctification-based model of purgatory (which he supports) from a satisfaction-based model of purgatory (which he continues to associate with Roman Catholicism and clearly rejects because he believes it to not acknowledge the total satisfaction rendered for every sin through Christ's death on the cross, and assumes that those in purgatory are continuing to be purified from "the penalty for sin or sin itself"),[87] and in turn proposes the sanctification model of purgatory as a possible solution to solving the Protestant problem of provisionism.

Although Barnard is not proposing a soul-making model of purgatory as such, his findings are significant in that they follow Brown in presenting a thorough account of the role and function of purgatory within current Protestant eschatological reflection. Moreover, Barnard's proposal effectively presents a vision of a sanctification-based model of purgatory that—whether aware of it or not—remains essentially compatible with the contemporary Catholic articulation of the doctrine. It is therefore unfortunate that the potential ecumenical potential of Barnard's conclusions is somewhat compromised by his mischaracterization of the Catholic understanding of the

---

84. Barnard, "Purgatory and the Dilemma of Sanctification," 314–15.
85. Barnard, "Purgatory and the Dilemma of Sanctification," 317–19.
86. Barnard, "Purgatory and the Dilemma of Sanctification," 327.
87. Barnard, "Purgatory and the Dilemma of Sanctification," 326.

doctrine. However, these ecumenical possibilities are apparently restored through the work of Neal Judisch, another Protestant, who, while agreeing with Barnard that a sanctification-based understanding of purgatory may indeed be fruitful within a Protestant context, further develops Barnard's work by proposing a rather simple argument that his and contemporary Catholicism's respective understandings of purgatory are in fact equivalent.

Judisch effectively renders moot Barnard's principal claim that Catholicism's supposedly satisfaction-oriented doctrine of purgatory is incompatible with his explicitly Protestant articulation of purgatory by following Brown in pointing to the Catholic concept of the "double consequence" of sin, a concept already touched upon,[88] according to which it is not God's residual fury over the sin itself that needs to be addressed, but rather the sin's consequent lingering effects that are still holding a person back from their own journey of sanctification—and it is in purgatory where the remaining post-mortem effects of those sins are expunged and where the process of sanctification is completed. Judisch thus concludes that from the Protestant perspective, Catholicism's so-called "satisfaction" model of purgatory (as characterized by Barnard) is indeed basically equivalent to the sanctification model that Barnard advocates as more amenable to Protestant thought.[89] And even though both Barnard and Judisch seem to overlook the categorical shift already present in Catholicism's current understanding of purgatory from a juridical, more satisfaction-based understanding to a more relational, sanctification-based understanding of how the residual effects of sin are experienced and purified, Barnard and Brown's conclusions are helpful to the extent that they clearly articulate a coherent "vision" of purgatory that seems to be emerging within the mainline Protestant tradition, and Judisch's argument is significant in that it demonstrates that there is a great deal of convergence between this and Catholicism's respective vision once the more juridical language of Catholicism's formal explanation is properly interrogated.

This is an opinion shared by Jerry L. Walls,[90] who has written extensively on the recent history of the doctrine of purgatory—both within the Catholic and Protestant contexts. Walls goes to great lengths in exploring how the sanctification-based model of purgatory has been developed within both traditions, and demonstrates how the particular theological themes and attitudes that have guided the development of these respective visions

---

88. This was first detailed in our exploration of Augustine's understanding of sin in chapter 3 of this book.

89. See Judisch, "Sanctification, Satisfaction," 178–79.

90. Walls, *Purgatory*, 90–91.

for purgatory have arrived at a present-day convergence in how this doctrine is understood and articulated. To this end, Walls's work may be of great benefit in helping to inform and frame further ecumenical conversations on the subject. However, while himself accepting a sanctification-based understanding of purgatory similar to the models already presented, and for many of the same reasons already listed, Walls goes on to propose an expanded view of purgatory that allows for post-mortem repentance and conversion "for those persons who were tardy in repentance, or complacent, or who pursued this relationship only halfheartedly in life."[91] Not ruling out the real possibility of an individual choosing to exist in perpetual alienation from God, Walls nevertheless maintains that due to God's universal salvific will, God desires to give every person every opportunity to gain salvation and will freely offer the grace necessary for each person to choose to enter into relationship with God, leaving Walls to wonder why these opportunities would end at the point of bodily death.[92] Thus, for those who were unable or simply unwilling to cooperate with that grace during their earthly life, Walls proposes that the opportunity for repentance and conversion continues into the afterlife, where their conscious dissatisfaction over their present state of alienation continuously encounters God's care for them and desire for relationship.

Although Walls himself admits that such an innovation deviates from the Catholic view,[93] he does not follow directly down the path of many of his contemporaries by advocating for universalism. Indeed, Walls's proposal seems to position itself as a sort of "hybrid" option between the hard universalism proposed by a number of Protestant theologians and the more traditional eschatological beliefs maintained within the Catholic and mainline Protestant traditions.[94] Thus, Walls's proposal aside, it would seem that while our analysis of the various contemporary Protestant articulations of purgatory does not necessarily provide any further contributions to consider within the context of our own soul-making project, it has nevertheless been useful for two principal reasons: firstly, by observing how some of the more problematic elements of Hick's thought has been further developed by subsequent theologians we are able to identify more clearly the possible extreme situations that might result in a contemporary soul-making

91. Walls, *Purgatory*, 126.
92. Walls, *Purgatory*, 127.
93. Walls, *Purgatory*, 137.
94. See Walls, *Purgatory*, 141. In his argument, Walls cites Catholic theologians whom he believes in their own work may be at least suggesting such a possibility, including Karl Rahner; see Rahner, "Purgatory," 191. This assertion invites further investigation, and may be further explored elsewhere, at another time.

understanding of purgatory if adhered to naively or left unaddressed. By reviewing these examples and arguments, our reasons for why we rejected these elements in the first place have been reinforced and it becomes even more apparent that a wholesale adoption of Hick's soul-making thought is simply unfeasible within a Catholic context.

Secondly, it seems clear that after reviewing the various contemporary Protestant voices in support of adapting some form of a post-mortem intermediate state into their eschatological beliefs, they too are motivated by the same spirit of generosity that served as the impetus for earlier reflection on the doctrine of purgatory.[95] Each individual—often to a very strong degree—emphasized an understanding of the intermediate state that was fundamentally hopeful, generally reflecting the current spirit guiding contemporary Catholic reflection as well. Thus, to the extent that these two eschatological spirits are converging, we become able to more clearly identify a possible field of ecumenical conversation that has long remained absent in Catholic-Protestant discussion. In outlining an understanding of purgatory that is able to satisfy many of the enduring theological sensibilities within the mainline Protestant tradition, the various voices that we have so far encountered provide a certain reassurance that a more robustly articulated sanctification-based understanding of purgatory within the Catholic tradition will hold strong ecumenical potential. These ecumenical upshots will be explored further in the concluding chapter, as we attempt to offer an articulation of a soul-making understanding of purgatory within the Catholic tradition and argue further that the specific soul-making insights we intend to incorporate will strengthen, rather than diminish, purgatory's ecumenical—as well as pastoral—potential.

---

95. See chapter 1 of this book.

6

A Soul-Making Concept of Purgatory within a Contemporary Catholic Context

IN IDENTIFYING VARIOUS ENCOURAGING prospects that a more robust and clearly articulated sanctification-based model of purgatory may offer in contemporary theological discourse, we are now able to return once again to John Hick's soul-making insights and come to some conclusions regarding the potential they might hold in developing an understanding of purgatory that is more clearly and comprehensively in accord with present Catholic eschatological themes. It has been the purpose of this book to determine if—and to what extent—John Hick's soul-making insights into the human person, the problem of evil, and the afterlife are able to inform the Catholic doctrine of purgatory as it is presently understood. Hick has been largely responsible for developing an understanding of the post-mortem intermediate state within a soul-making context, and we believe that a measured interaction with his conclusions can in turn effectively augment the sanctifying elements that recent Catholic theologians have attempted to cultivate in their own attempts to better understand purgatory's role and function.

OVERVIEW

Throughout the course of our exploration, two basic theological themes or propositions undergirding purgatory's existence have been encountered: the universal and enduring presence of sin in creation that perpetually estranges humanity from God, and God's universal call to perfect holiness for all persons. These two themes—the former centering around Augustine's articulation of the doctrine of original sin (and its enduring effects upon each person) as part of his theological response to the problem of evil, and the latter, which although present in some form throughout the history of Christianity, would eventually be made more explicit in the decrees of the Second Vatican Council—remain entrenched within the present Catholic theological context. They directly inform what Catholicism currently teaches regarding its understanding of humanity's fallen condition, its transformation, and eventual salvation.

Yet even a cursory review of these themes would seem to suggest that they exist in apparent opposition to one another, that the experience of sin would make impossible any person's attempt to fully respond to (and progress in) that divine call to perfection. However, as theologians developed an increasingly sophisticated understanding of sin and its implications, the question of resolving sin's lingering effects upon the human person and their ability to respond to that call remained in need of an answer. In our survey of purgatory's doctrinal history, we have seen how a coherent understanding of its eschatological role would emerge from a crude folk-based attempt at responding to this question, in which it functioned as the means by which the good-yet-not-perfect were able, through God's grace, to experience the transformation necessary in order to be fully received into heaven, to something that was eventually seized upon and systematized by the hierarchy of the Catholic Church according to the understanding that it functioned as the realm in which the lingering effects of a person's sins are to be purified, so as to no longer impede their journey toward perfect union with God.

As such, a path has been traced detailing how the doctrine of purgatory came to serve as an indispensable component within Catholic eschatological thought, in which its defined role ultimately helped to bridge the two seemingly opposing propositions mentioned above. Yet in our survey of purgatory's doctrinal history, we have also seen how purgatory's understood function within its assigned role has been largely predicated upon the context in which the secondary effects of sin have themselves been understood, in light of an individual's call to salvation. For example, when the doctrine of purgatory was first formalized during the thirteenth century, its function was notably articulated according to the juridical concepts of the time, which emphasized a reading of Augustine's understanding of sin's secondary effects as an unsatisfied personal injustice against God's perfect goodness and as such had to be satisfied in a post-mortem context if they were not already satisfied here on earth. Later, we were able to see how this historical understanding of the secondary effects of sin began to be influenced by a contemporary—if not fully developed—spiritual emphasis upon the relational qualities of sin and salvation, resulting in an understanding of purgatory's function as the means by which the lingering effects of an individual's collected sins are purified so as to achieve an end of personal sanctification and deeper relationship with God (and not necessarily as a means to satisfy God's divine sense of justice).

Thus, while purgatory's ultimate role (as the venue for the post-mortem purification of the secondary effects of sin) has remained basically unaltered throughout its doctrinal history, there has been a more recent and clearly identifiable attempt to adapt how the doctrine is understood to function in this role to new spiritual and theological contexts. By briefly touching upon the existential and relational qualities of the human person's relationship with sin, we have noted that the decrees of the Second Vatican Council have offered some guidance toward interpreting how purgatory may actually function in its role regarding the post-mortem purifications of sin's secondary effects. And while current interpretations of the doctrine's function have indeed emphasized a shift away from retributory, satisfaction-based concepts and vocabulary to reformational, sanctification-based concepts and vocabulary, it is apparent that this shift has not yet been able to adequately tie this new-found functional understanding clearly back to its basic role of providing the purification of the secondary effects of sin. Thus, while proposals regarding new ways of understanding purgatory's transformative dynamics within its sanctifying function have been offered, these proposals have yet to fully articulate a corresponding understanding of sin whereby it is capable of being transformed through the process of sanctification.

On the other hand, we have encountered demands by some theologians, such as Dermot A. Lane, that any eschatological consideration, including that of post-mortem purification, must provide a means of resolving the lived realities, anxieties, and hopes carried by the people of God, or risk theological and pastoral irrelevancy. A credible eschatology, according to Lane, "must be able to chart a course that contains some degree of continuity between past, present, and future, while at the same time leaving room for the important elements of change and transformation."[1] As we have seen, Lane believes that any such eschatology must necessary encompass what he calls the "new pressures" on eschatology, including the existence of poverty in the developing world, "the permanency of the nuclear threat, the ongoing ecological crisis, and a new awareness of the finiteness of our small blue planet."[2] Lane also includes the existence of mass death, which he claims "raises questions about the destiny of the whole human species,"

---

1. Lane, *Keeping Hope Alive*, 13.
2. Lane, *Keeping Hope Alive*, 7.

forcing us to "go beyond questions about my individual death, enabling us to realise that individual destiny is bound up with the destiny of the whole human race."[3] Yet while it has been suggested that these concerns may be considered within the context of purgatory's transformative role, it would also seem that these demands have not yet been fully considered in relation to its function in contemporary articulations of the doctrine. As such, there continues to exist in these contemporary articulations a seeming disconnect between purgatory's traditionally understood role (the post-mortem purification of the secondary effects of sin) and certain ideas about how purgatory ought to function within its role, and what it ought to include in its purview. This is manifested in an overall inability to be more explicit in outlining an understanding of how sin's secondary effects correspond with a more explicitly sanctification-based understanding of purgatory's function, which has seemingly led to a certain present confusion regarding purgatory's actual eschatological role and function, as well as perhaps a corresponding decline in its pastoral and theological significance. Without a clearly expressed articulation of how secondary effects of sin are understood to exist and be purified within a more robust sanctification-based context informed by present anthropological, theodical, and eschatological concerns, an understanding moreover that is grounded within the Catholic theological tradition, it appears that a satisfactory description of how these sanctifying forces operate to purify a person within a post-mortem context may indeed remain elusive.

We have turned to the thoughts and ideas of John Hick in order to see if his unique soul-making understanding of the human person, theodicy, and the afterlife is able to offer any new theological insights into how these secondary effects of sin can be better understood within the Catholic tradition, so as to both more fully reflect the complexities of the contemporary human condition and, ultimately, explain how that condition can eventually be transformed through God's grace within a post-mortem context. As we have pointed out, Hick has been uniquely able to develop a sanctification-based understanding of the post-mortem intermediate state that is essentially predicated upon his soul-making understanding of the human person and that person's unique relationship with sin within their own spiritual journey toward God.[4] As such, we have been able to observe how the intermediate state forms an integral—and fully integrated—component within his soul-making project. And through our exploration of his soul-making worldview, we are now able to show how it is indeed able to inform our

3. Lane, *Keeping Hope Alive*, 8.
4. This point was initially raised in chapter 4 of this book.

understanding of sin's secondary effects and consequently, in the interest of our project, offer an expanded understanding of how purgatory can function within its purificatory role. Hopefully, these insights may in some small measure help the doctrine of purgatory return to its earlier, basically hopeful, roots and in so doing, regain some of its lost theological and pastoral relevance by offering a more compelling vision of how it might be situated within the current Catholic eschatological context.

To demonstrate this conclusion, it will be helpful to outline the necessary components of a more robust, sanctification-based, particularly soul-making influenced, understanding of purgatory: firstly, by recalling soul-making's conceptual roots within the broader Catholic tradition (which was earlier explored in chapter 3) and detailing how a recovery of these insights can serve to develop Catholicism's traditional understanding of the secondary effects of sin to better reflect current theological and spiritual emphases. Secondly, with an expanded soul-making-influenced understanding of sin's secondary effects established, we will offer some conclusions regarding what impact this might have on the currently existing sanctification-based understanding of purgatory; this will include revisiting the particular insights found in Hick's application of soul-making concepts to eschatological reflection (as outlined in chapter 4), as well as observing, through the insights of certain contemporary theologians, how these insights can be adapted—and even further strengthened—for a Catholic theological context (which was further explained in chapter 5). Finally, we will conclude by assessing how well a soul-making model of purgatory is capable of strengthening its currently understood sanctification-based role by evaluating its ability to better respond to the demands of what John E. Thiel describes as the Pauline eschatological culture inaugurated by the reforms of the Second Vatican Council,[5] as well as any implications such an understanding may have in further Catholic and, more broadly speaking, Christian eschatological reflection.

In so doing, it will be demonstrated that the soul-making insights offered by John Hick can indeed develop already-existing elements within the Catholic understanding of the human person and their relationship with sin, and consequently add greater clarity and depth to the present sanctification-based understanding of purgatory, thereby more effectively integrating it within the present Catholic eschatological system. As such, it is hoped that the conclusions found in this chapter will ultimately provide some modest contribution in helping the doctrine to reengage with the early—if primitive—hopeful impulses that enabled its initial emergence and

---

5. See chapter 2 of this book.

widespread acceptance (as we identified to be present in the early Christian communities in chapter 1). The point ought to be made, therefore, that if we are successful in showing how Hick's soul-making insights help the doctrine to more fully reengage its religious roots, we are at the same time contributing to its ongoing relevance in contemporary theological reflection, and vice-versa. But to help facilitate this dual process, it is necessary to revisit an earlier question: namely the suitability of the very concept of soul-making within the Catholic context.

SOUL-MAKING WITHIN A CATHOLIC THEOLOGICAL CONTEXT

As we have seen, a soul-making understanding of creation basically entails that (a) God created humanity as mutable, dynamic creatures, in possession of an imperfect freedom over its own mutability, (b) God desires for humanity, over the course of time, to come to moral maturity and spiritual perfection, which will ultimately find its full realization in the eschaton, and (c) God has created ante-mortem and post-mortem environments, both ideally suited to facilitate this process of growth in perfection.

We have also seen the great lengths to which Hick goes in order to distinguish his so-called Irenaean understanding of the human person over and against an Augustinian understanding. Identifying the concept of soul-making exclusively with the former approach, Hick firmly believes that its insights can only be authentically developed outside of the mainstream Western theological tradition. Yet, with the assistance of Paul W. Gooch, it has been argued that in spite of Hick's beliefs to the contrary, these key principles of soul-making are indeed present in the sources of both the Irenaean and Augustinian anthropological perspectives, with each approach offering distinct yet ultimately non-contradictory emphases that together can uniquely help to inform and color further reflection on this question. This realization is of great importance. Firstly, it allows for an explicit examination of the concept of soul-making within a Catholic setting, thereby allowing soul-making's unique insights to more fully interact with the richness and depth of the Catholic tradition, and indeed, to further enrich the tradition's anthropological and eschatological conceptual frameworks of sanctification. Secondly, it in turn establishes a foundation upon which the insights identified within Hick's soul-making understanding of the post-mortem intermediate state can be further developed within a Catholic context.

As Neal Judisch reminds us, the point of distinction between a so-called satisfaction-based understanding of purgatory and a sanctification-based understanding of purgatory is how sin's effects are approached and understood. While sin's secondary effects (and their ultimate resolution) were for a great deal of time considered within the satisfaction model's legalistic framework of justice and punishment, the existential and developmental framework of the sanctification model suggests that they be considered as something more akin to the "corrosive effect of sin itself upon the individual's soul," resulting in that person's "enduring through and struggling to rectify the disorder of [their] soul and the spiritual ill health that sinful behavior brings in its wake."[6] In so doing, Judisch is essentially describing the secondary effects of sin as it is presently understood within the sanctification-based model of purgatory within the Catholic context; however, it has already been pointed out that this shift could in fact be more accurately characterized as a retrieval and reemphasizing of certain sanctifying themes already present in Augustine, in terms of his concept of healing and transcending our fallen natures by withstanding and overcoming the trials of disordered concupiscence. When Augustine's articulation of the secondary effects of sin is read through the post-Vatican II hermeneutic of relationality and sanctification, one can already find strong parallels between it, its direct and more broadly considered effects upon the individual and creation, and the soul-making narrative offered by Hick.

Once acknowledged, it is possible to envision sin's secondary effects shaping a world in which the divine presence is obscured from human lives and in which an epistemic distance remains between the human person and God. It is also possible to envision that obscurity to slowly dissipate as the person strives to overcome the lingering state of sin that these secondary effects have helped to create—both at a personal and communal level. One can also envision this journey of personal and communal transcendence ultimately requiring an eschatological resolution. And finally, one can conceivably envision the created world in which we live to be intentionally suited to facilitate and abet this journey of transcendence (although with the caveat that this suitability nevertheless remains *in spite* of the effects of sin in the world).

If one is to agree that a soul-making interpretation of creation and the human person remains possible within both Hick's Irenaean understanding and Catholicism's seemingly Augustinian understanding, it would therefore seem that Augustine's understanding of sin's double effect may also provide the basis for such an interpretation within the Catholic context. In

---

6. Judisch, "Sanctification, Satisfaction," 176.

emphasizing personal growth in holiness and relationship through a process of striving and prevailing over various forms of adversity, one finds in the so-called Augustinian understanding of both sin's residual effects on creation and the nature of creation's journey of transcending those effects not just the kernels of a sanctifying-based understanding of the human person, but also the same basic content of the soul-making themes Hick believed to be exclusive to Irenaeus. As such, it is specifically within the context of understanding sin's secondary effects that these soul-making themes can be developed to further enhance the already established sanctifying-based understanding of the human person present in contemporary Catholic thought.

As pointed out earlier, there exist profound insights into the human condition within Augustine's understanding of the residual effects of sin, insights that can constructively contribute to any soul-making understanding of the human person within a Catholic context.[7] Augustine specifically demonstrates a deep knowledge of the pervading effects of residual sin, and consequently, a particular attentiveness to the frailty and inconsistency of fallen human nature as it embarks on a volatile and arduous journey of transcending those effects. And in reminding us of just how delicate and precarious a personal process soul-making can oftentimes be, Augustine is able to effectively offer a word of caution against what can sometimes become an overly exuberant and optimistic reading of soul-making offered by Hick's interpretation of Irenaeus. Perhaps writing out of his own well-documented experience of attempting to overcome the enduring, disordering effects of sin experienced in his own life, Augustine, for whatever reason, demonstrates a clear awareness that the process of moral and spiritual growth ought not to be romanticized or glossed over as an inevitability, but indeed remains both messy and difficult with many twists, turns, and setbacks.

While sometimes decried as an overly pessimistic assessment of the human person and its capabilities, it can, on the other hand, be argued that although Augustine's understanding may seemingly avail itself to more pessimistic interpretations than Irenaeus's, his assessment of the fallen human condition nevertheless possesses a certain uncomfortable accuracy, which has been validated throughout the recorded events and experiences of human history. It can be said that Augustine indeed demonstrates a realistic understanding of just how powerful, subtle, and pervading the reality of sin actually is in both our world and our personal lives, and likewise offers a realistic assessment of how difficult it ultimately is to surmount it. And yet, it can also be said that Augustine nevertheless believed that given our sinful

---

7. See chapter 3 of this book.

reality, we, as individuals and as a species are indeed better off with this struggle than without. Returning to a passage of Augustine's cited earlier, we find him offering a rallying cry, of sorts, for each person to fully engage themselves in this struggle: "If there is no war there will be no victory. And if we do not obtain victory over the faults that strip against us there will not be any cleansing from faults, for, if we conquer temptation in these snares of our body, we are purged of the strife of passions that war against us."[8]

With this in mind, we must, however, return to Hick's soul-making interpretation of Irenaeus, and again highlight certain thematic elements present in this particular understanding that remain less developed in Augustine's, namely a compassionate understanding regarding the immaturity of primordial humanity and an optimism regarding its ability for growth and development. Interpreters of Irenaeus have tended to focus on his understanding of the human condition as it existed in its spiritual infancy, which appears to highlight humanity's innate—if lost—innocence, impressionableness, ignorance, and perhaps even helplessness, as it engages the world around itself (characteristics which have also endured, in some relative form, to a greater or lesser extent, in each human person throughout history). Yet while these characteristics can—and of course have—contributed to the state of sin in which each person (and indeed all of humanity) finds itself, Irenaeus indicates that it is possible for these characteristics to also be positively and constructively developed throughout the course of a person's life. As we have seen, Irenaeus's reference to humanity's primitive child-like nature highlights an important feature of Hick's understanding: that the soul-making path of sanctification involves more than just a journey of transcendence from a state of sin in all of its varieties. It also involves a journey of transcendence from a state of ignorance and immaturity. Thus, if one is to recall Augustine's initial insight that the residual effects of sin leave humanity with the task of transcending the forces of concupiscence that continue to rage inside each person, we are able to add to that Irenaeus's insight that these same sinful effects leave humanity with the task of transcending its ignorance and lost innocence, so as to progress toward the likeness of God. The distinction, it seems, in our interpretation of Augustine and Irenaeus's respective understandings of the human spiritual journey is subtle but crucial: Augustine's emphasis primarily lies in our journey of transforming that which is disordered within us, whereas Irenaeus primarily emphasizes our journey of transcendence into that which we are called to be. It is only when both of these saints are considered in tandem that we are able to grasp more clearly their individual contributions toward more

---

8. Augustine, "Against Julian," bk. 2, ch. 6.

fully understanding the process of personal sanctification: namely that it amounts to more than simply an expulsion or transformation of what is evil in our lives, or a continual cultivation and flourishing of what is good, but indeed a combination of the two.

In providing a basis with which one can understand the process of soul-making in light of the secondary effects of sin, Augustine and Irenaeus together offer a more comprehensive backdrop with which one can reapproach a sanctification-based understanding of the human person within a Catholic context. When observed together, both individuals are able to present a more complex and nuanced treatment of the human person and their relationship with both God and creation than if interpreted in isolation; likewise, when observed together, both individuals are able to offer a more complex and nuanced treatment of the forces of sanctification at work in an individual. We are able to interpret from their insights a vision of a human person who was fundamentally created to engage in a process of sanctification in a world designed to abet that process. Moreover, we are also able to interpret from their insights an understanding that although a person is created to grow into relationship with God, human immaturity and frailty is such that this task remains arduous at best; nevertheless, God, in God's wisdom, has accounted for this reality by allowing for opportunities by which human striving against these limitations and obstacles can indeed cooperate in the advancement of the very process of sanctification.

We are therefore able, like Hick, to identify early within the tradition a sanctification-based understanding of the human person's relationship to sin that in turn can serve as a foundation for exploring a sanctification-based understanding of purgatory. As we have observed, purgatory's understood role and function has been predicated upon one's approach to understanding more broadly the process of how the secondary effects of sin come to be purified and resolved. Just as the purpose and mechanics of the doctrine were systematized centuries ago according to the juridical concepts of sin present at that the time, we now have for ourselves the basis for returning to the doctrine and reengaging it according to the more relational, developmental, psychological, and social concepts of sin of our time. We are now able to see that together, both Irenaeus and Augustine provide the means for such an understanding of the human person and its relationship with sin, as well as the basis for a comprehensive, expanded sanctification-based understanding (specifically, a soul-making influenced, sanctification-based understanding) of how the human person is able to eventually break free from that relationship. This is an understanding that incorporates key soul-making elements from Hick, and yet remains grounded firmly within the Catholic tradition that it seeks to further enrich. By following Hick's lead in exploring an understanding of the human person created for a soul-making process of sanctification, we are able to expand our sense of sin's secondary effects and turn our reflections toward how people might continue that journey in an afterlife that is specifically designed to further encourage that process and ultimately bring it to completion.

A SOUL-MAKING UNDERSTANDING OF THE HUMAN PERSON

Although John Hick presented a number of views which proved themselves at odds with various positions held within the Catholic tradition, we have been able to identify certain insights in his understanding of the human person and the afterlife that stand to further inform and strengthen a Catholic understanding of how the sanctifying dynamics that have guided a person throughout their earthly life continue in the afterlife. These include: (a) an increase in the awareness of the purgation of the secondary effects of sin to include the purgation of isolating self-regard and with it a proportionally increasing awareness of one's place in the Mystical Body of Christ, leading to (b) a more positive understanding of what is meant by purgatorial "purifications" within a sanctifying context, which includes increased awareness of how the purgation of the secondary effects of sin can include a growth in personal authenticity and right-relationship, and, finally, (c) an increased awareness that a person's transition to the afterlife need not necessarily be an anxiety-inducing event but rather something to be welcomed as the next stage in an individual's progress toward perfect relationship with God and all of creation.[9]

It has been argued that these points are indeed consistent with certain spiritual and eschatological themes and concerns identified during the Second Vatican Council, and consequently hold great potential in developing an understanding of purgatory that better reflects these themes. However, as we have seen, Hick is unique in using the concepts and vocabulary of soul-making to further develop a particular understanding of how those secondary effects that were present on earth continue to linger—both personally and collectively—within a post-mortem context, as well as a corresponding understanding of the nature of the purifications required for their eventual resolution and definitive transcendence. These contributions, it seems, can greatly contribute to our historical understanding of the human person's relationship to sin and its effects, which can in turn offer a far richer

---

9. See chapter 4 of this book.

understanding of purgatory as the venue where these secondary effects are ultimately resolved.

Through his understanding that the process of soul-making takes place in an environment that stands at an epistemic distance from God, Hick is able to further develop a key interpretive insight in a sanctification-based reading of Augustine and Irenaeus's respective understandings of living in a fallen world that struggles with the enduring presence of sin: namely, that its effects do not just manifest themselves as internal compulsions or dispositions to be mastered, but can also appear as externally imposed dilemmas, situations and environments to be overcome, thereby becoming opportunities for further moral and spiritual growth. As such, an emphasis on soul-making is able to effectively illuminate the reality of the many ways in which the effects of sin remain present in the world and may be encountered by a person. Existing in need of personal and communal transformation, these effects not only include the lingering consequences of an individual's personal actions, but also those lingering manifold consequences of other people's actions, which all together contribute toward the creation of the moral environment in which a person finds themselves. As such, this communal dynamic found in Hick's soul-making understanding effectively develops an essential point already present within then-Cardinal Joseph Ratzinger's description of how the person ought to be considered within eschatological consideration: "Every human being exists in himself and outside himself: everyone exists simultaneously in other people. What happens in one individual has an effect upon the whole of humanity, and what happens in humanity happens in the individual. 'The Body of Christ' means that all human beings are one organism, the destiny of the whole is the proper destiny of each."[10] It is precisely this intermingling of personal and collective sin's lingering effects upon social, cultural, economic, ecological, and political spheres of existence that together make up the environment out of which a person's moral and spiritual character is uniquely formed, for better or for worse. Indeed, such an understanding of sin's secondary effects more readily complements the post-conciliar emphasis on a universally felt experience of sin, which, as we have seen, is often included in contemporary theological discourse as a primary component of the Pauline non-competitive dynamics of how we understand salvation.[11]

In applying the insights of Hick's soul-making theology to the existing Catholic notion of the double effect of sin, we are able to add greater depth to this understanding by pointing out the fact that sin does not just

---

10. Ratzinger, *Eschatology*, 190.
11. See Thiel, *Icons of Hope*, 67.

exist as a clear and obvious opposing force to personal sanctification, experienced by every person in varying degrees along their path of moral and spiritual growth. Its presence in a person's life is much more subtle, evasive, yet ubiquitously felt. It exists as complex overlapping of layers or "worlds" of sin toward which that person—or other persons—have contributed to a greater or lesser extent, within which each person lives (again, to a greater or lesser extent, although not necessarily as a direct consequence of their actions), and from out of which each person must work out their own salvation.

This universal experience of sin is indeed unique to each person according to how the totality of its layers is composed in their own life and as such will have a unique bearing on their own character, with which they must uniquely interact and ultimately transcend in order to complete their own soul-making journey. Such an expanded understanding of sin and of sin's secondary effects—which includes both those which have resulted as direct consequences of a person's own actions, as well as those which have resulted as the consequences of the actions of other persons—is able to more convincingly explain how everyone, including someone of genuine moral and spiritual goodness, is still able to live "in a world of sin," that has in turn affected every aspect of their spiritual character (which would include religious, moral, psychological, and relational aspects, among others), and in spite of that person's innocence and goodness nevertheless remains in need of purification. And in so doing, such an understanding also provides the means for dramatically expanding both the scope of understanding purgatory's purifying role, and, as we shall see, purgatory's sanctifying function.

By interpreting Hick's soul-making insights into how the human person and the process of their moral and spiritual development can be understood within Catholicism's already-existing theological framework of sin's secondary effects, we are thus presented an opportunity for regarding purgatory as not just the venue for post-mortem purification of our personal defects, but also, more broadly, as a venue to develop and grow in every aspect of our personal character, through a process of building upon, transcending and integrating the manifold lingering effects—be they of personal or circumstantial origin—that sin has had regarding how we relate to ourselves, how we relate to the world, and how we relate to God. In other words, we are now presented with an opportunity to more deeply appreciate how purgatory functions within its essential role in the transformation of a person's entire spiritual character that emerged and developed during their time on earth.

A SOUL-MAKING UNDERSTANDING OF PURGATORY'S ESSENTIAL ROLE

Within his soul-making worldview, the role which John Hick initially assigned the post-mortem intermediate state was that of an opportunity for a person to continue, through the workings of God's grace, their own spiritual journey to the point of completion. Although Hick remained emphatically against any notion of a singular "final decision" for or against God to be irrevocably determined at the moment of death,[12] he nevertheless appears to have acknowledged that a person's basic spiritual character is indeed heavily influenced through certain "great" choices, which, he writes, are "normally made through innumerable small choices. And the unique set of human interactions in time, which we call history, is the sphere within which these vital choices are made." Accordingly, Hick continues, "the kind of belief in a life after death which I shall now argue . . . is one which postulates a further history, a post-mortem history, in which the work of attaining to self-transcendence is continued to its completion."[13] The intermediate state functions for Hick as a venue in which a person may continue and conclude their moral, psychological, spiritual, and social development, in which a person is guided, graced with the benefit of time and perspective, in the integration of previous life experiences—including traumatic and personally destructive experiences—wherein these experiences (along with their various direct and indirect effects) are purified and transformed, so as to constructively abet their own divinely directed growth in sanctification. As such, the image of the intermediate state ultimately conjured by such an understanding is not that of a looming, excruciating, impersonal realm by which the person was made to conform to an objective ideal of perfection, but rather as a realm where God's grace is able to uniquely meet that person wherever they were, morally, spiritually, and psychologically, at the time of death, and work within that person to allow them to become their own ideal self.

If the function of Hick's soul-making intermediate state is largely defined according to how a person's decisions taken under the shroud of epistemic distance are understood and integrated within the post-mortem person in light of person's destiny of uniquely entering into an ever-deepening relationship with God, then the basic content of his understanding also becomes available to interpretation according to the structures found within present articulations of the Catholic doctrine of purgatory, whose function has in turn been largely defined according to how the secondary

---

12. Hick, *Death and Eternal Life*, 240.
13. Hick, "Present and Future Life," 8.

effects of decisions taken under the shroud of fallen human nature are understood and integrated within the post-mortem person in light of their ever-deepening relationship with God. As such, we now have the foundations to more systematically explain—and more robustly articulate—how Hick's soul-making insights may contribute toward a revisited "sanctification-based" model of purgatory within a contemporary Catholic context.

Firstly, this is a model of purgatory that ought to be considered as a continuation of the doctrine's historical understanding through its upholding of a point made earlier by Ratzinger regarding its essential nature: namely, that throughout its history, "the Church held fast to one aspect of the idea of the intermediate state, insisting that, even if one's fundamental life-decision is finally decided and fixed in death, one's definitive destiny need not necessarily be reached straight away. It may be that the basic decision of a human being is covered over by layers of secondary decisions and needs to be dug free."[14] This statement bears remarkable similarity to the one earlier made by Hick. Therefore, assuming that Ratzinger's "secondary decisions" is basically synonymous with the term "secondary effects of sin," that has been used throughout this book, we now find ourselves in a position to consider the implications of Hick's insights into how these secondary decisions/secondary effects that remain in need of purification can include both personal, and—crucially—communal, environmental, and circumstantial dimensions. They interconnect and overlap in a near-infinite variety of ways so as to impede or even arrest a person's journey of spiritual growth and/or stimulate or perpetuate their estrangement from God. In this view, we are invited to consider an understanding of purgatory that is capable of responding to the various overlapping layers of negative secondary decisions/effects of sin that have built up around an individual, to gradually transform them so that they no longer serve as barriers between the person and the divine. In other words, we are presented with a model of purgatory that offers to expand our understanding of how it might function according to its traditionally held role in the purification of the accrued negative secondary decisions/effects of sin from a person's identity: this model regards these decisions or effects not simply within a strictly personal context, that is, as the direct consequences of their personal actions (of which the person bears personal responsibility), but rather within the context of the totality of their human experience—with all of its contributing factors. This can include the circumstances in which that person lived, the way in which those circumstances have sometimes impressed themselves upon that person's moral and spiritual character (and perhaps

---

14. Ratzinger, *Eschatology*, 219.

still do), and the sometimes-often difficult decisions that person has had to make within those circumstances.

Likewise, this understanding of purgatory also encourages consideration of the gravity that relational and communal realities play in the formation of a person's self-identity. This point was identified earlier as one of the real contributions that Hick's soul-making worldview can provide for our ongoing eschatological reflections, as an acknowledgment of the multivalent role that the relational dynamic can play in the formation of our identities. It consequently broadens both our understanding of the human person's need for purification, and how purgatory functions in its role in carrying out that purification and providing an ultimate resolution. It emphasizes the basic fact that one's identity is not formed in isolation but rather is conditioned by the relationships that one has had and the society in which one has lived (and the effects thereof) for better or for worse. It takes into account the undeniable influence and lasting imprint of familial (perhaps even ancestral) relationships, friendships, partnerships, neighborhoods, groups, and communities, along with their respective hopes, dreams, anxieties, and traumas, that have been shared with and/or imparted on a person and have helped to form—again, for better or for worse—a person's journey of moral and spiritual growth.

As such, we are therefore proposing an understanding of purgatory that, within its role of encompassing, engaging, and purifying the secondary effects of sin that have been carried by a person into the afterlife, ultimately encompasses and engages the totality of a person's experience, in all of its complexity, and is able to discover within that complexity the person's basic decision. It is an understanding of purgatory that is predicated upon a deep awareness of the critical and intricate connectedness between the person's basic and secondary decisions in the composition of their own spiritual identity, reinforcing the notion that the communal and environmental factors affecting their lived spiritual life must too be part of any eschatological resolution.

It is just such an understanding of purgatory that Cardinal Ratzinger and recent Catholic documents have appeared to point toward in their relatively brief statements on the doctrine. And while perhaps traces of this particular expanded sense of purgatory's role can already be implicitly found in current sanctification-based models of purgatory, little attention has been given to systematic accounts that would be able to ground such an understanding squarely within the greater Catholic tradition or to address how purgatory's sanctifying function might be understood in light of an expanded and more nuanced understanding of sin's secondary decisions/effects. For this view also maintains that these secondary layers are more than simply superfluous chaff to be burned away, thereby allowing the essential core of the person to emerge. Rather, they represent that the person's own history, for better or for worse, is inextricably woven into their own identity. Indeed, it would seem that any attempt to undermine or eliminate the significance that these accumulated effects have had on a person's identity would ultimately have a destructive effect upon that person, whereupon they might be considered simply as a perfected—but isolated and characterless—"monad," purged of all their unique yet supposedly superfluous characteristics, relationships, and experiences.[15] Such a reductionist and regressive conception of purgatory's transformative dynamics would ultimately result in a distortion of the person's sense of their own identity, thereby threatening their basic integrity within a post-mortem context.

By contrast, we have seen that one of the beliefs that undergirds Hick's soul-making understanding of the human person is that its final state of blessedness is not to be gained by stripping away key aspects of a person's history and personal characteristics, thereby attaining the essential perfection of an idealized past, but rather will be gained according to a process of realization and integration, of discovering more fully one's true self, and of gradually becoming who one is called to be in both a pre- and post-mortem person-making environment.[16] Hick's insight, therefore, is significant: that within a sanctification-based understanding of the afterlife, the purgation of these secondary decisions/effects does not involve their sudden obliteration but rather their gradual transformation and redemption.

A SOUL-MAKING UNDERSTANDING OF HOW PURGATORY FUNCTIONS

Due to the interconnected relationship that we have observed between a person's so-called basic spiritual identity and the various secondary decisions/effects that have helped to form that identity, it may seem at times—at least superficially to an external observer—that the basic truth of this identity can become overshadowed by these manifold secondary decisions, to the extent that these distortions may appear to dominate that person's moral and spiritual narrative and obscure the basic truth of their own basic identity. But if we return again to a point made by Ratzinger, it is important to remember that "in terms of the sum total of decisions from out of which an entire life is constructed, this final direction may be, in the end, a fumbling

15. See Ratzinger, *Eschatology*, 232, wherein he warns against the notion to consider one's purgatorial experience as something taking place in strict isolation.
16. See Hick, "Irenaean Theodicy," 66.

after readiness for God, valid no matter what wrong turnings have been taken by and by."[17] In light of this, it would seem that within purgatory's defined role, its sanctifying dynamics of purification basically seek to identify this (however dim) basic affirmative decision that is resting within the depths of a person's innermost being (and often buried under the weight of their myriad secondary decisions), and work to coax out and develop its essential truth so that all of the secondary decisions eventually become reordered in light of the content of that basic decision.

This can only be a gradual process that must touch upon every aspect of the human person, wherein God's grace continues the work that begun (or not yet had the chance to begin) during that person's earthly life, labouring to bring it to completion. And as this grace shines upon the totality of a person's experiences, history, relationships, as well as their psychological, spiritual and moral dispositions, the affirmative response of their basic life-decision is progressively revealed and magnified, thereby allowing for a personal response of gradual realization of its heretofore obscured existence, accompanied by an ever-deeper reclamation of it for themselves. This can occur through a variety of means. Presumably, for most individuals, the experienced grace of post-mortem purifications would involve periods of sober self-reflection regarding how that person related to themselves, to others, and to God, during their earthly life. It would offer opportunities for them to better understand how their own attitudes and actions, for better or for worse, have resulted in a series of secondary effects—or have perhaps led to a series of secondary decisions taken—that have come to inform both their own personal identity, and that of others. Indeed, a soul-making environment should support a deeper personal and communal awareness, wherein a person is able to realize just how intimately connected their own spiritual journey has been to that of others. In so doing, such a person would become able to more clearly observe the way in which secondary effects created through their actions, and/or experienced through the actions of others, have informed the content of their own basic identity, so as to be able to more fully reclaim these secondary effects in light of that basic identity. Ultimately, this ongoing journey of self-discovery will inevitably conclude with a full appreciation of the totality of their own history as understood through the lens of a person loved by God intimately bound to other persons loved by God.

This period may be incredibly painful for some, as the delusions and artifice of their imperfect understandings and perspectives gradually recede and the truth emerges regarding the full effect that they have had in the

---

17. Ratzinger, *Eschatology*, 209.

world, and the full effect that the various forces of the world have in turn had upon them, again, for better or for worse. The sanctifying purifications within this context may perhaps take on their more traditionally perceived role, as they assist the person in their divinely guided journey of self-discovery by carrying out the sometimes unpleasant process of peeling away voluntary and imposed obstructions, in order to gain a full appreciation of why and how they in fact related to themselves, to the world, and to God. But it must be stressed that this is ultimately a constructive experience, as a more perfect realization of who that person has been in all of their complexity will eventually allow that person to more perfectly transcend, through the process of integration, all of that which, for one reason or another, has been impeding their journey of becoming who they truly are, and who they are ultimately called to be.

Additionally, within a soul-making sanctifying context, purgatory's post-mortem purifications may take the form of a sustained educational experience, touching upon the moral, spiritual, and intellectual aspects of a person's character, which would naturally seem to accompany any process of self-realization and development of their basic identity. Again, such an experience would be particular to each person, in which divine grace would uniquely build upon whatever skills, virtues, experiences, and maturity levels that already are present, invariably creating in that person a more perfect understanding of right-relationship, of love, and ultimately, of who God really is. As such, this becomes an opportunity to further develop any aspects of a person's character that fall short of perfection, including their possibly immature or rudimentary understanding of God, or perhaps any of their own misconceived notions regarding the moral and spiritual laws with which God governs the universe, or even any ignorance on their own part concerning the manner in which God desires for a person to authentically relate to those around themselves. Inevitably, purifications in this context will continue to develop and expand a person's consciousness, enabling them to gain a deeper spiritual, moral, and intellectual appreciation of what it means to be a person in love by—and in intimate relationship with—God. This post-mortem context must support this process of personal growth, of helping the person to eventually perfect the virtues already present within themselves, so that they may be adequately prepared to comprehend an experience of God's direct presence.

Finally, the sanctifying purifications of purgatory can alternatively, or even at the same time, take on the form of an experience of compassion and healing for those who might have had to carry profound experiences of pain, trauma, and suffering throughout their earthly lives, which have in turn impressed themselves—seemingly irretrievably—upon their basic identity. As initially proposed by Michael Stoeber,[18] this appears to be an immensely important if a not yet fully explored aspect of the post-mortem dynamics of purification. Stoeber writes:

> If the victims of destructive suffering are not to be unfairly removed from this possibility [of redemption through spiritual transformation], there must be contexts of healing which give them further opportunities for transforming purification. What is required is a life-condition suitable to healing and continued spiritual development, so the destructive horror does not unjustly remove the victim finally or permanently from the redemptive dynamic.[19]

It seems clear that for some, their moral and spiritual world may be more conditioned by the secondary effects of sin than for others—in particular, effects that were not of their own making. Their particular experience of these effects may be so acutely destructive that no increase in self-awareness or instruction will fundamentally alter the destructive nature of their effect. For such persons, it would seem that the possibility for any sort of transcendence over these secondary effects requires an especially tender grace of supportive healing of the trauma that they may be carrying, so that they may first discover that at the core of their own basic identity that they are—above all else—a person who is loved and is of great intrinsic worth.

As mentioned earlier, this point has since been developed by Nathan O'Halloran, who also draws upon past theologians—both inside and outside of the Catholic tradition—to persuasively argue for an expanded understanding of the purgatorial experience as one that "includes both the purifying of the effects of one's own sin as well as the healing of the other-inflicted wounds of sin."[20] O'Halloran also notes that while much attention has been paid to the eschatological rehabilitation and transformation of those who may be deemed "sinners," very little attention has been paid to the eschatological healing and transformation of those who may be considered "victims," commenting (and in so doing, echoing a number of theologians already cited) that "the Catholic Church's eschatological teaching has failed to speak to the growing contemporary 'self-understanding' that circumstances of violence, oppressive poverty, and abusive relationships ... do in fact constitute major obstacles to receiving God's love, including heavenly

---

18. See Stoeber, *Reclaiming Theodicy*, 73–78. See also chapter 5 of this book for reference to Stoeber's work on this question.

19. Stoeber, *Reclaiming Theodicy*, 74.

20. O'Halloran, "Purgatory," 724.

love."[21] O'Halloran's analysis offers considerable precision in how this post-mortem healing may be experienced, identifying that this particular grace will specifically touch upon a person's intellect and will. Pointing out that a person's ability to will can often be manipulated so as to become attracted to—and even identify with—the will of a powerful external force (such as that of a perpetrator or abuser), O'Halloran postulates that post-mortem healing in such instances would involve "the healing of the victim's will so that it can be fully reoriented and thus fully participate in choosing its own good in union with Christ."[22] On the other hand, the healing of the intellect, for O'Halloran, would include a healing of modes of recognition and self-identification that have become co-opted and warped by feelings of shame and self-incrimination.[23]

In both instances, O'Halloran envisions a process that would necessarily take place over an extended period of time, for by its very nature, healing itself requires an extended period of time.[24] In envisioning this process, O'Halloran draws particular inspiration from Miroslav Volf, notably his insistence that any eschatological resolution of such experiences of sin will necessitate a true reconciliation between both perpetrators and victims: "If sin has an inalienable social dimension . . ." Volf writes, "then the divine embrace of both the victim and the perpetrator (justification) must be understood as leading to their mutual embrace. Persons cannot be healed without the healing of their specific socially constructed and temporarily structured identities."[25]

For O'Halloran, such a focus on the post-mortem needs of the victim, and of the wounds and wounded relationships that the victim may carry, indeed offers crucial insight into the how the communal eschatological reality as emphasized by the Second Vatican Council may be reconsidered within the existing doctrine of purgatory. Indeed, he believes that such an understanding of purgatorial graces ultimately allows for a more comprehensive response to the particular claim O'Halloran cites by then-Cardinal Ratzinger that all of the "question marks" that inevitably linger behind instances of human suffering must also be overcome in order for the joy of heaven to be considered truly complete.[26] At the heart of such a response, for O'Halloran, is a process that involves the healing of a person's memory.

21. O'Halloran, "Purgatory," 705.
22. O'Halloran, "Purgatory," 710.
23. O'Halloran, "Purgatory," 711.
24. O'Halloran, "Purgatory," 724.
25. Volf, "Enter into Joy!," 262. Quoted in O'Halloran, "Purgatory," 707.
26. See Ratzinger, *Eschatology*, 189. Quoted in O'Halloran, "Purgatory," 722.

Turning to examples in Scripture, O'Halloran notes the effects of personal encounters with Jesus in the Gospel stories, in which Jesus would not just heal this or that particular person, but would also remove the effects of sin from their lives.[27] Although O'Halloran specifically explores the effects of these encounters from the perspective of the victim, his point could perhaps be restated more generally as follows: healing interpersonal encounters with Jesus effectively allows persons to definitively "move on" from the effects of the sins that they have been carrying; it "liberates" persons from no longer being tied to the sins of their past through perpetual bonds of guilt (in the case of perpetrators) or forgiveness (in the case of victims).

Extending the reach of this liberating dynamic into the afterlife, O'Halloran identifies purgatory as the post-mortem location for such an encounter, remarking that at its conclusion, with the lingering "question marks" of sin finally resolved, those healed and liberated persons in heaven will "need no longer recall the effects of sin upon them."[28] Like Volf, it would also appear that O'Halloran holds to some form of a "non-remembrance" understanding of the relationship between those in heaven and the since-resolved sinful effects that they have been carrying throughout their existence. Although there are some who have taken issue with this position, arguing instead for a redemption and transformation of certain memories instead of non-remembrance,[29] it seems quite possible that the conclusions offered by Volf and O'Halloran deserve further exploration as a potential "middle ground" between the extreme positions of a total transformation of memories of destructive suffering (as advocated by Adams) and a simplistic mere "forgetting" of those memories. However, to engage in such exploration now would be outside the scope of this present project. What is important to highlight at this moment is simply that both O'Halloran and Volf posit that before a person is ready to enter into heaven—at which point their memories of suffering may no longer be remembered—those memories must first be touched upon by God's compassionate grace, so that that person may somehow become fully reconciled to themselves, with others, and ultimately, with God. Crucially, O'Halloran understands that this will necessarily take some time, thus his insistence for a post-mortem temporal reality (purgatory) that can allow for a *process* of reconciliation to take place. And in so doing, O'Halloran (and to a lesser extent, Volf) serves to highlight one of the essential features, already identified, of our soul-making understanding of purgatory: that purgatory's sanctifying dynamics

---

27. O'Halloran, "Purgatory," 721.
28. O'Halloran, "Purgatory," 723.
29. See Hauerwas, "Why Time," 42–46; and Horne, "Reservation," 325–28.

of transformation do not simply function to engage a person existing solely as a "person-in-isolation," but rather engages a person who has been existing as "a person-in-the-world," "a person-in-community," and, perhaps most basically, "a person-in-relationship."

Thus, we return once again to the eschatological communal dynamic that naturally becomes emphasized in any soul-making understanding of purgatory. Within such an understanding, purgatory's sanctifying function does not shine its metaphorical spotlight solely upon the person and all of their perceived and actual faults and virtues, but rather casts itself over the entirety of their spiritual landscape, illuminating it for them in its full reality. Inevitably, as each person is uniquely touched by God's grace, they will uniquely experience a peeling away of whatever inward-looking self-regard that remains, while simultaneously experiencing an opening up of their being toward the source of this grace, gradually becoming, as Hick states, "so transparent to the divine life that we no longer live as separate self-enclosed individuals."[30] Presumably, as this spiritual gaze is gradually directed outwards, that person will gradually become aware of this illuminated landscape, transfigured by grace and now co-populated with countless other persons within a new creation, held in God's benevolent embrace. This, it seems, must be the final result of purgatory's transformative forces of sanctification. This is what those forces have prepared the person for, and this is what those same forces will allow them to ultimately see. After the process of spiritual maturing and integration through increased self-awareness, continued personal development, and healing is complete, the person is left with a perfected awareness of who they really are as a person held in God's love, and of where and among whom they are ultimately dwelling. And it is at this point that they are finally ready to enter into the eternity of the divine life.

To illustrate perhaps better just how radical the dynamics of a soul-making understanding of purgatory might function, we can perhaps conjure an especially horrific hypothetical example of suffering and healing: that of a small child who was raped and murdered after a very short lifetime in which they experienced a variety of abuse. One can say that through no fault of her own, that child died under very sinful circumstances after living a life that one can reasonably conclude was dominated by sin's presence. Though not of that child's own doing, these secondary effects and/or results of another person's sinful actions pervaded that child's life and violently forced themselves upon that child's own personal identity, to the extent that the two have become inseparable. Yet, trusting in a loving, compassionate

---

30. Hick, *Death and Eternal Life*, 446.

God, we can hope with confidence that these sinful circumstances did not totally corrupt this child's basic goodness and close them off from relationship with God, even if the trauma holds the child's personal identity in a stranglehold, rendering their basic decision all but invisible. Purgatory for that child might initially become an opportunity for that domination upon their personal identity to loosen through an ongoing experience of God's compassionate healing—to learn, perhaps for the first time, what love actually is, and to know what a loving relationship might actually feel like. As this child gradually experiences and grows in love, their understanding of themselves as a person who is loved is also magnified. Hopefully, this realization eventually becomes so strong that they are able to confront the undeniably horrific aspects of their own history and identity, and somehow regard them with the perspective of someone who fundamentally knows that they are truly loved, respected, and cared for in a community of the redeemed in fellowship with the Creator. That child's history is not immediately expunged or somehow contorted into a retroactive "good"; rather this history, for what it is, is gradually regarded, appropriated, and integrated into the child's emerging basic identity as a person of infinite value who is loved by God, to the extent that they are able to do so, and this process of integration will continue to the point of total realization and total transparency between that child and the divine life.

On the other hand, we can perhaps take this example further and explore what might perhaps be an equally unpalatable scenario: the eventual salvation of that child's abuser. Even though this hypothetical individual committed a series of heinous acts, we can imagine that the abuser eventually experienced a conversion-event, repented from their past sins, underwent the various penances demanded by civil and divine justice, and died essentially reconciled to God. We can assume that within purgatory's role of transforming the negative secondary effects of sin carried by a person, the sanctifying transformative forces experienced by this abuser will take on a dramatically different character, and will include a lengthy period of self-realization, during which they will come to terms with the full extent of the suffering that they imparted upon their victims, the victims' families, the various relationships that have been fractured through the abuser's actions, the destabilizing effect they have had on society at large and upon the world in which they have lived. This journey of unvarnished self-realization will undoubtedly be extremely difficult and at times very painful. Yet, hopefully, with this full realization will also eventually come the full awareness that this person is someone who has been forgiven, that in spite of their actions they are still a person who is loved, and who is still capable of rejoining the same community that they had previously sought to destroy. In short, this hypothetical abuser is able to realize that they, too, are a member of God's new creation as this progressive experience of redemption gradually reorients their being toward full fellowship with God and neighbor.

These two examples are intentionally extreme so that the potential breadth and depth of the transformative dynamics available to a soul-making understanding of purgatory's transformative function may be demonstrated. Through them, we are able to speculate about the radical tenderness and sheer audacity of God's grace, and in so doing, we also find an understanding of the doctrine that is able to respond to Dermot A. Lane's earlier demand that any credible eschatological response must take into account the lived concerns and struggles of the people of God.[31] Soul-making's ability to expand our understanding of the effects of sin and the method of its purification makes it possible to clearly communicate an understanding of purgatory that responds directly to the breadth of a person's experience of sin, embracing as well whatever traumas, concerns, and anxieties they may be carrying, and bring them to a positive resolution. Thus, we are able to state with confidence that a qualified application of John Hick's soul-making insights can indeed stand to inform the Catholic doctrine of purgatory by grounding these insights more firmly within the Catholic tradition, and in turn by allowing these insights to expand our appreciation for how purgatory's presently understood sanctifying elements are able to function within its existing purificatory role. In so doing, these insights carry with them the potential to help strengthen the doctrine's pastoral and theological relevance, and perhaps most fundamentally, the potential to help the doctrine more authentically embody the simple spirit of hope that precipitated its initial emergence in religious belief and practice. We will now conclude this investigation by briefly outlining this conclusion and exploring its various implications.

---

31. See Lane, *Keeping Hope Alive*, 7. See also chapter 2.

Conclusion

AFTER A DETAILED REVIEW of both the Catholic doctrine of purgatory and a soul-making understanding of the human person and the afterlife principally inspired by the work of John Hick, we have been able to conclude that due to the basic feasibility of the concept of soul-making within the Catholic tradition, it would seem that Hick's soul-making insights indeed remain capable of constructively contributing toward an understanding of purgatory that is able to better situate itself within the current Catholic eschatological context, thereby affording it a greater overall theological and pastoral relevancy.

Starting with its religious origins in chapter 1, we have traced the history of the role and function of the doctrine of purgatory within Catholic eschatological thought, including its prevailing cultural and spiritual themes that emphasized a hierarchical and legalistic understanding of the doctrine, up to the point of the reforms of the Second Vatican Council. In chapter 2, we were able to identify the development, in spite of notable efforts made by a number of current theologians in emphasizing certain reformational and sanctifying themes, of a disconnect between the core theological values guiding contemporary Catholic eschatological reflection that emerged from the Second Vatican Council and those that stubbornly remain in the present understanding of the doctrine of purgatory. To that end, the principal point made earlier by John Thiel was highlighted as being particularly helpful, namely that Catholicism's more recent approach toward eschatological questions has seemingly been guided by a spiritual culture that focuses less on anxiety-inducing issues surrounding personal adequacy and soteriological uncertainty, and instead is characterized by an emphasis upon the importance of an authentic personal relationship with a merciful, loving God, a renewed social awareness, communal emphasis, and, ultimately, a more emphatic soteriological hopefulness.[1]

---

1. See Thiel, *Icons of Hope*, 63–70, 93–105.

In response to this problem, we have looked to certain theologians outside of the Catholic tradition who have offered unique insights of their own regarding how purgatory—or what they might describe as a "post-mortem intermediate state" (or some variation thereof)—might be approached or understood as an essential component within their own respective eschatological systems. Specifically, John Hick's "soul-making" understanding of the human person, theodicy, and the afterlife has been identified as having great potential for further developing the current sanctification-based model of purgatory. After demonstrating the basic compatibility between soul-making and the Roman Catholic theological tradition in chapter 3, we explored his understanding of the "intermediate state" in chapter 4, noting its ability to develop the current Catholic model of purgatory in a manner that is able to respond to Thiel's principal concerns.

After listing and resolving a number of issues pertaining to the adoption of Hick's insights within a Catholic setting, we were able to identify within chapter 5 a number of relevant contemporary Protestant thinkers, and explored to what extent their respective conclusions might contribute toward our project of developing soul-making themes of the afterlife within a Catholic context. This exploration culminates with chapter 6, which has offered certain conclusions on how the present Catholic doctrine of purgatory can be approached and understood once informed by Hick's soul-making insights.

As was already mentioned above (and developed at greater length in chapter 2),[2] Thiel has pointed out that one of the leading causes for purgatory's decline in theological and pastoral relevance has been its functional inability to reflect the eschatological concerns and realities of the present dominant spiritual culture (termed by Thiel as "Pauline") found within the Catholic Christianity, which includes the diminution of an individual sense of eschatological anxiety due to an increasing awareness of the universal presence of sin—as well as the universal availability of God's grace—in our lives, and an accompanying focus upon personal authenticity in questions pertaining to soteriology. While purgatory within the earlier "Matthean" spiritual culture was understood to assuage the fears of the faithful who believed that God's grace was highly selective, and that their own sins were perhaps such so as to exclude them from any chance of receiving that grace, its relevance declined as the faithful gradually came to terms with sin's presence in their lives and came to rely on more expansive notions of God's grace, which was understood to meet them and care for them directly in

---

2. See also chapter 2 for a description on how this transition has affected the practical status of purgatory in recent history.

the afterlife (thus leaving no need for purgatory as a mediating venue for an encounter with that grace). And as the faithful became less preoccupied by the soteriological implications of personal sin and more trusting in God's freely given grace, the belief in a purgatory predicated on addressing the fears associated with personal sin diminished through an inability to constructively reflect this new-found emphasis upon both sin and grace's universal presence, leaving Thiel to conclude that "purgatory disappears where strong grace prevails."[3]

Therefore, based upon Thiel's analysis of the relationship between the doctrine of purgatory and Pauline spiritual culture, we were able to arrive at the conclusion that purgatory's eschatological relevance within both contemporary theological thought and popular religiosity hinges upon its functional ability to relate to the question of how sin is basically understood to exist in creation, and how it is understood to be purged from creation. And with regard to the Pauline spiritual context, the question that could be asked is: How is purgatory understood to function when both sin and grace take on more universal qualities? For Thiel, it would seem that such an understanding has yet to be articulated satisfactorily. This can be evidenced in the present expressions of a sanctification-based models of purgatory, which, as we have seen, have continued to rely predominantly upon the more traditional categories of personal sin and its effects when describing the nature of post-mortem purifications, and/or have yet to offer a coherent explanation regarding how purgatory's sanctifying function can be expanded to encompass the present spiritual concerns.

However, John Hick's soul-making worldview has helped us to uncover insights into the doctrine that allows for a systematic articulation of a sanctifying function that more explicitly responds to a heightened awareness of the forces of sin and grace operating within our personal and collective lives. As such, it is able to support concepts of purgatory that more constructively reflect the theological and pastoral demands of our present Pauline spiritual culture. Hick, as we have seen with his notions of primordial human immaturity and epistemic distance from God, has developed an understanding of the intermediate state predicated upon a concept strikingly similar—and, as we have argued, basically compatible—with the Pauline emphasis upon the universal reality of sin. He has also successfully explained how the transformative dynamics of God's grace function according to this spiritual reality within a post-mortem context. As we have seen in soul-making understandings of purgatory, each person is uniquely affected by the universal reality of sin, which necessarily includes manifestations of

---

3. Thiel, *Icons of Hope*, 99. Found in chapter 2.

sin within their personal and/or environmental circumstances. And these effects are transformed through a continued, all-pervading experience of—and growth in—God's grace, to the point of eventual resolution. By expanding the understanding of the nature of a person's relationship with sin, and what, accordingly, remains in need of purification, we are subsequently able to conceive of a purgatory in which we find operating the very strong sense of grace, such as the kind that Thiel has spoken of, a grace capable of embracing the breadth of this world, including all of the personal *and* collective experiences therein, and slowly bringing them to perfection.

Hick's soul-making insights provide greater clarity and consistency to the sanctifying themes already present in the doctrine, thereby allowing them to be more forcefully emphasized in present articulations. Moreover, we have also shown how a such an understanding of purgatory's sanctifying function is still able to find its roots within the Roman Catholic tradition, remaining basically consonant with purgatory's traditionally defined theological role. In so doing, we have hopefully offered an understanding of purgatory that more comprehensively satisfies Thiel's questions regarding purgatory's relevancy within its relationship with the present Pauline spiritual culture. Able to directly encompass and transform contemporary concerns and realities, such an understanding is not something that has been haphazardly revised through a simple change in vocabulary, or vaguely expressed as a desired possibility in a half-hearted attempt to adjust it to current theological and spiritual realities. Rather, in reference to Hick's work, we have shown that it is indeed possible to look back into the tradition and develop a coherent understanding of the doctrine that maintains its historical integrity, and yet can assertively engage current needs, hopes, and fears of the faithful, providing for them a compelling vision of eschatological resolution.

A soul-making understanding of purgatory is able—perhaps more than present articulations of the doctrine—to make clear God's unceasing care for individuals and make even more apparent for them the real possibility of salvation. Due to its openness in considering more fully the history of individuals, its more nuanced understanding of the human condition, and its ability to offer a more compassionate and constructive means for personal transformation, it is clear that the pastoral potential of the doctrine so conceived is significant. It clearly articulates an understanding of the doctrine that fundamentally respects each person's identity and history, and through an intimate experience of God's providential care, allows them to grow in whatever graces they may need in order to become whomever they were called to be, in full fellowship with God. Consequently, it now becomes a far simpler task to represent purgatory as an instrument of God's compassionate love that exists for a person's spiritual benefit, rather than simply as a venue that exists to exact the outstanding demands of God's justice.

In its ability to unequivocally articulate this essential feature, we are able to draw one final conclusion regarding the effects that soul-making insights can have on the doctrine of purgatory: it assumes an eschatological character that represents less the worries—either a worry over the possibility of entering into heaven or a worry over what the post-mortem sufferings may consist of—on the part of the faithful, and offers a more hopeful anticipation of the spiritual possibilities (such as healing, consolation, and transformation) that may await each person and their loved ones in the afterlife. It more readily reflects a loving and compassionate God eager to impart whatever grace is necessary to bring to completion their journey of becoming a human person fully alive. It can thus be thought of as something to look forward to with great hope, as an opportunity to both grow as a person in a community of the redeemed, and, ultimately, in intimacy with the Lord.

It would therefore appear that such an understanding of the doctrine would offer an opportunity for it to more fully recapture aspects of purgatory present at its emergence, when it reflected the basic hopes of the early Christians that, in spite of the formally juridical culture in which they lived, the God whom they worshiped nevertheless remained merciful at heart, desiring the salvation for them and their loved ones. Moreover, in a certain sense, it also marks a continuation of the work of preceding theologians, who have consciously sought to channel that same spirit of hopeful optimism into a more formally articulated and coherent theological principle. Accordingly, efforts were taken within this project to develop an understanding of purgatory that remains within the received parameters of the Catholic eschatological tradition and yet is able to more comprehensively reflect the long-held notion within Catholic theology that God desires the salvation of all persons. By shedding further light onto how God's mercy is able to envelop the totality of the human person (with all of their experiences and history) in order to bring that person to salvation, it seems even more difficult to speculate on the population of—or on the sort of person who may populate—an eternal hell, even if its existence remains a real possibility for all.

Thus, after thoroughly reviewing the intentions behind—and the implications of—a soul-making based understanding of the doctrine, one is able to discern just how such a conception of purgatory, as outlined above, successfully embodies these early spiritual impulses and their legacy, and serves once again as an extension of the basic, authentic hope that they carried. Yet it is able to do so as a fully integrated component of the Catholic eschatological system, continuing its history and bound to its theological tradition. This perhaps becomes soul-making's most fundamental contribution to how the doctrine is popularly and theologically considered: its ability to honor both the doctrine's initial religious intention and ongoing theological tradition within an articulation that successfully responds to the hopes, fears, and sensibilities of the present age. Moreover, in being able to articulate an understanding of the doctrine that does not rely—in whole or in part—upon either hierarchical or merit-based explanations regarding its basic function, there also emerges a number of ecumenical possibilities. We can recall Protestantism's enduring suspicion of the doctrine from chapter 5, owing particularly to confusion over the language of outstanding "satisfaction" and purgatorial "punishment" in explaining the doctrine, which indicates that Christ's death on the cross was less than meritorious for all persons. We are able to see that by choosing to intentionally develop an explanation of purgatory's function that is more explicitly based around the theological principle of sin's double effect, clear parallels can be found between the assumptions and conclusions found within such an understanding and those reached within understandings of the doctrine as found within the work of certain contemporary Protestant theologians.[4] Such an emphasis, it would seem, is able to by-pass occasions for further confusion regarding purgatory's underpinning theological assumptions,[5] and offers in itself a foundation upon which conversation and perhaps a mutual understanding can develop.

Indeed, we have already seen glimpses of where this conversation can take place in the work of such authors, theologians, and theological bodies as C. S. Lewis, John Macquarrie, John Polkinghorne, and the United Church of Canada's document on the intermediate state. Even though these various proposals vary in depth, detail, and eventual conclusions, they all seem to share with our soul-making understanding of purgatory a similar understanding of how the intermediate state functions in the purification of the effects of sin, how it basically operates for an individual's spiritual development, and how it represents a fundamentally optimistic eschatological outlook. And thus, while our respective understandings of the intermediate state may have developed toward different conclusions, it nevertheless seems possible that clearer agreement may now be found on both certain theological fundamentals and points of spiritual emphasis when such an agreement was perhaps not as possible—or perhaps not as clearly discernable—before. As such, we are left with the conclusion that a soul-making understanding of purgatory allows for further opportunities for discussion and possible

4. See chapter 5.
5. See chapter 5.

convergence with certain segments of Protestant Christianity, where people may be presently curious or even maintain their own idea of the postmortem intermediate state, and yet may be hesitant to engage the Catholic position on the doctrine due to certain misgivings over its often tumultuous and controversial history, or how it might still be theologically understood within the Catholic context. By offering an understanding of purgatory that accounts for these concerns by providing a constructive, theologically sensitive interpretation of the doctrine's role and function, it is possible to envision opportunities in which potential areas of understanding—or even agreement—may be explored in future ecumenical discussions.

Thus, as our exploration of these soul-making insights has helped to reveal purgatory's constructive theological, pastoral, and ecumenical potential, it would seem that it has also able to provide a clear response to Dermot A. Lane's earlier question of whether purgatory "is worth retrieving," or whether it ought to be "quietly forgotten about."[6] By demonstrating how the expanded sanctifying capabilities of a soul-making understanding of purgatory are able to strengthen its capacity for providing a constructive, compassionate, eschatological response to the needs and realities of the faithful, our findings ultimately advance the argument for a deeper appreciation of purgatory's current place in continuing eschatological reflection—that, in other words, the doctrine is indeed worth retrieving and that such a retrieval is in fact possible.

---

6. See Lane, *Keeping Hope Alive*, 146.

Bibliography

Adams, Marilyn McCord. *Christ and Horrors: The Coherence of Christology*. Cambridge: Cambridge University Press, 2006.
———. *Horrendous Evils and the Goodness of God*. Ithaca, NY: Cornell University Press, 1999.
———. "Horrors in Theological Context." *Scottish Journal of Theology* 55.4 (2002) 468–79.
———. "Ignorance, Instrumentality, Compensation, and the Problem of Evil." *Sophia* 52.1 (2013) 7–26.
Alighieri, Dante. *The Divine Comedy*. Translated by Allen Mandelbaum. New York: Knopf, 1995.
———. *The Divine Comedy*. Translated by John Ciardi. New York: New American Library, 2003.
Anglican Church of Canada. "39 Articles of Religion." https://www.anglican.ca/about/beliefs/39-articles/.
Atwell, R. R. "From Augustine to Gregory the Great: An Evaluation of the Emergence of the Doctrine of Purgatory." *The Journal of Ecclesiastical History* 38.2 (1987) 173–86.
Augustine of Hippo. "Against Julian." *The Fathers of the Church: A New Translation* 35. Translated by Matthew A. Schumacher. Edited by Roy Joseph Deferrari. New York: Fathers of the Church, 1957.
———. *The City of God*. Translated by Henry Bettenson. London: Penguin Books, 2003.
———. "De Natura Boni." In *Corpus Scriptorum Ecclesiasticorum Latinorum*. Vienna, Austria: Tempsky, 1865.
———. *Enchiridion of Faith, Hope, and Love*. Translated by J. B. Shaw. Washington, DC: Regnery, 1996.
———. "On Marriage and Concupiscence." In *Anti-Pelagian Writings: Nicene and Post-Nicene Fathers of the Christian Church, Part 5*. Translated by Peter Holmes and Robert Ernest Wallis. Edited by Philip Schaff, 263–308. Peabody, MA: Hendrickson, 1995.
———. "On Nature and Grace." In *Anti-Pelagian Writings: Nicene and Post-Nicene Fathers of the Christian Church, Part 5*. Translated by Peter Holmes and Robert Ernest Wallis. Edited by Philip Schaff, 121–51. Peabody, MA: Hendrickson, 1995.
———. "On the Grace of Christ, and on Original Sin." In *Anti-Pelagian Writings: Nicene and Post-Nicene Fathers of the Christian Church, Part 5*. Translated by Peter

Holmes and Robert Ernest Wallis. Edited by Philip Schaff, 213–55. Peabody, MA: Hendrickson, 1995.

Barnard, Justin D. "Purgatory and the Dilemma of Sanctification." *Faith and Philosophy* 24.3 (2007) 311–30.

Barrett, Peter. "Love Almighty and Horrendous Evils—Recent Theodicy in Light of the Sciences." *Journal of Theology for Southern Africa* 129 (2007) 99–115.

Bede. *The Historical Works: Ecclesiastical History of the English Nation, Books IV-V.* Translated by J. E. King. Edited by Jeffrey Henderson. Loeb Classical Library Cambridge, MA: Harvard University Press, 1994.

Beer, Peter J. "What Price Indulgence? Trent and Today." *Theological Studies* 39.3 (1978) 526–35.

Benedict XVI. "General Audience." January 12, 2011. Vatican website. http://www.vatican.va/holy_father/benedict_xvi/audiences/2011/documents/hf_ben-xvi_aud_20110112_en.html.

———. "General Audience." March 28, 2007. Vatican website. https://w2.vatican.va/content/benedict-xvi/en/audiences/2007/documents/hf_ben-xvi_aud_20070328.html.

———. *Spe Salvi*. San Francisco: Ignatius, 2007.

Bonner, Gerald. *St. Augustine of Hippo: Life and Controversies*. Norwich, UK: Canterbury, 1986.

Bounds, Christopher T. "Irenaeus and the Doctrine of Perfection." *Wesleyan Theological Journal* 45.2 (2010) 161–76.

Brown, David. "No Heaven without Purgatory." *Religious Studies* 21 (1985) 447–56.

Burkert, Walter. *Greek Religion*. Translated by John Raffan. Cambridge, MA: Harvard University Press, 1985.

Calvin, John. *Institutes of the Christian Religion*. Translated by Ford Lewis Battles. Edited by John T. McNeill. Philadelphia: Westminster, 1960.

———. *Soul Sleep*. Translated by Henry Beveridge. Middletown, DE: Legacy, 2011.

Casey, John. *After Lives: A Guide to Heaven, Hell, and Purgatory*. Oxford: Oxford University Press, 2009.

Catherine of Genoa. *Purgation and Purgatory, the Spiritual Dialogue*. Translated by Serge Hughes. Mahwah, NJ: Paulist, 1979.

Catholic Church. *Catechism of the Catholic Church*. Ottawa: Publications Service, Canadian Conference of Catholic Bishops, 1994.

Cheetham, David. *John Hick: A Critical Introduction and Reflection*. Aldershot, UK: Ashgate, 2003.

The Committee on Christian Faith of the United Church of Canada. *Life and Death: A Study of the Christian Hope*. Edited by A. G. Reynolds. Toronto: The Board of Evangelism and Social Service and The Board of Christian Education, 1959.

Cumont, Franz. *After Life in Roman Paganism*. New York: Dover, 1959.

de La Soujeole, Benoît-Dominique. "The Universal Call to Holiness." In *Vatican II: Renewal within Tradition*, edited by Matthew L. Lamb and Matthew Levering, 37–53. New York: Oxford University Press, 2008.

Denzinger, Heinrich. *Enchiridion symbolorum definitionum et declarationum de rebus fidei et morum: Compendium of Creeds, Definitions and Declarations on Matters of Faith and Morals*. Edited by Peter Hünermann et al. 43rd ed. San Francisco: Ignatius, 2012.

Domning, Daryl P., and Monika K. Hellwig. *Original Selfishness: Original Sin and Evil in the Light of Evolution*. Hampshire, UK: Ashgate, 2006.

Donovan, Mary Ann. *One Right Reading? A Guide to Irenaeus*. Collegeville, MN: Liturgical, 1997.

Drever, Matthew. "Redeeming Creation: *Creatio ex nihilo* and the *Imago Dei* in Augustine." *International Journal of Systematic Theology* 15.2 (2013) 135–53.

Egan, Harvey D. "In Purgatory We Shall All Be Mystics." *Theological Studies* 73.4 (Dec 2012) 870–89.

English, Adam C. "Mediated, Mediation, Unmediated: 1 Corinthians 15:29: The History of Interpretation, and the Current State of Biblical Studies." *Review and Expositor* 99 (2002) 419–28.

Fenn, Richard K. *The Persistence of Purgatory*. Cambridge: Cambridge University Press, 1995.

Gill, Joseph. *The Council of Florence*. Cambridge: Cambridge University Press, 1959.

Gleeson, Andrew. "On Letting Go of Theodicy: Marilyn McCord Adams on Good and Evil." *Sophia* 54 (2015) 1–12.

Gooch, Paul W. "Augustinian and Irenaean Theodicies: Reconciling a Rivalry." Unpublished manuscript, 1–13.

Greggs, Tom. "Exclusivist or Universalist? Origen the 'Wise Steward of the Word' (*CommRom*. V.1.7) and the Issue of Genre." *International Journal of Systematic Theology* 9.3 (2007) 315–27.

Hauerwas, Stanley. "Why Time Cannot and Should Not Heal the Wounds of History But Time Has Been and Can Be Redeemed." *Scottish Journal of Theology* 53.1 (2000) 33–49.

Hick, John. *An Autobiography*. Oxford, UK: Oneworld, 2002.

———. "An Irenaean Theodicy." In *Encountering Evil: Live Options in Theodicy*, edited by Stephen T. Davis, 39–55. Atlanta: John Knox, 1981.

———. *Death and Eternal Life*. Louisville, KY: Westminster John Knox, 1994.

———. *Evil and the God of Love*. New York: Palgrave Macmillan, 2010.

———. *The New Frontier of Religion and Science: Religious Experience, Neuroscience and the Transcendent*. Basingstoke, UK: Palgrave Macmillan, 2006.

———. "Present and Future Life." *The Harvard Theological Review* 71.1–2 (1978) 1–15.

———. "The Problem of Evil in the First and Last Things." *Journal of Theological Studies* 19.2 (1968) 591–602.

Holsinger-Friesen, Thomas. *Irenaeus and Genesis: A Study of Competition in Early Christian Hermeneutics*. Winona Lake, IN: Eisenbrauns, 2009.

Horne, Jon. "A Reservation about Miroslav Volf's Theory of Non-Remembrance." *Theology* 114.5 (2011) 323–30.

International Theological Commission, under the leadership of Rev. Candido Pozo, S.J. "Some Current Questions in Eschatology." 1992. http://www.vatican.va/roman_curia/congregations/cfaith/cti_documents/rc_cti_1990_problemi-attuali-escatologia_en.html.

Irenaeus of Lyons. *Against Heresies*. Translated by Alexander Roberts and W. H. Rambaut. Edited by Alexander Roberts and James Donaldson. LaVergne, TN: Ex Fontibus, 2010.

———. *On the Apostolic Preaching*. Translated by John Behr. Crestwood, NY: St. Vladimir's Seminary Press, 1997.

John XXIII. *Humanae Salutis.* 1962. Vatican website. https://w2.vatican.va/content/john-xxiii/la/apost_constitutions/1961/documents/hf_j-xxiii_apc_19611225_humanae-salutis.html.

John Paul II. "General Audience." August 4, 1999. Vatican website. https://www.vatican.va/content/john-paul-ii/en/audiences/1999/documents/hf_jp-ii_aud_04081999.html.

Judisch, Neal. "Sanctification, Satisfaction, and the Purpose of Purgatory." *Faith and Philosophy* 26.2 (2009) 167–85.

Jugie, Martin. *Purgatory and the Means to Avoid It.* Translated by Malachy Gerard Carroll. Westminster, MD: Newman, 1949.

Keats, John. *The Letters of John Keats.* Edited by M. B. Forman. London: Oxford University Press, 1952.

Kelly, Anthony. *Eschatology and Hope.* Maryknoll, NY: Orbis, 2006.

Lamberigts, Mathijs. "A Critical Evaluation of Critiques of Augustine's View of Sexuality." In *Augustine and His Critics: Essays in Honour of Gerald Bonner*, edited by Robert Dodaro and George Lawless, 175–96. London: Routledge, 2000.

Lane, Dermot A. *Keeping Hope Alive: Stirrings in Christian Theology.* Eugene, OR: Wipf & Stock, 2005.

Le Goff, Jacques. *The Birth of Purgatory.* Translated by Arthur Goldhammer. Chicago: Scolar, 1990.

———. *Your Money or Your Life: Economy and Religion in the Middle Ages.* Translated by Patricia Ranum. New York: Zone, 2001.

Lewis, C. S. *Letters to Malcolm: Chiefly on Prayer.* New York: Harcourt Brace Jovanovich, 1964.

Luther, Martin. "The 95 Theses." https://www.luther.de/en/95thesen.html.

———. *Luther's Works.* Vol. 4, *Lectures on Genesis, Chapters 21–25.* Translated by George V. Schick. Edited by Jaroslav Pelikan. Saint Louis, MO: Concordia, 1964.

———. "In Defence and Explanation on All the Articles (1521)." In *Luther's Works*, Vol. 52, *Career of the Reformer II*, translated by Charles M. Jacobs. Revised by George W. Forrell. Edited by George W. Forrell and Helmut T. Lehman, 3–99. Philadelphia: Muhlenberg, 1958.

Mackie, J. L. "Evil and Omnipotence." In *The Problem of Evil*, edited by Marilyn McCord Adams and Robert Merrihew Adams, 25–37. Oxford: Oxford University Press, 1990.

Macquarrie, John. *Principles of Christian Theology.* London: SCM, 1966.

Malkovsky, Bradley. "Belief in Reincarnation and Some Unresolved Questions in Catholic Eschatology." *Religions* 8.9 (2017) 1–11.

Minns, Denis. *Irenaeus: An Introduction.* London: T. & T. Clark International, 2010.

Moltmann, Jürgen. *The Coming of God.* Translated by Margaret Kohl. Minneapolis, MN: Fortress, 2004.

———. "Is There Life after Death?" In *The End of the World and the Ends of God: Science and Theology on Eschatology*, edited by John Polkinghorne and Michael Welker, 238–55. Harrisburg, PA: Trinity, 2000.

Moreira, Isabel. *Heaven's Purge: Purgatory in Late Antiquity.* New York: Oxford University Press, 2010.

Nichols, Terence. *Death and the Afterlife: A Theological Introduction.* Grand Rapids, MI: Brazos, 2010.

Nilsson, Martin P. *Greek Folk Religion.* New York: Harper Torchbooks, 1961.

Novello, Henry. "Eschatology Since Vatican II: Saved in Hope." *The Australasian Catholic Record* 90.4 (2013) 410–23.
O'Halloran, Nathan W. "Purgatory and the 'Time' of Eschatological Healing of Victims." *Modern Theology* 38.4 (2022) 704–28.
Origen. *On First Principles.* Translated and edited by John Behr. Oxford: Oxford University Press, 2017.
Pasulka, Diana Walsh. *Heaven Can Wait: Purgatory in Catholic Devotional and Popular Culture.* New York: Oxford University Press, 2015.
Paul VI. *Indulgentiarum Doctrina.* January 1, 1967. Vatican website. https://www.vatican.va/content/paul-vi/en/apost_constitutions/documents/hf_p-vi_apc_01011967_indulgentiarum-doctrina.html.
Phan, Peter C. "Contemporary Context and Issues in Eschatology." *Theological Studies* 55.3 (1994) 507–36.
———. *Eternity in Time: A Study of Karl Rahner's Eschatology.* Cranbury, NJ: Associated University Presses, 1988.
———. *Living into Death, Dying into Life: A Christian Theology of Death and Life Eternal.* Hope Sound, FL: Lectio, 2014.
Pius XII. *Mystici Corporis Christi.* Encyclical letter. June 29, 1943. Vatican website. http://w2.vatican.va/content/pius-xii/en/encyclicals/documents/hf_p-xii_enc_29061943_mystici-corporis-christi.html.
Plato. "The Republic." In *Plato: Complete Works*, translated by G. M. A. Grube and revised by C. D. C. Reeve. Edited by John. M. Cooper, 971–1223. Indianapolis, IN: Hackett, 1997.
Polkinghorne, John. "Eschatology: Some Questions and Some Insights from Science." In *The End of the World and the Ends of God: Science and Theology on Eschatology*, edited by John Polkinghorne and Michael Welker, 29–41. Harrisburg, PA: Trinity, 2000.
Rahner, Karl. "The Intermediate State." In *Theological Investigations 17: Jesus, Man, and the Church*, translated by Margaret Kohl, 114–24. New York: Crossroad, 1981.
———. *On the Theology of Death.* Translated by Charles H. Henkey. New York: Herder and Herder, 1961.
———. "Purgatory." In *Theological Investigations 19: Faith and Ministry*, translated by Edward Quinn, 181–93. New York: Crossroad, 1983.
Ramelli, Ilaria R. E. *The Christian Doctrine of Apokatastasis: A Critical Assessment from the New Testament to Eriugena.* Leiden, Neth.: Koninklijke Brill NV, 2013.
Ratzinger, Joseph. *Eschatology: Death and Eternal Life.* Translated by Michael Waldstein. Washington, DC: The Catholic University of America Press, 1988.
Rowe, William. "Paradox and Promise: Hick's Solution to the Problem of Evil." In *Problems in the Philosophy of Religion: Critical Studies of the Work of John Hick*, edited by Harold Hewett Jr, 111–24. Basingstoke, UK: Macmillan, 1991.
Sacred Congregation for the Doctrine of the Faith. "Letter on Certain Questions Concerning Eschatology." May 17, 1979. Vatican website. http://www.vatican.va/roman_curia/congregations/cfaith/documents/rc_con_cfaith_doc_19790517_escatologia_en.html.
Scott, Mark S. M. "Guiding the Mysteries of Salvation: The Pastoral Pedagogy of Origen's Universalism." *Journal of Early Christian Studies* 18.3 (2010) 347–68.
———. "Suffering and Soul-Making: Rethinking John Hick's Theodicy." *Journal of Religion* 90.3 (2010) 313–34.

Second Vatican Council. *Gaudium et spes*. In *Vatican Council II: The Conciliar and Post Conciliar Documents*, edited by Austin Flannery. Dublin, Ire.: Dominican, 1988.

———. *Lumen gentium*. In *Vatican Council II: The Conciliar and Post Conciliar Documents*, edited by Austin Flannery. Dublin, Ire.: Dominican, 1988.

Steenberg, M. C. *Irenaeus on Creation: The Cosmic Christ and the Saga of Redemption*. Leiden, Neth.: Koninklijke Brill, 2008.

Stoeber, Michael. *Reclaiming Theodicy: Reflections on Suffering, Compassion and Spiritual Transformation*. Houndmills, UK: Palgrave Macmillan, 2005.

Swinburne, Richard. *Providence and the Problem of Evil*. Oxford: Oxford University Press, 1998.

Tallon, Philip. *The Poetics of Evil: Toward an Aesthetic Theodicy*. Oxford: Oxford University Press, 2012.

Thiel, John E. *Icons of Hope: The "Last Things" in Catholic Imagination*. Notre Dame, IN: University of Notre Dame Press, 2013.

———. "Time, Judgment, and Competitive Spirituality: A Reading of the Development of the Doctrine of Purgatory." *Theological Studies* 69 (2008) 741–85.

Trigg, Joseph W. *Origen*. New York: Routledge, 1998.

———. *Origen: The Bible and Philosophy in the Third-Century Church*. Atlanta: John Knox, 1983.

Volf, Miroslav. *The End of Memory: Remembering Rightly in a Violent World*. Grand Rapids, MI: Eerdmans, 2006.

———. "Enter into Joy! Sin, Death, and the Life of the World to Come." In *The End of the World and the Ends of God: Science and Theology on Eschatology*, edited by John Polkinghorne and Michael Welker, 256–78. Harrisburg, PA: Trinity International, 2000.

———. "The Final Reconciliation: Reflections on a Social Dimension of the Eschatological Transition." *Modern Theology* 16.1 (2000) 91–113.

———. "Love Your Heavenly Enemy." *Christianity Today* 44.12 (2000) 94–97.

Vorster, Nico. "The Augustinian Type of Theodicy: Is It Outdated?" *Journal of Reformed Theology* 5 (2001) 26–48.

Walls, Jerry L. *Purgatory: The Logic of Total Transformation*. New York: Oxford University Press, 2012.

Wingren, Gustaf. *Man and the Incarnation: A Study in the Biblical Theology of Irenaeus*. Translated by Ross Mackenzie. Eugene, OR: Wipf & Stock, 2004.

Zagzebski, Linda. "Critical Response [In Response to William Rowe]." In *Problems in the Philosophy of Religion: Critical Studies of the Work of John Hick*, edited by Harold Hewett Jr, 125–29. Basingstoke, UK: Macmillan, 1991.

Index

Adams, Marilyn McCord 99, 170–75
Alighieri, Dante: *The Divine Comedy* 50–53
Atwell, R. R. 35, 39, 41
Augustine of Hippo, Saint 8, 34–38, 39–41, 43–44, 90–91, 191–94
    anthropology and theodicy of 100–106, 107–11, 113–17, 122, 190
    Enchiridion 37–38, 115

Barnard, Justin D. 180–82
Bede, Venerable 42–45
Benedict XVI, Pope 70 n.40, 74–76, 82; *see also* Joseph Ratzinger
Bonner, Gerald 100
Bounds, Christopher 92, 95
Briggs, Charles A. 88
Brown, David 180*ff.*
Buddhism (specifically the concept of *bardo*) 135
Burkert, Walter 17

Calvin, John 166–67
Casey, John 16, 20
Catechism of the Catholic Church 2–4, 69, 137, 142–43
Catherine of Genoa, Saint 80–81
Cheetham, David 133, 153–54, 159
Church Militant 39
Clement of Alexandria 29–30

communion of saints 27, 38
Council of Florence 48
Council of Trent 49

Donovan, Mary Ann 92, 93

Egan, Harvey D. 80
eschatology (Catholic) 56–64, 64–65, 139, 143–45, 148, 187, 211, 214; *see also* purgatory, Second Vatican Council
evil, *see* theodicy

Fenn, Richard K. 25
fire, purgatorial, relative temperature of 27
free will 155–60, 161–63, 173–74; *see also* theodicy, Linda Zagzebski

Gleeson, Andrew 174–75
Gooch, Paul W. 107–9
Greco-Roman afterlife beliefs, *see* purgatory, pre-Christian antecedents to
Gregory the Great, Pope 40–41, 43–44

Hick, John ix, 6–10, 87–91, 107, 113, 122–37, 138, 140–50, 153–54, 158–60, 162–63, 195*ff.*, 198, 212–13:
    Death and Eternal Life 133
    Evil and the God of Love 118–21, 133
Homer 17

imago Dei 104, 106; *see also* Saint Augustine of Hippo, anthropology and theodicy of

INDEX

indulgences, *see* Pope Paul VI, *Indulgentiarum Doctrina*
Irenaeus of Lyons, Saint 6, 8, 89, 91, 193–94
  anthropology and theodicy of 92–99, 107–9, 111–14, 116–17, 122, 131, 190
  On the Detection and Overthrow of Knowledge Falsely So Called (Against Heresies), 28–29

John Paul II, Pope 74
Judisch, Neal 182, 191

Keats, John 86–87

Lane, Dermont A. x, 57–58, 79–80, 81, 84, 187
  Keeping Hope Alive: Stirrings in Christian Theology 3
La Soujeole, Benoît-Dominique de 61–62 n.19
Le Goff, Jacques 1–2, 16, 22, 26–27*ff*., 43 *ff*.,
"Letter on Certain Questions Concerning Eschatology" 71–72
Lewis, C. S. 168–69
Luther, Martin 165–66

Macquarrie, John: *Principles of Christian Theology* 168–69
Malkovsky, Bradley 137–38
"Matthean" style of faith, *see* eschatology, John E. Thiel
Minns, Denis 94, 95, 98–99, 109
Mitchell, Stephen ix
Moltmann, Jürgen 176–77
Moreira, Isabel 14, 15, 36, 42*ff*.:
  Heaven's Purge 44

Nichols, Terence 4
Novello, Henry 63

O'Halloran, Nathan 179, 204–7
Origen 30–34, 43–44, 130–31
  De Principiis 32–33
Orpheus, *see* Orphism

Orphism 18

"Pauline" style of faith, *see* eschatology, John E. Thiel
Paul VI, Pope: *Indulgentiarum Doctrina* 70–71
personal sanctification, *see* sanctification
Phan, Peter 79
Pius XII, Pope: *Mystici Corporis Christi* 61, 83
Plato 18–19
  Gorgias 19
Polkinghorne, John 176
post-mortem intermediate state, *see* purgatory, John Hick
purgatory xi–xii, 1–6, 9–10, 69, 128–32, 134–36, 139–42, 143–50, 163–64, 186–87, 188–90, 198, 211–16:
  contemporary Protestant reconsideration of 167–84, 215–16
  early Anglican understanding/rejection of 167
  early Christian understanding of 22–28
  early Greek/Eastern formulations of 28–34, 39–40
  early Latin/Western formulations of 34–45
  early Protestant Reformers understanding/rejection of 165–67
  ecumenical potential of 184, 216
  full (medieval, pre-Second Vatican Council) formalization of 45–50, 56–57
  Judaic foundations of 20–22, 39–40
  possible opportunity for healing in x, 9, 10, 13, 56, 130, 140, 147, 148, 163–64, 172–74, 203–8, 214
  possible process of the purifications experienced in 202–9
  (post-)Second Vatican Council developments of 55, 58–59, 62, 64, 64–65, 67–68, 69–71, 83–84

pre-Christian antecedents to 15–20
recent papal engagements of 72–76
role of categories of sin in defining
    40–41, 46
sanctification-based understanding
    of 80–81, 88–89, 114, 115–16,
    120, 146–48, 181–83, 189, 194,
    199–201, 212; *see also* John Hick
satisfaction-based understanding
    1–2, 3, 26–40, 54, 72, 79, 115–
    16, 120, 147, 166, 181–82, 191
see also, sin, post-mortem
    purification of the secondary
    effects of

Rahner, Karl 71 n.43, 77–79
Ramelli, Illaria 31
Ratzinger, Joseph 16, 19, 21, 76, 196,
    199, 201–2, 205
reincarnation 137–38

Scott, Mark S. M. 30
Scriptural references for the existence
    of purgatory 20–21, 23–24,
    165–66
Second Vatican Council 2–3, 5, 54,
    57–56, 65, 68, 143–45
Gaudium et spes 61, 64
Lumen gentium 59–60, 61–62,
    61–62 n.19, 141–42
see also purgatory, (post-)Second
    Vatican Council developments
sin
    double effect of 4, 75, 103–4, 115,
        180, 192, 191–92, 196–97, 199,
        215
    juridical concept of 1–2, 8, 24,
        35–36, 46–47, 53, 71–73, 100,
        182, 186, 191
    post-mortem purification of the
        secondary effects of 1, 4, 5, 8,
        36, 70, 71, 115–16, 146–47, 180,
        182, 186–89, 191–95, 195–201,
        201–4, 207–9

relational concept of 2–3, 4–5, 47,
    52, 54, 62, 73, 76, 145, 187,
    191–92, 195–97, 200
see also, purgatory, role of
    categories of sin in defining
"Some Current Questions in
    Eschatology" 72–73
soul-making x, 6–10, 86–88, 90*ff*., 109–
    11, 116, 119, 124–29, 131–32,
    134–36, 140–42, 147, 155,
    164–65, 183–84, 189–90, 195–201,
    209, 212–16; *see also* theodicy,
    John Hick, *and* purgatory
Stoeber, Michael: *Reclaiming Theodicy:
    Reflections on Suffering,
    Compassion and Spiritual
    Transformation* 161, 163–65,
    204
St. Patrick's Purgatory 45

theodicy ix, 6–8, 84, 86–87, 89–91,
    118–19, 122, 124–29, 131, 162;
    see also Saint Augustine of
    Hippo, Saint Irenaeus of Lyons
Thiel, John E. 25, 64, 65–68, 139–41,
    211–12
Thirty-Nine Articles of Religion 167, 168

United Church of Canada, Committee
    on Christian Faith of: *Life
    and Death: A Study of the
    Christian Hope* 169–70; *see
    also* purgatory, contemporary
    Protestant reconsideration

Vatican II, *see* Second Vatican Council
Volf, Miroslav 177–79, 205, 206
Voster, Nico 103

Walls, Jerry L. 16, 38, 182–84
Weil, Simone ix
Wingren, Gustaf 94, 97–99

Zagzebski, Linda 154–60

www.ingramcontent.com/pod-product-compliance
Lightning Source LLC
Chambersburg PA
CBHW051640230426
43669CB00013B/2381